Parallel Lives in Painting

JANE AND JOHN ROBERTSON

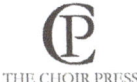

THE CHOIR PRESS

Copyright © 2022 Jane and John Robertson

All rights reserved. No part of this publication may be reproduced or transmitted in any form or by any means, electronic or mechanical including photocopying, recording or any information storage or retrieval system, without prior permission in writing from the publishers.

The right of Jane and John Robertson to be identified as the author of this work has been asserted by them in accordance with the Copyright, Designs and Patents Act 1988

First published in the United Kingdom in 2022 by
The Choir Press

ISBN 978-1-78963-310-8

Contents

FLOWERS 9

PAINTING SIDE BY SIDE 15

ENGLISH LANDSCAPES (JOHN) 40

SCOTTISH LANDSCAPES (JOHN) 70

ENGLISH LANDSCAPES (JANE) 91

SCOTTISH LANDSCAPES (JANE) 99

PORTRAITS 132

Parallel Lives in Painting

The world is becoming a busy noisy place and it is good to find a pastime that creates a different space, another dimension. Our paintings mean a lot to us because they remind us of lovely places we have visited and enable us to remember them in detail.

It takes time to study the colours and contours of a scene. It may be that the drawing is an inadequate representation of the three dimensional scene spread out before us, how can it be anything else, but the process of trying to represent it on the two dimensions of the blank page is intellectually rewarding. The emerging picture is not just about the scene before you but also about your response to it at the time. Painting gives pleasure, a pleasure that is seen in every brush stroke. The picture records a moment in time. The scene can change, sometimes quite dramatically over time, as when a new forest is planted, but then new possibilities present themselves.

A photograph enables you to capture the scene with the press of a button but without requiring you to spend time there to absorb the landscape. These are pictures you can find in a holiday album. Photography can be different. If the photographer spends a lot of time getting to know the subject of interest he or she will return at different times to study the light and shade and get to know the subject intimately. The resulting picture will demonstrate that much care and time has been taken to enable others to share his efforts.

The activity of painting makes time slow down. The news is so full of sad thoughts and of an evolving dystopic society. Better to switch the television off and create your own good news. People are increasingly seeking ways to distance themselves from the stress and noise of work. Apparently week day evensong is increasingly popular in some cathedrals because there is a real need to find a more peaceful dimension. For some, the same may be true of a game of golf. When you paint on canal tow paths and on the foot paths linking villages you have to adopt a different pace, and you discover how peaceful and beautiful the countryside is.

But painting is not just about therapy and escape, it is a creative act. Its product will be unique, a personal response to the subject. It may not be well executed, it may fail to meet the artist's own criteria, that's part of the learning process, but when it succeeds it will be rewarding. Often serendipity plays its part.

In the poem "*Leisure*", William Henry Davies (1871–1940) wrote:

> "What is this life if, full of care,
> We have not time to stand and stare."

Most of us are kept busy doing what is necessary for our survival, mostly dictated by events and duty. What Davies is talking about is private time, and that's what painting is for us. Most of the paintings in this collection took about an hour, were not revisited, they are not consciously composed, they are a spontaneous reaction to the scene before us. Roads feature in a lot of them because we frequently paint from the car, sitting side by side, one perhaps taking the view to the left the other to the right. It is a restricted style of painting, not allowing much flourish, not forgiving of mistakes. In the latter respect watercolour doesn't help either but it was a practice developed out of necessity when time to stare was at a premium and water colour is less messy in a restricted space. Until we retired output was a few paintings a year, only afterwards would it reach a few a week.

What is the value of a painting? We've talked about the therapeutic effects of painting, we get a lot of mileage from just looking at our paintings, that's the value to us. A long time ago we entered a painting in an amateur painter competition. The gallery asked us to put a price on it. The cost to us of framing the painting and the gallery charge for displaying the painting were about the same and we thought a similar amount might reasonably be our share. When we added it up we got a figure which didn't seem to represent it's true value to us and began to regret that we'd agreed to sell it. Fortunately, nobody wanted to buy it and we could take it home after the display period. We're still enjoying having it.

We had to conclude, looking back, that if the work was any good we'd want to keep it and if it wasn't we wouldn't want to sell it. Not the right commercial attitude!

Van Gogh paintings didn't enjoy, in his life time, the commercial success that they do today. Artists live to paint but in order to live they have to pay the grocer. Traditionally, they have had to seek the patronage of rich individuals or institutions who usually had their own reasons for commissioning their work and their own ideas of what they wanted. Later, art dealers like Theo Van Gogh, and Durand Ruel began to promote artists as a commercial venture and to democratise the ownership of art. Dealers like these seem genuinely to have admired the paintings they sold but often it seems that the name of the artist is more important than the work and dealers are more interested in the provenance of paintings than the content. Expert bodies exist to authenticate works and however impressive without authentication the work will not command anything like the price of the "genuine" article. The high end art market thrives on rarity.

Fortunately for us the Art Print has now evolved to a high degree of sophistication. Just as the written word passed from the preserve of states and institutions and classic works of literature could be purchased by the general public from bookshops, newsagents and railway station kiosks, so art is no longer restricted to palaces and galleries. Good quality art reproductions can now be bought for sums affordable by the not so rich. This also solves our own dilemma, we can keep the original and pass on the print copy: the criterion still applies, we still have to feel that the original painting is worth keeping and if not we wouldn't want to sell the print. The ownership of literature and art has been democratised.

The United Kingdom is a collection of beautiful islands. No one has far to travel to find a picturesque spot that will rival any other on the planet. Monet in his later years painted in his garden, Lowrie captured the streets and factories and people of the city in which he lived and worked, Cezanne painted wonderful still lives within the confines of a room.

Our early landscapes were painted in and around Staffordshire, later ones in Scotland.

The paintings are arranged in seven sections. The section "Painting side by side" may require further explanation. We are not competing or collaborating, we are simply responding to a shared subject, choosing that aspect of it which appealed to us as individuals. Consequently some of the scenes selected will be recognisably the same while others may not. Learning from each other comes later in sharing and comparing the results or reliving a shared enjoyment.

Flowers

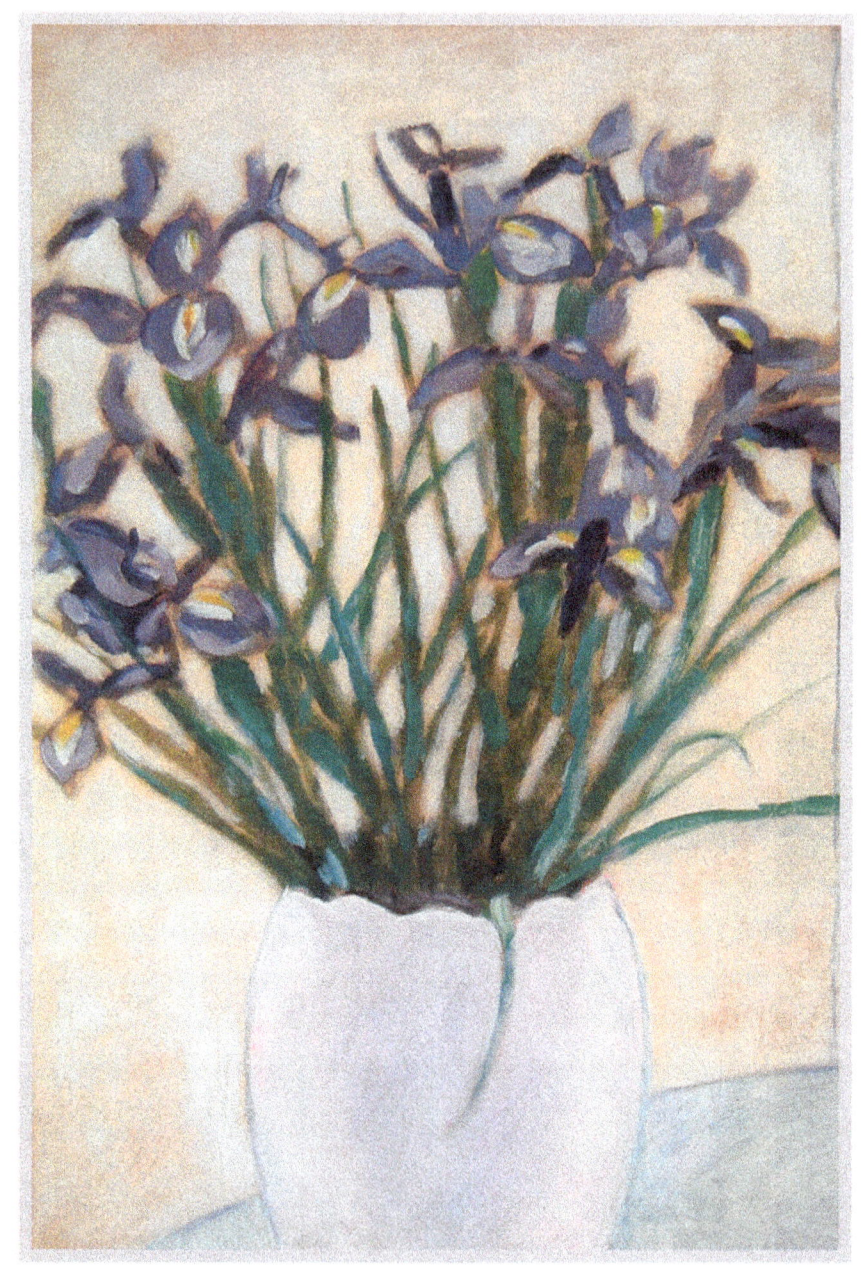

Irises
By John Robertson
Pre 2007 Acrylic on Board 20" x 16"

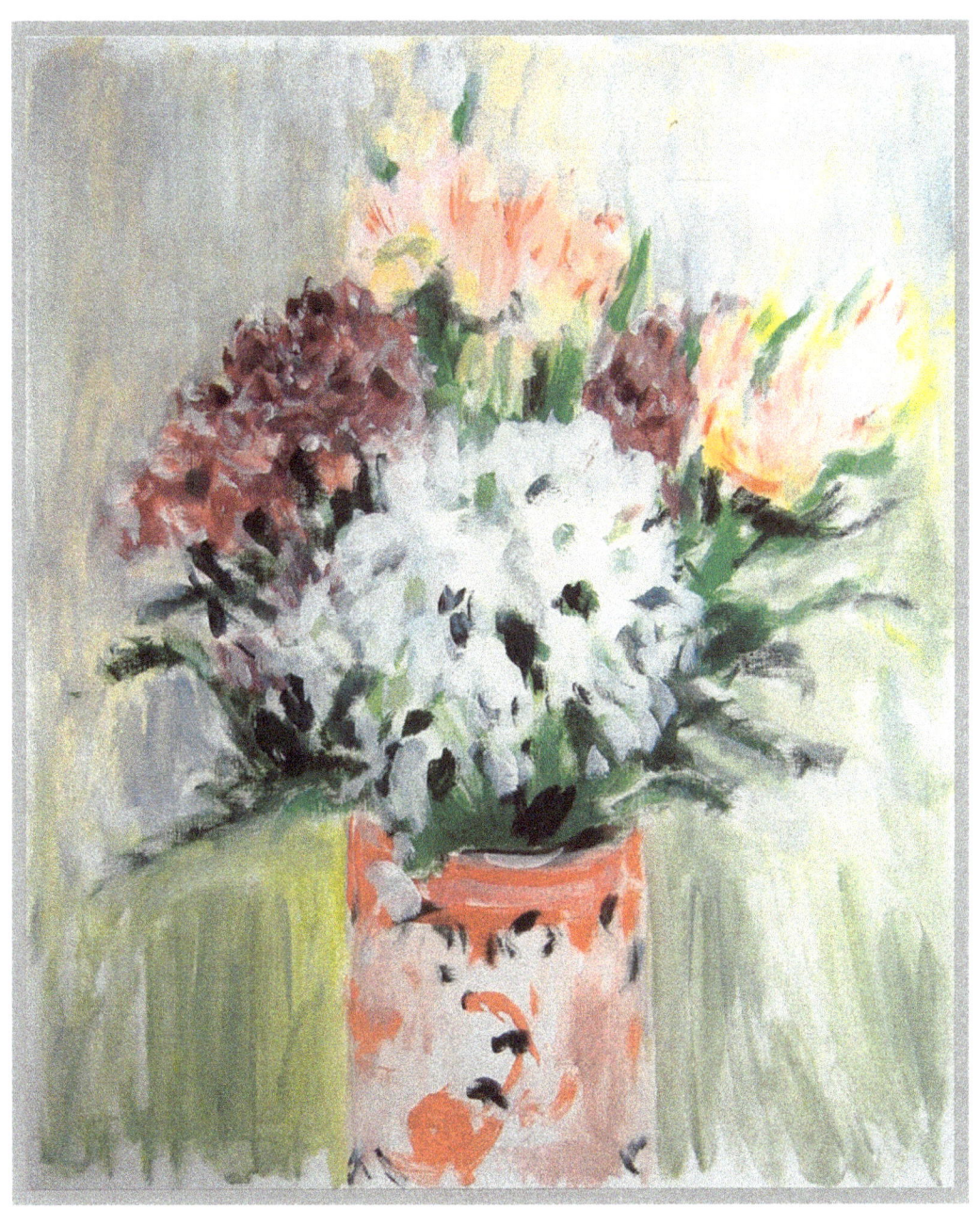

Chrysanthemum and Alstroemeria
By John Robertson
Pre 2007 Acrylic on Board 20" x 16"

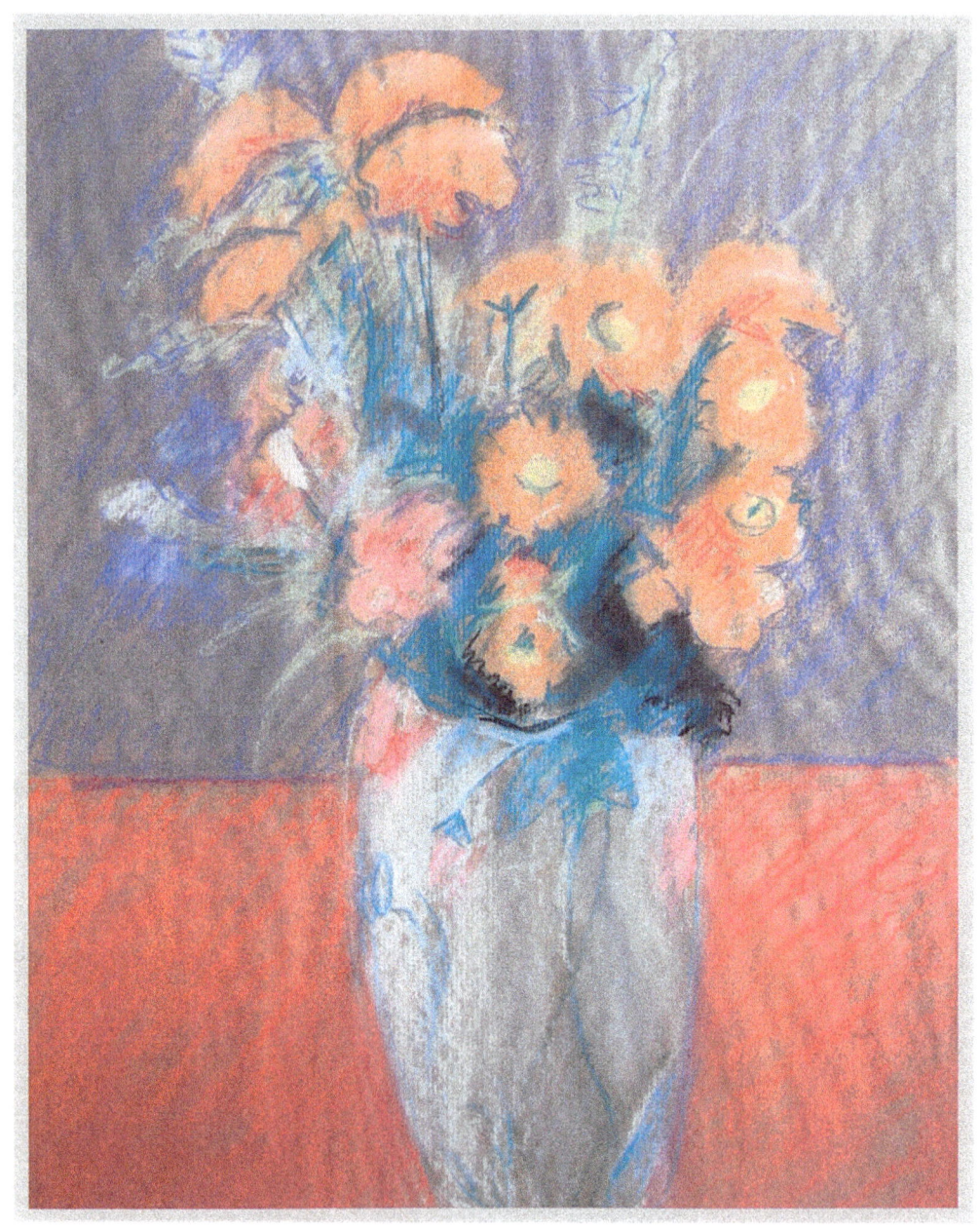

Helianthus and Gypsophila
By John Robertson
Pre 2007 Pastel 20" x 16"

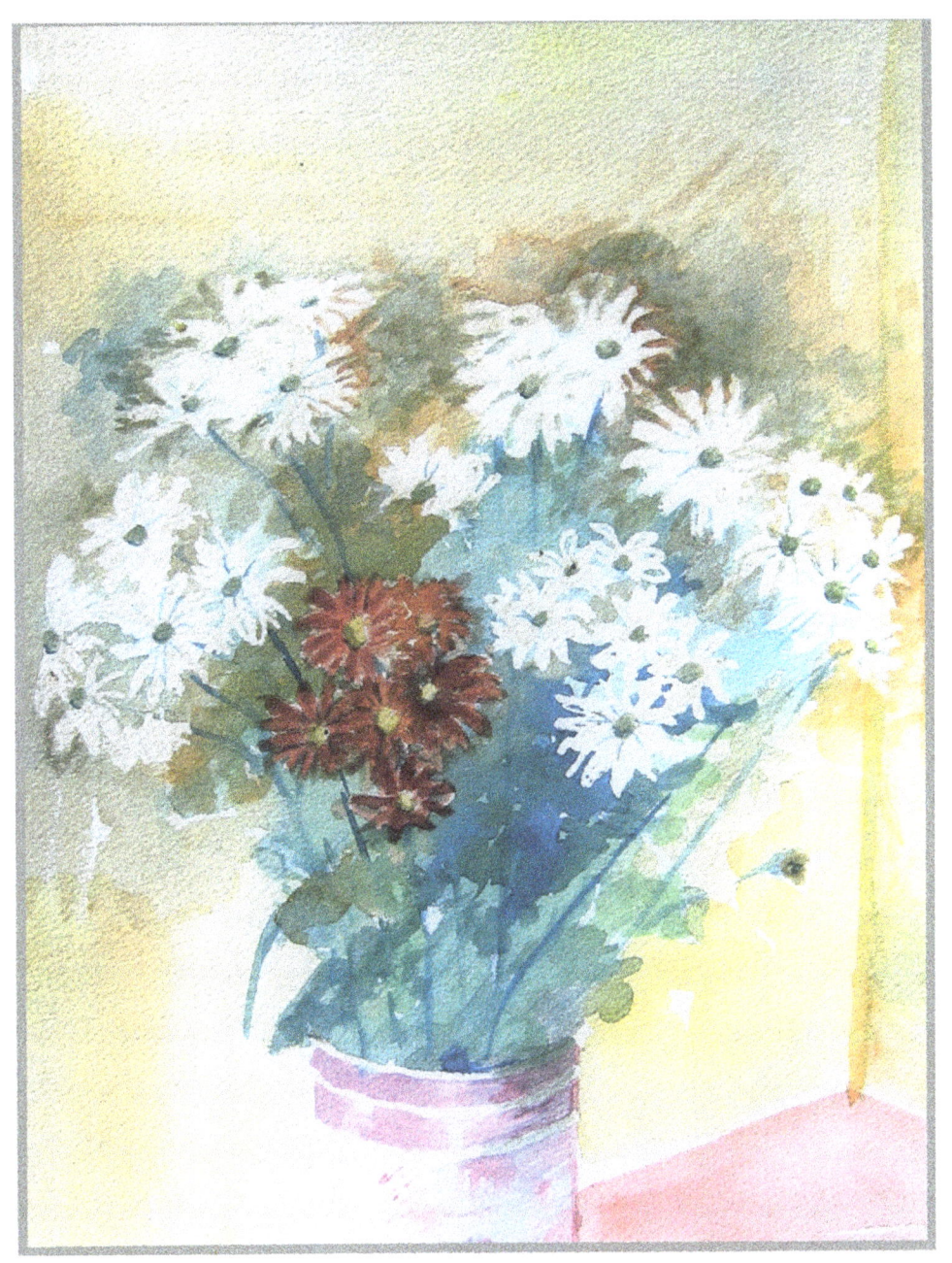

Daisies
By Jane Robertson
2005 Watercolour 16" x 12"

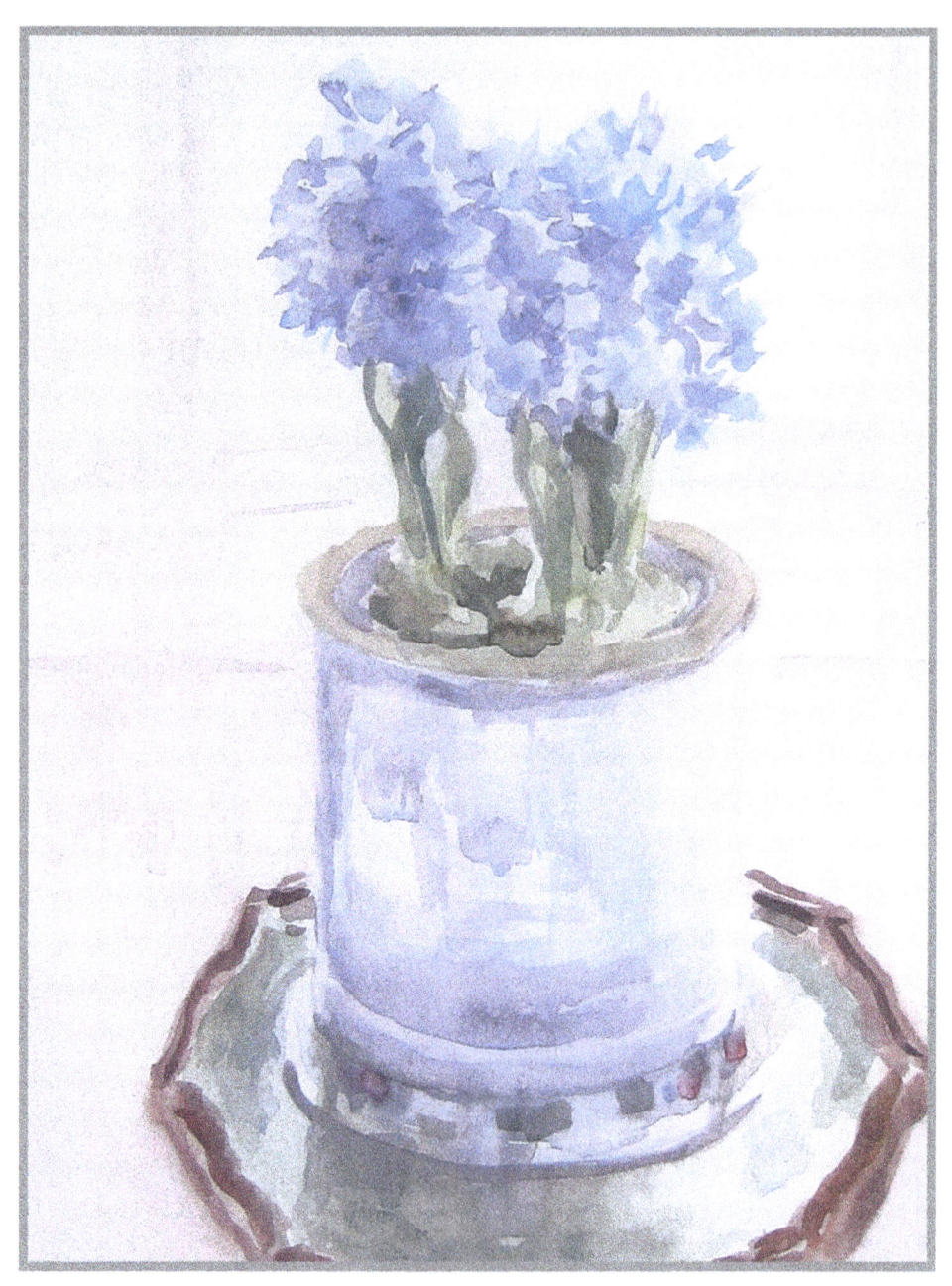

Hyacinths
By John Robertson
22.03.1992 Watercolour 20" x 16"

Painting Side by Side

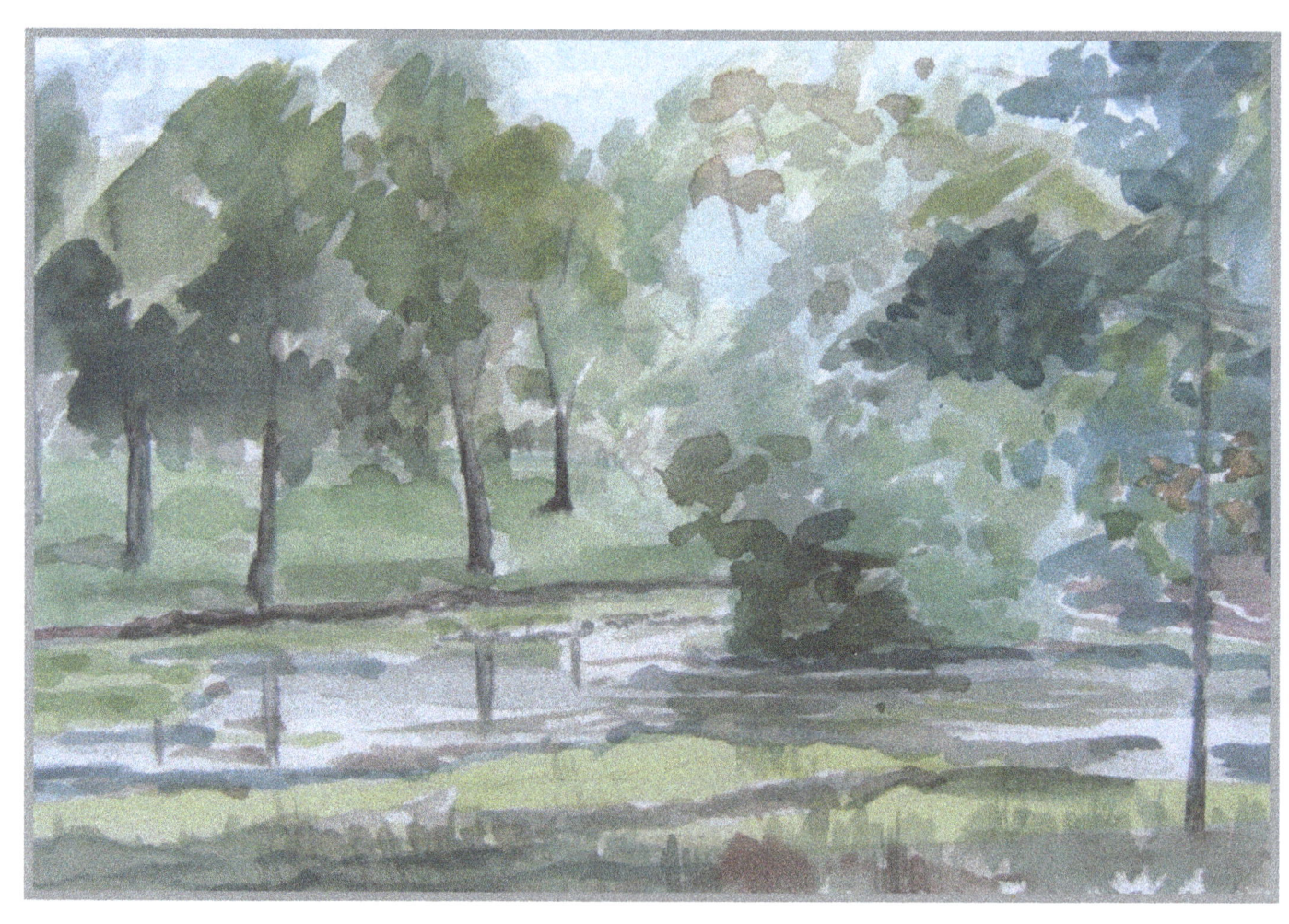

Dunstall
By Jane Robertson
2004 Watercolour 16" x 12"

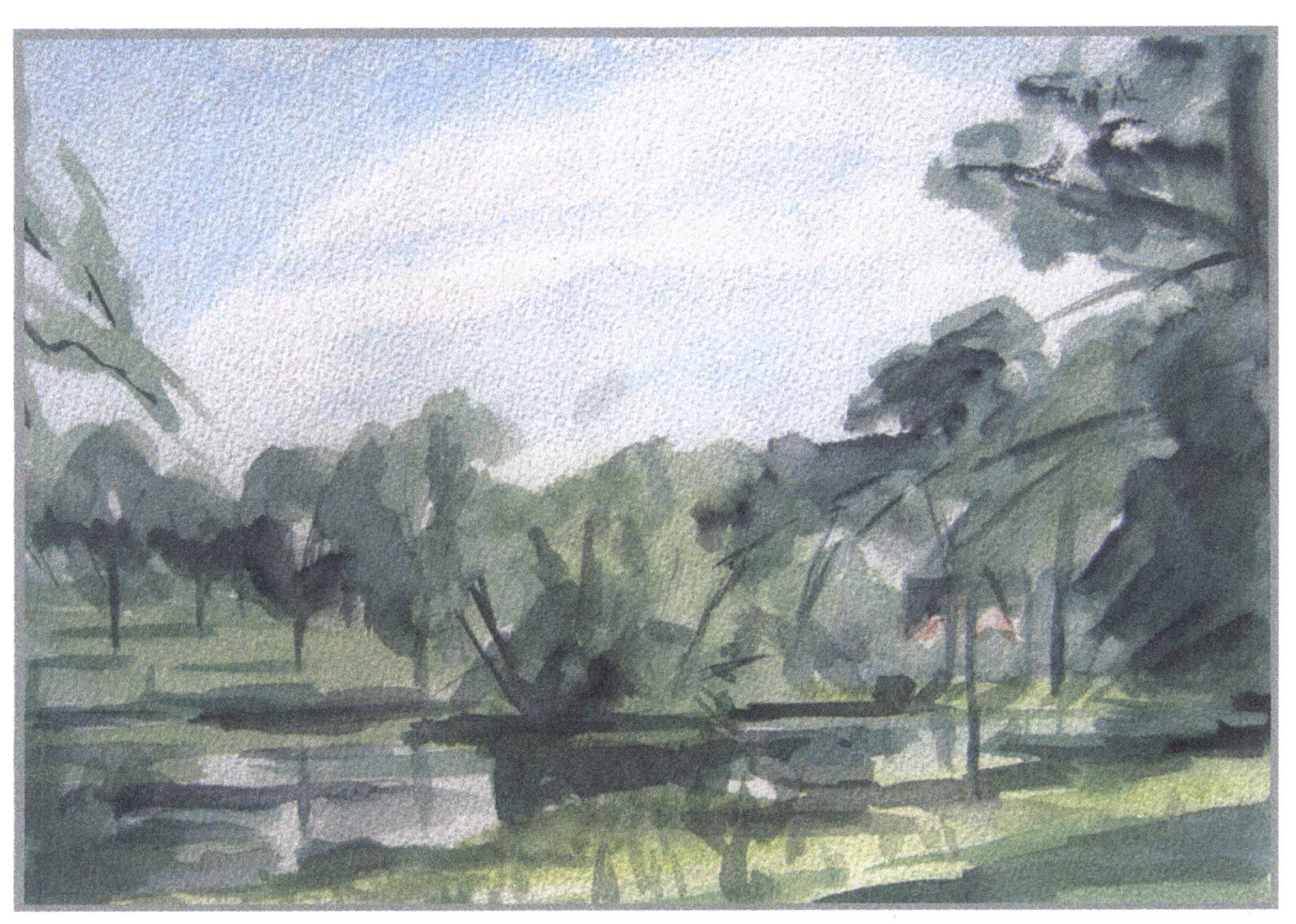

Dunstall
By John Robertson
04.09.2004 Watercolour 20" x 16"

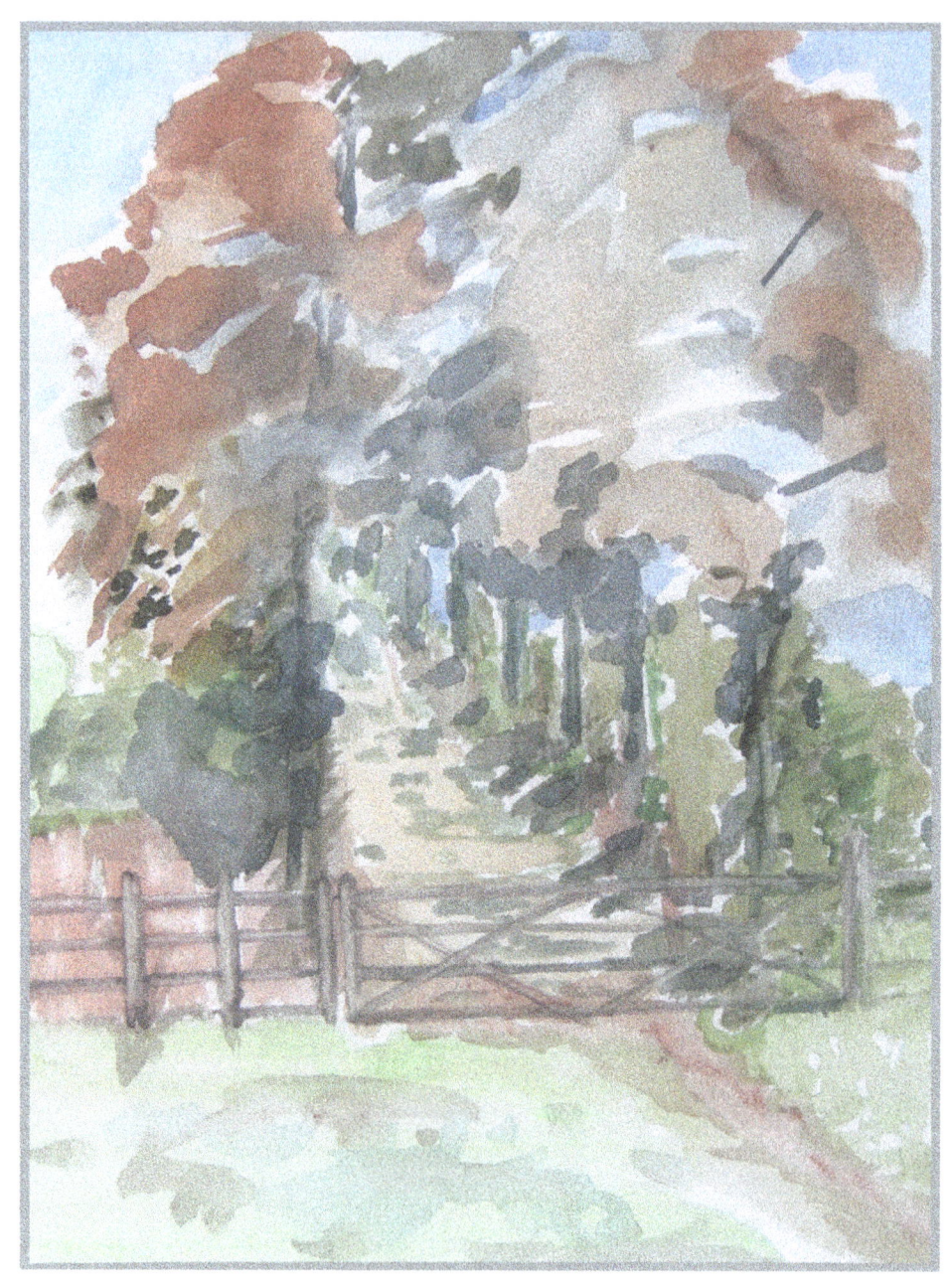

Path to Dunstall
By Jane Robertson
2004 Watercolour 20" x 16"

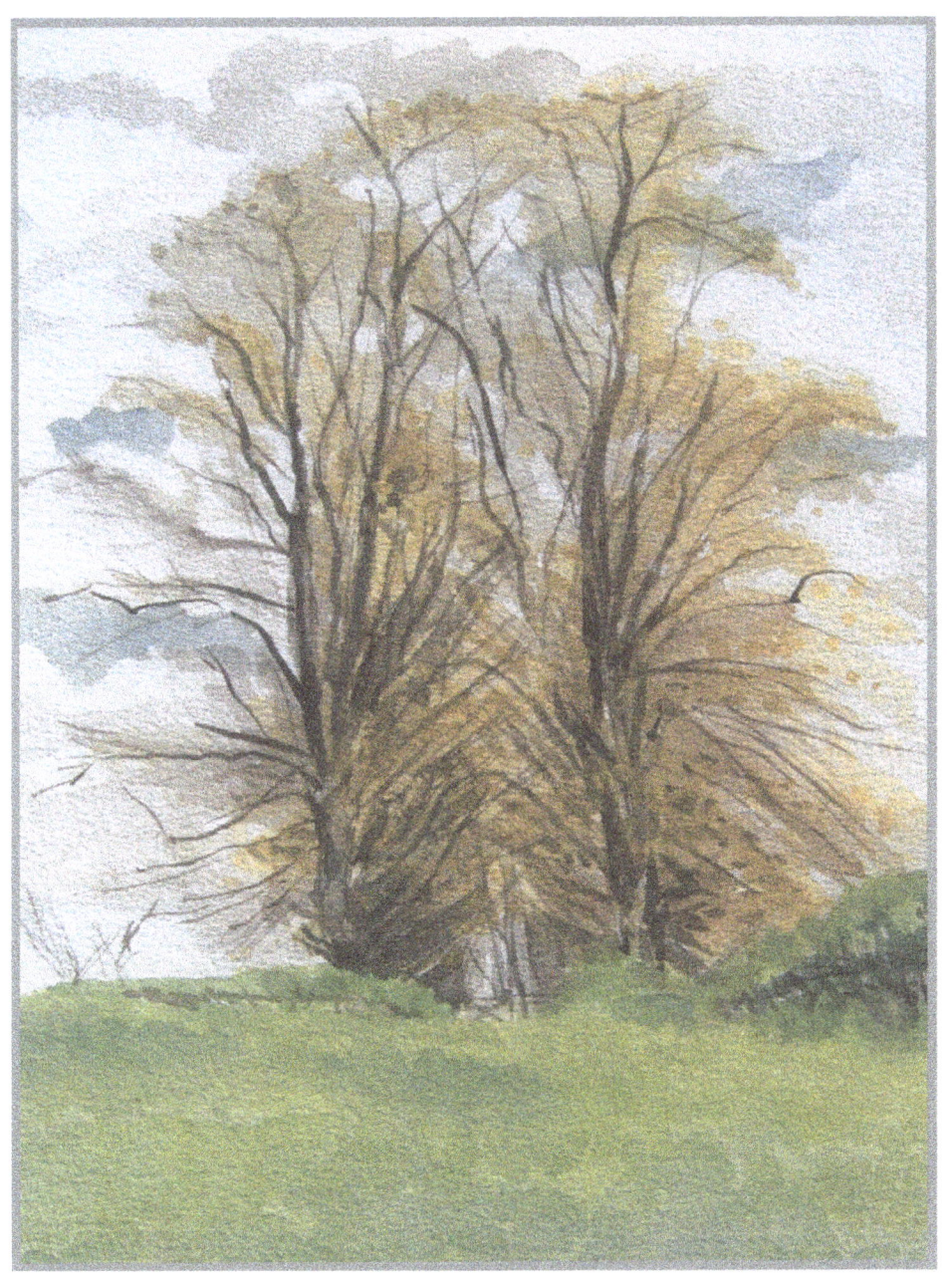

Path to Dunstall
By John Robertson
1980 Watercolour 14" x 10"

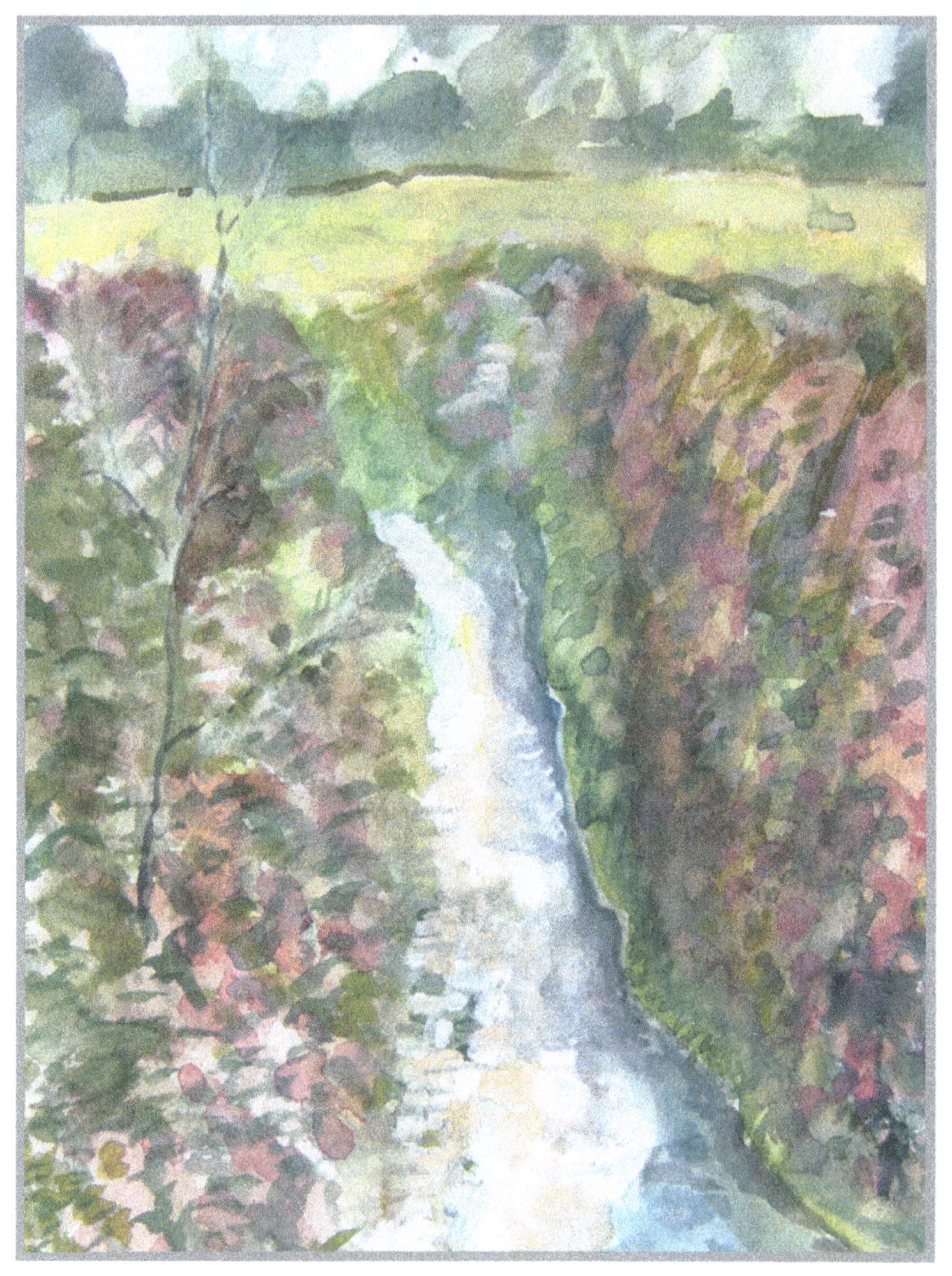

Himalayan Balsam
By Jane Robertson
2004 Watercolour 16" x 12"

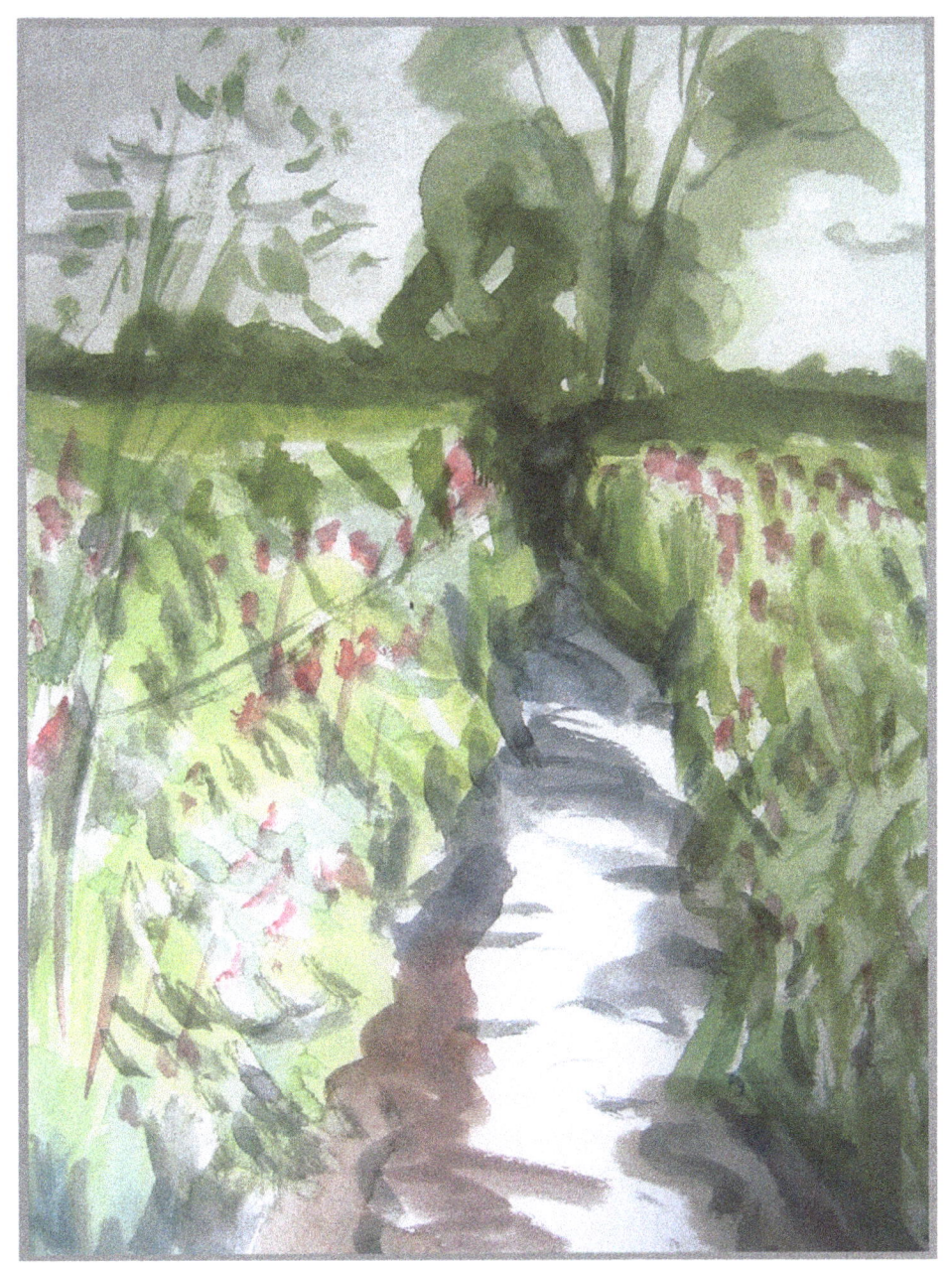

Himalayan Balsam
By John Robertson
07.07.2004 Watercolour 20" x 16"

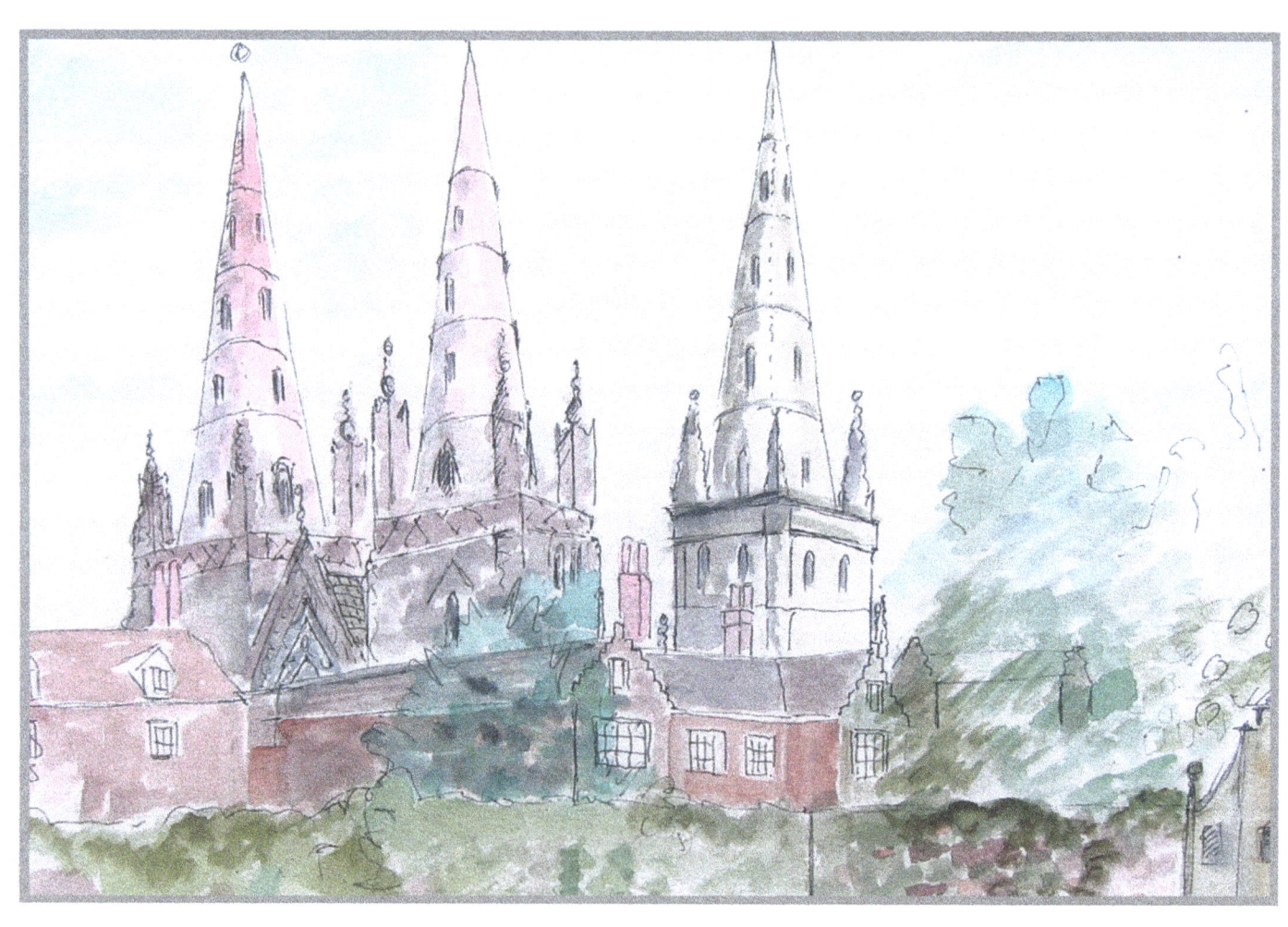

Lichfield Cathedral
By Jane Robertson
30.09.2004 Watercolour 16" x 12"

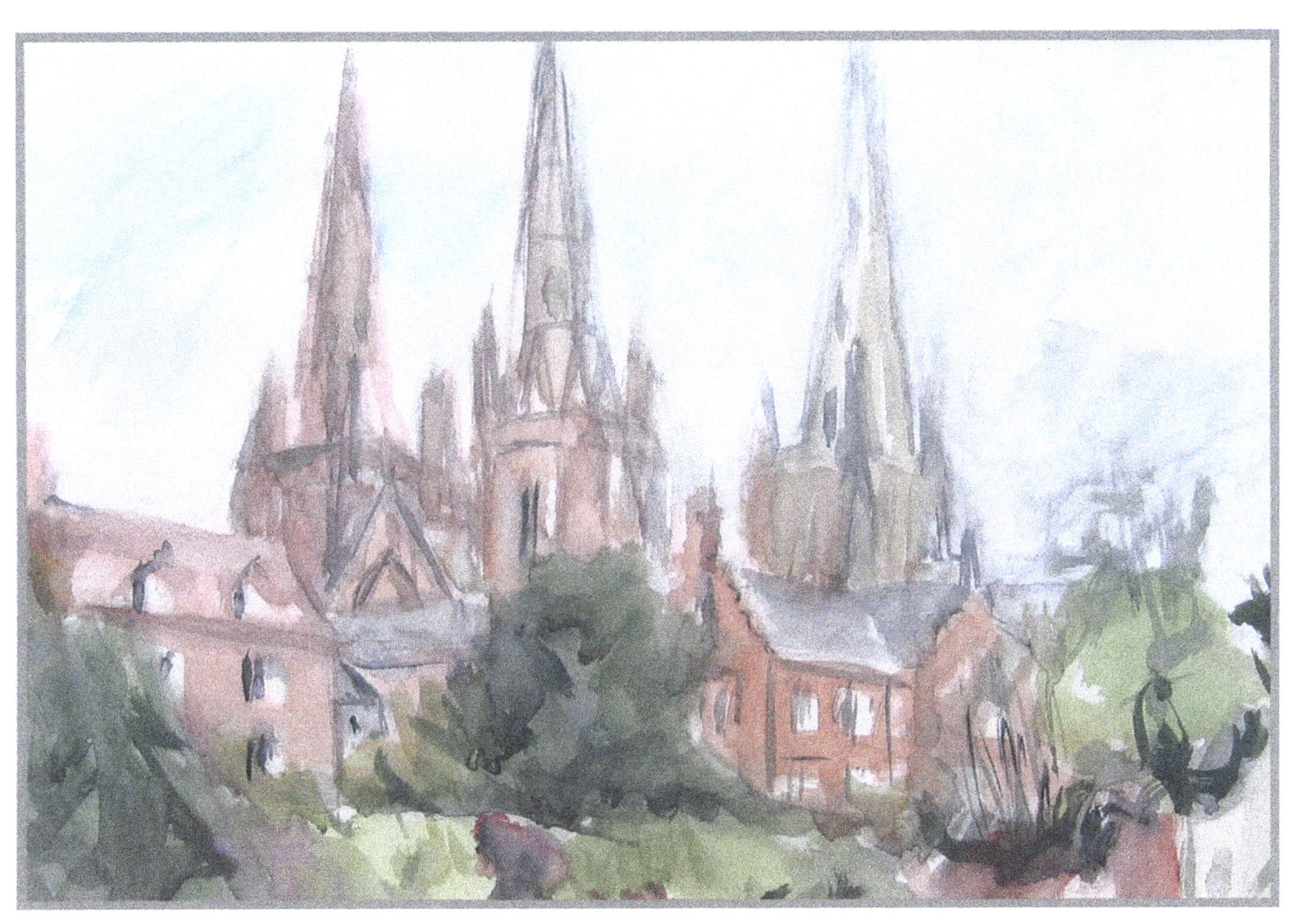

Lichfield Cathedral
By John Robertson
30.09.2004 Watercolour 20" x 16"

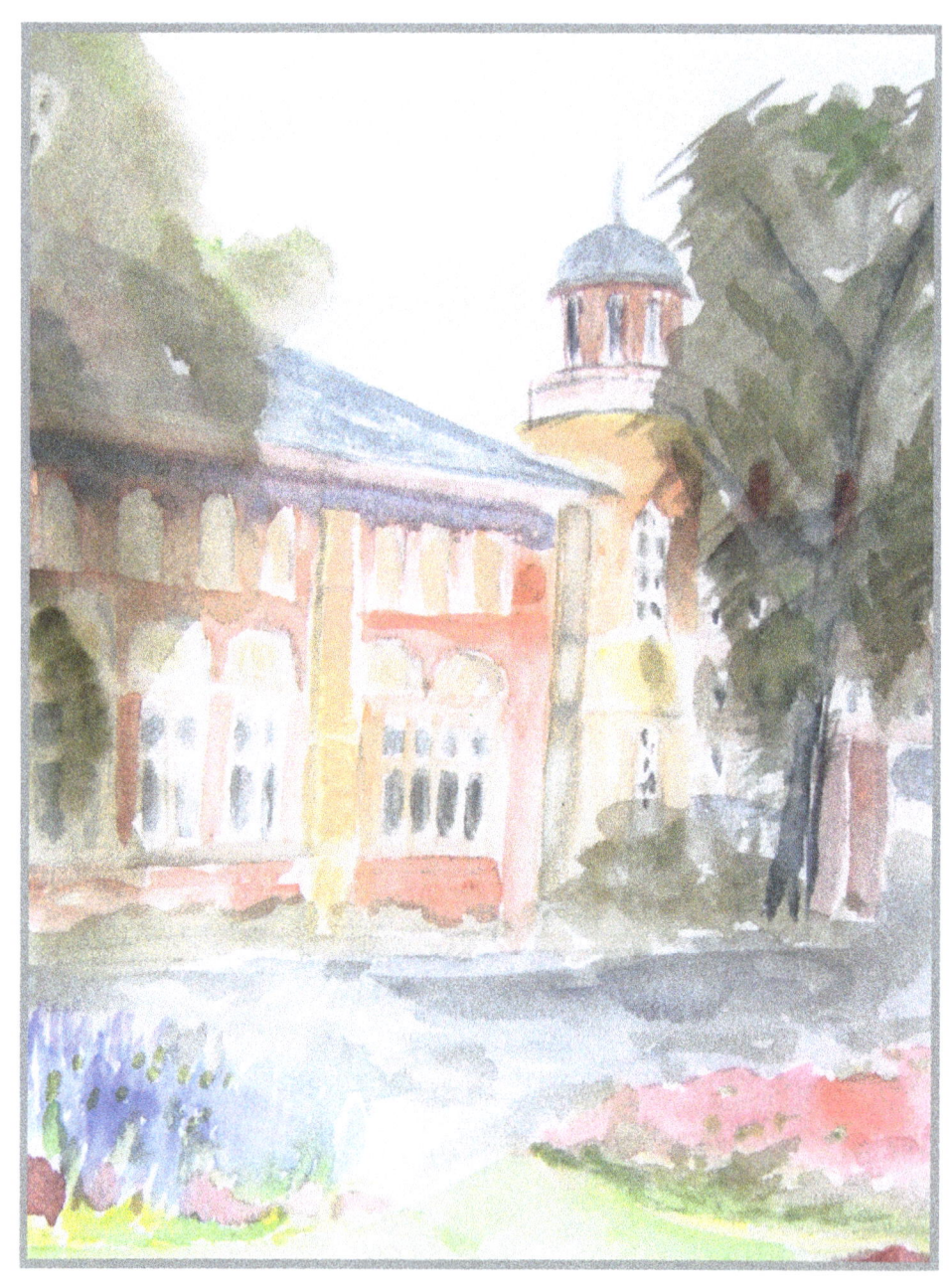

Lichfield Library
By Jane Robertson
2006 Watercolour 16" x 12"

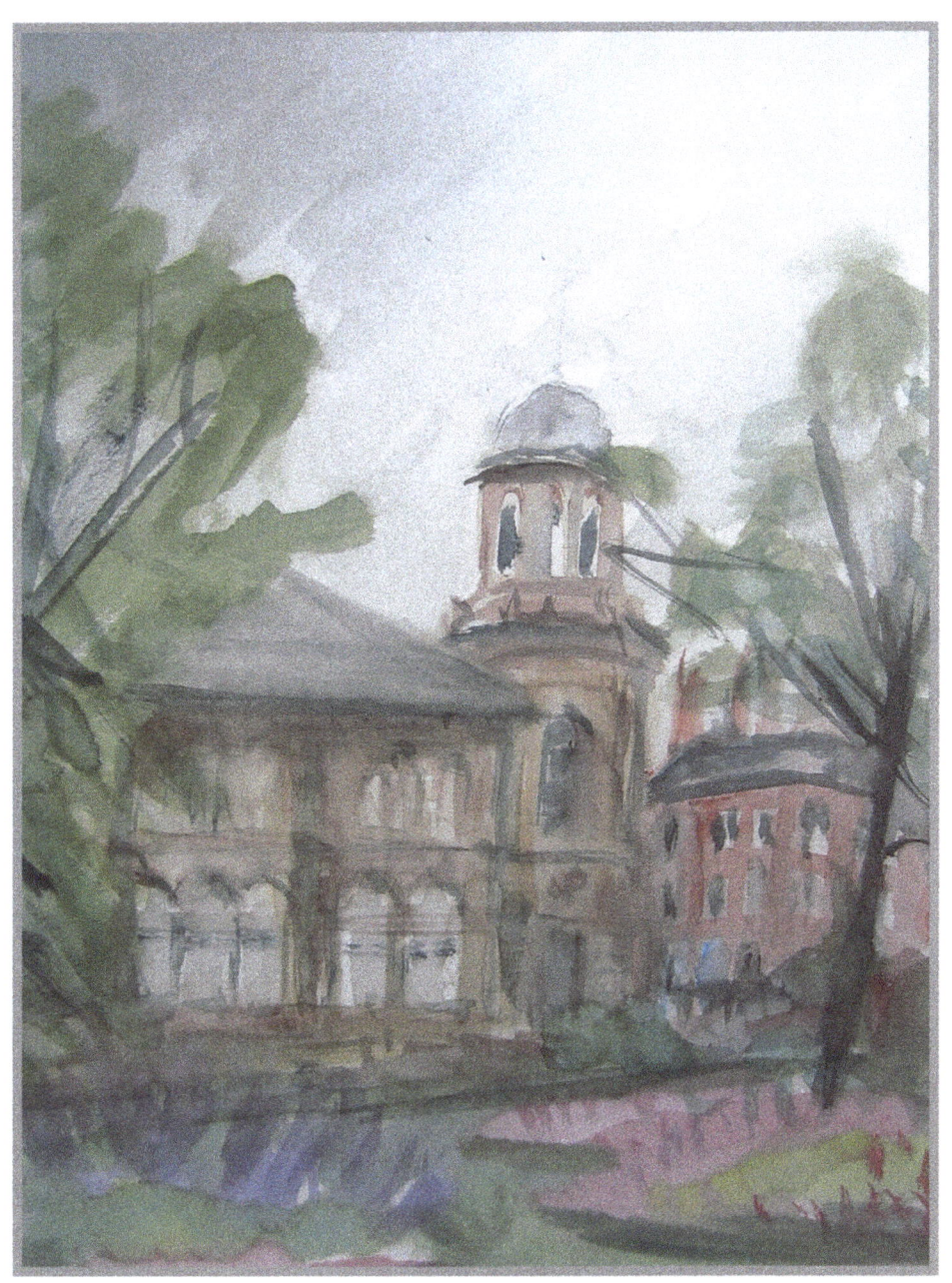

Lichfield Library
By John Robertson
28.09.2004 Watercolour 20" x 16"

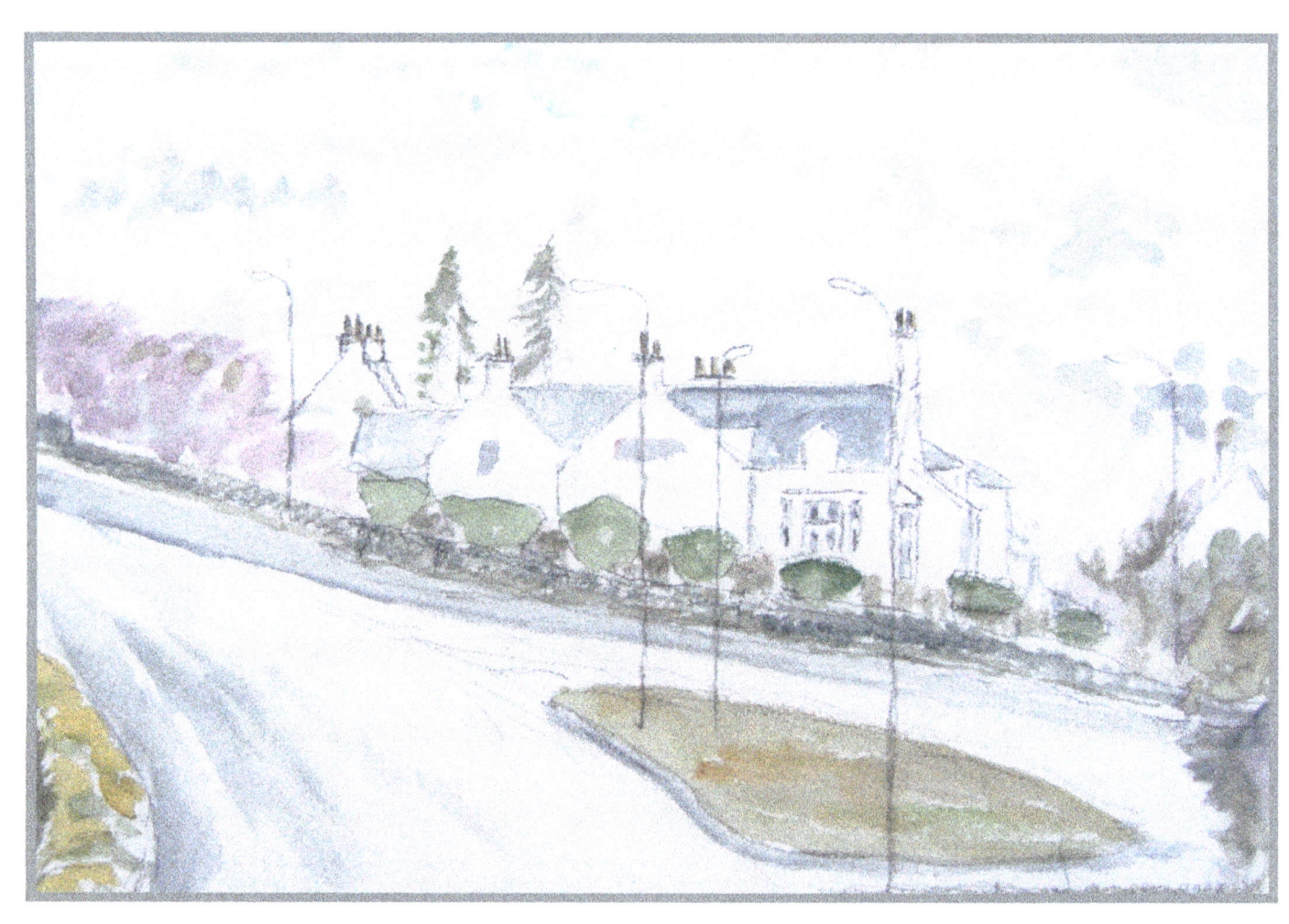

Dunvegan
By Jane Robertson
2018 Watercolour 16" x 12"

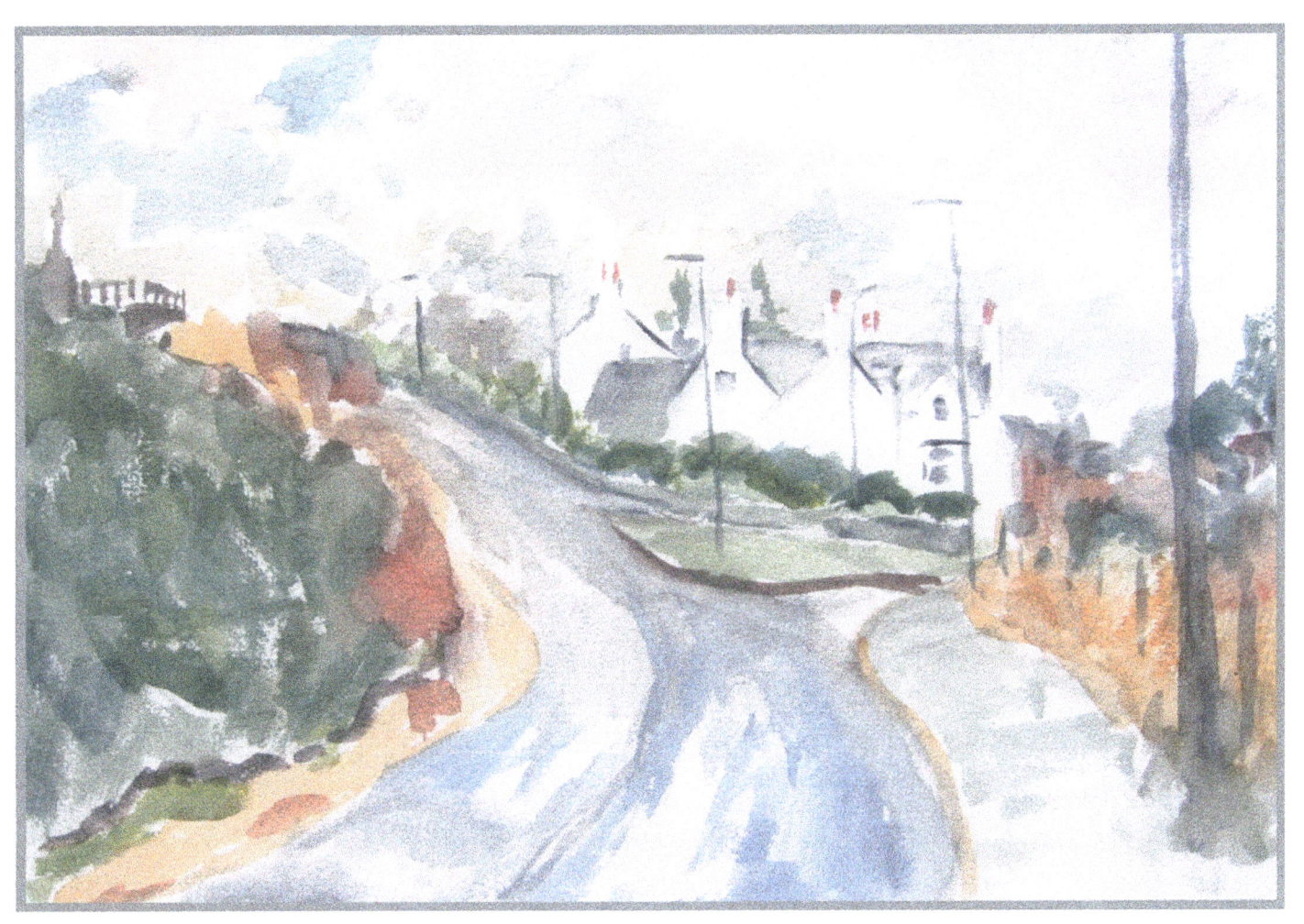

Dunvegan
By John Robertson
08.02.2018 Watercolour 20" x 16"

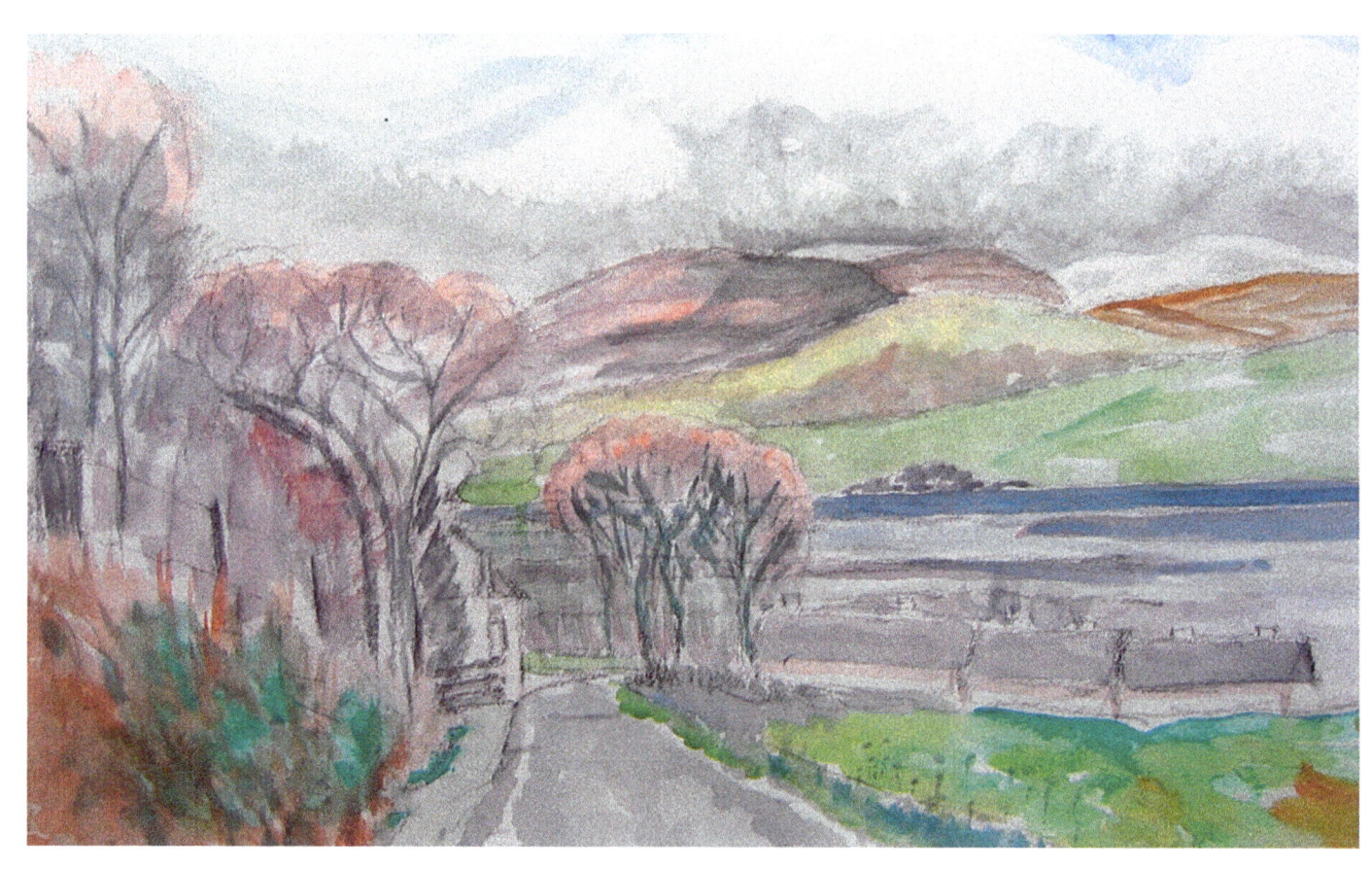

Bernisdale
By Jane Robertson
2018 Watercolour 16" x 12"

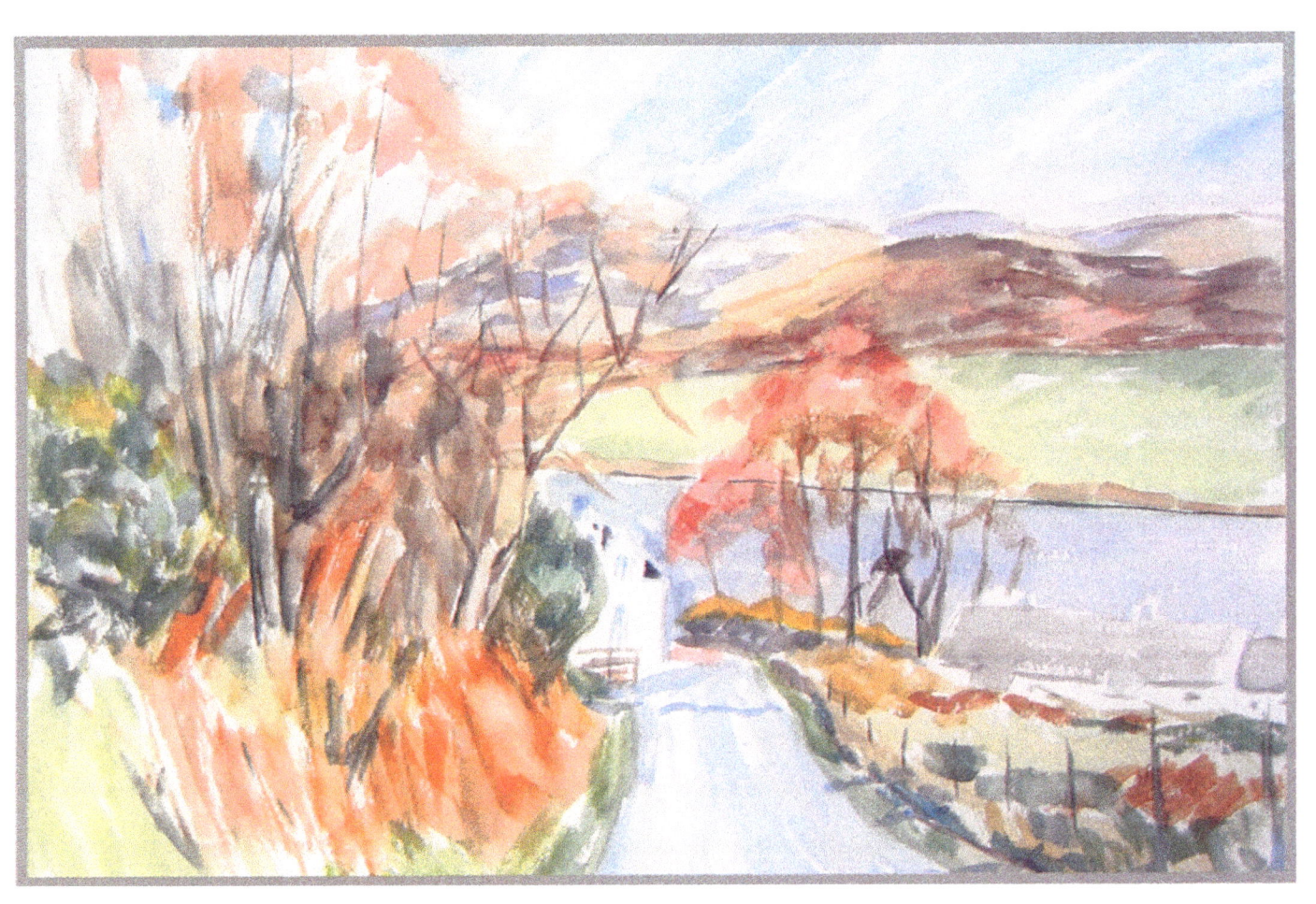

Upper Bernisdale
By John Robertson
2018 Watercolour 20" x 16"

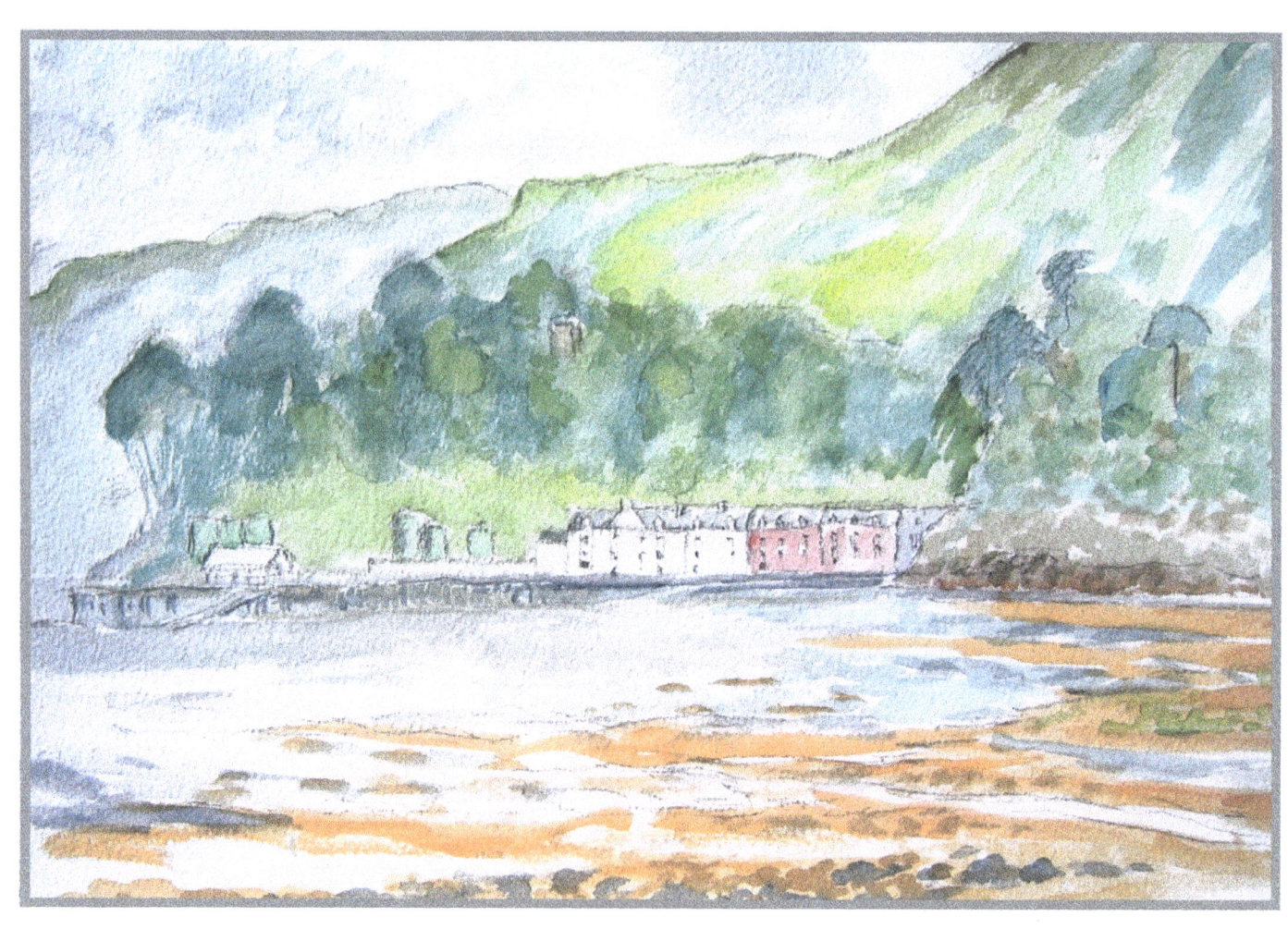

Portree Harbour
By Jane Robertson
2019 Watercolour 16" x 12"

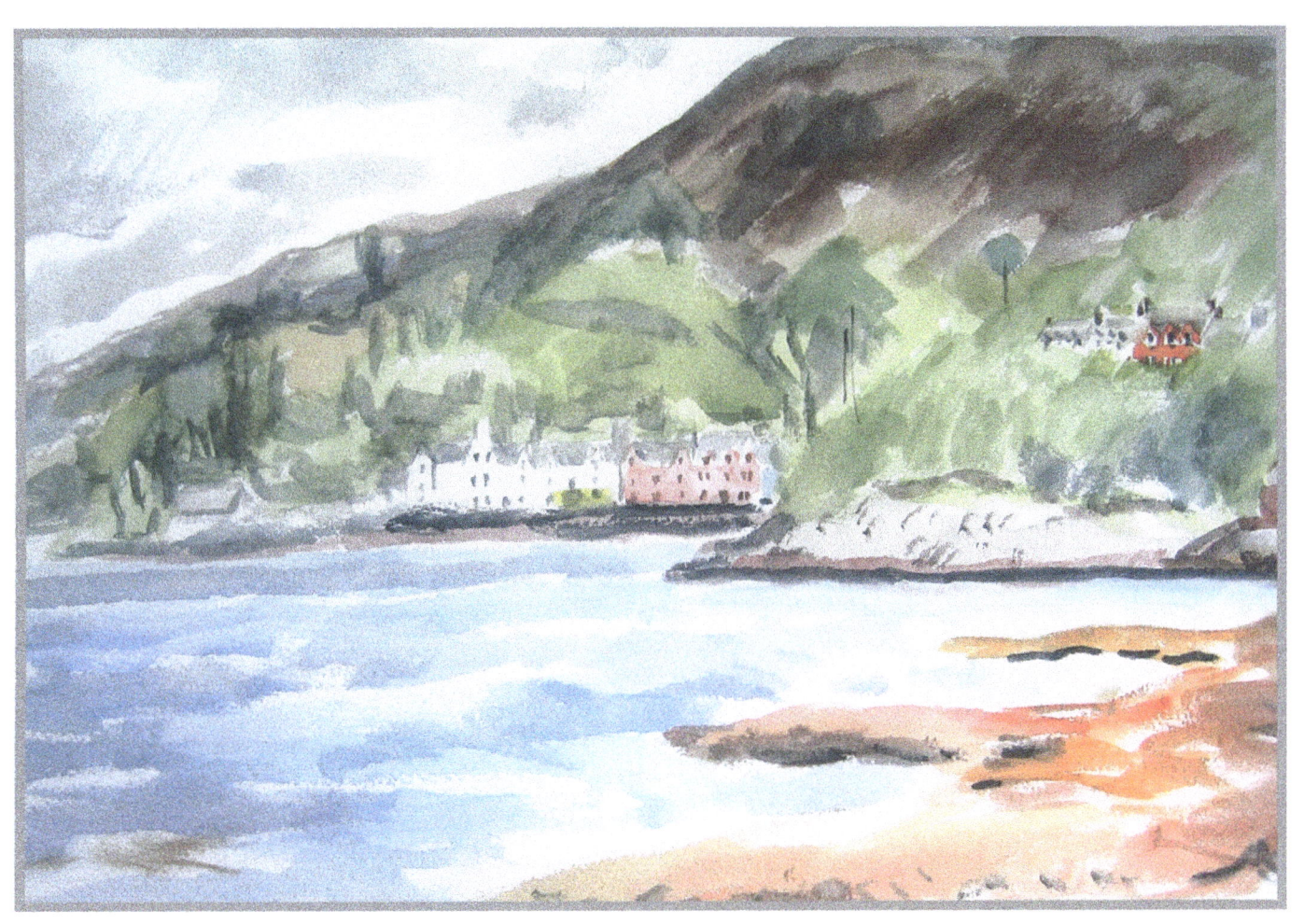

Portree Harbour
By John Robertson
13.06.2013 Watercolour 20" x 16"

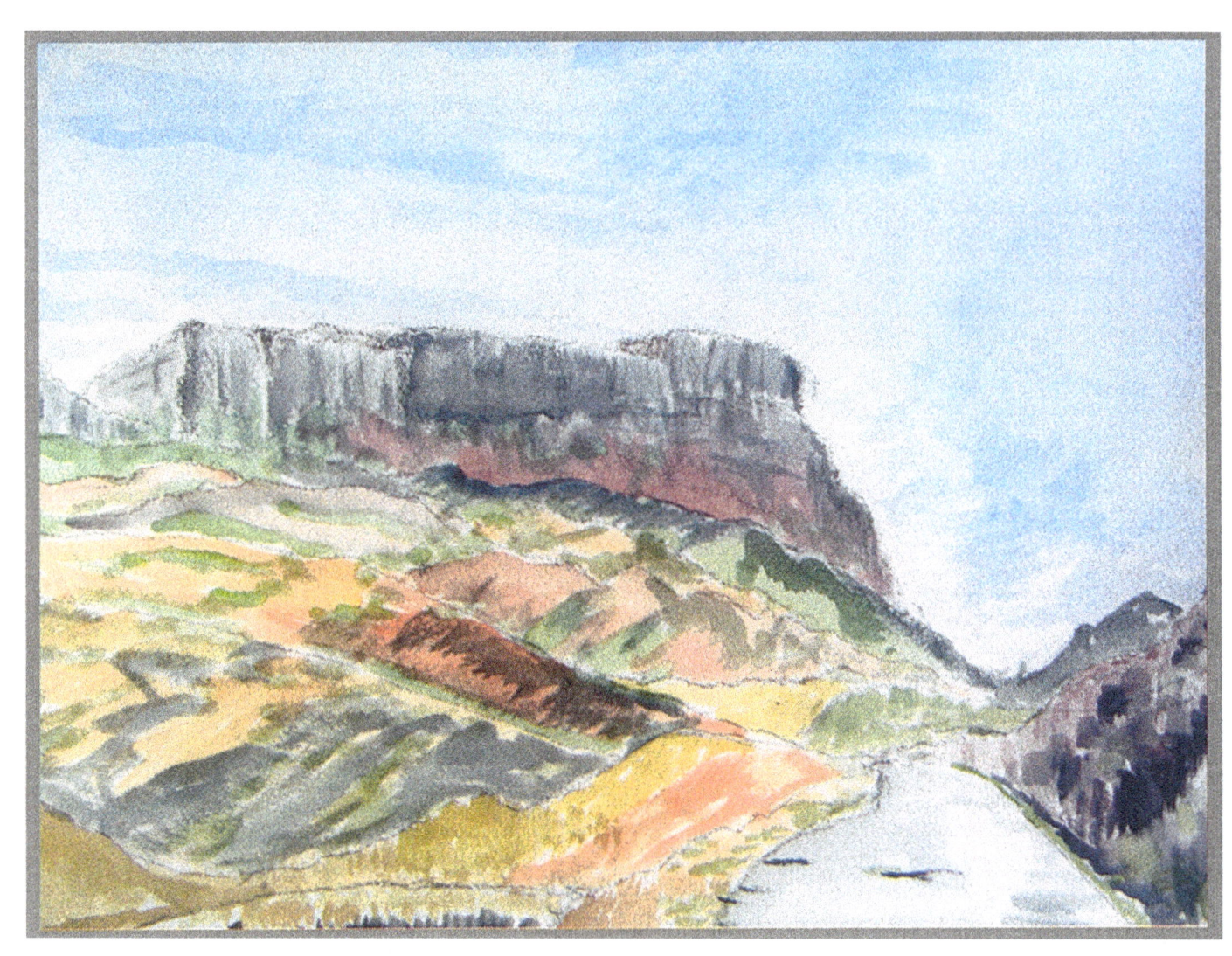

Quiraing Flodigarry
By Jane Robertson
2017 Watercolour 16" x 12"

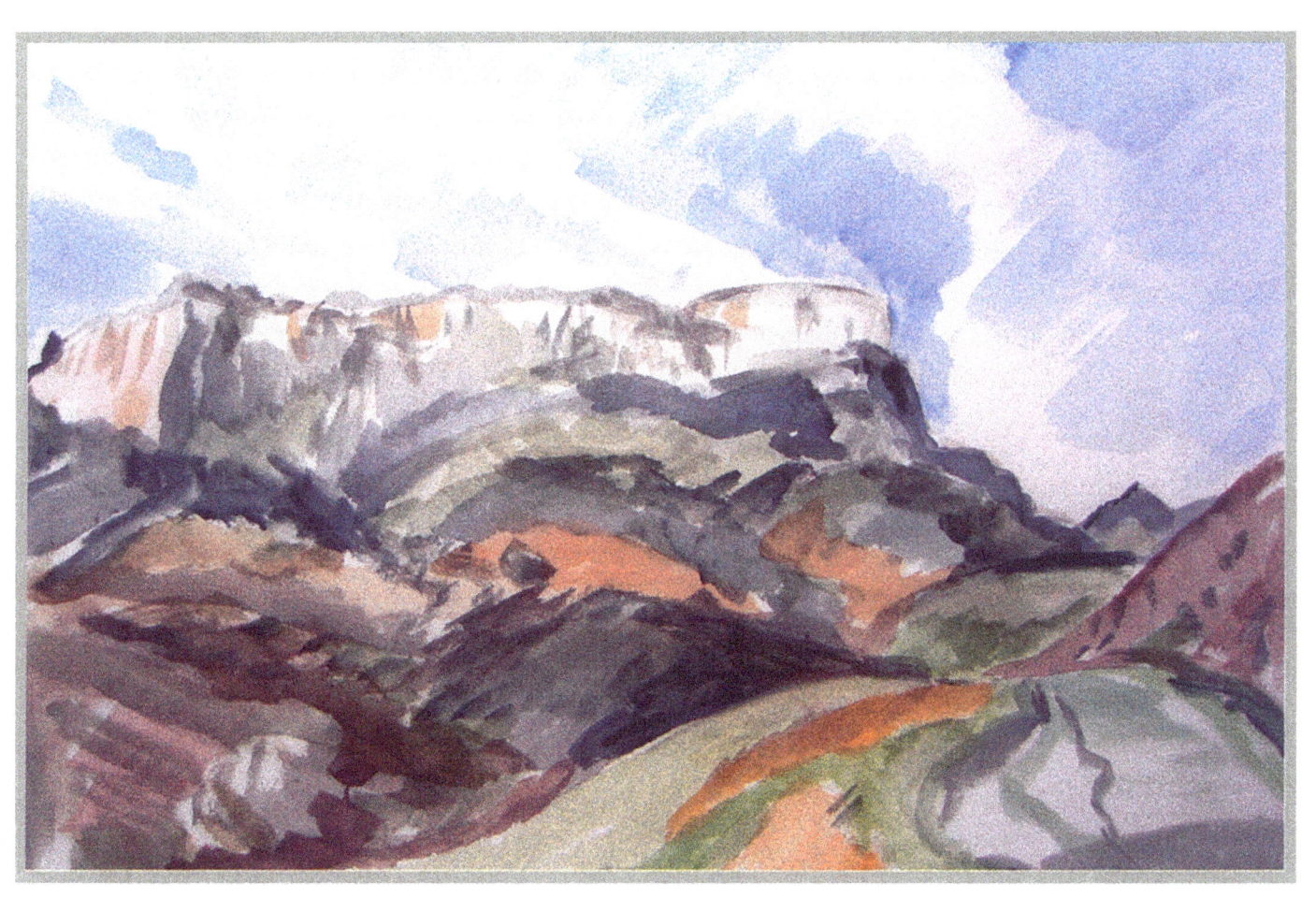

The Quiraing
By John Robertson
2017 Watercolour 20" x 16"

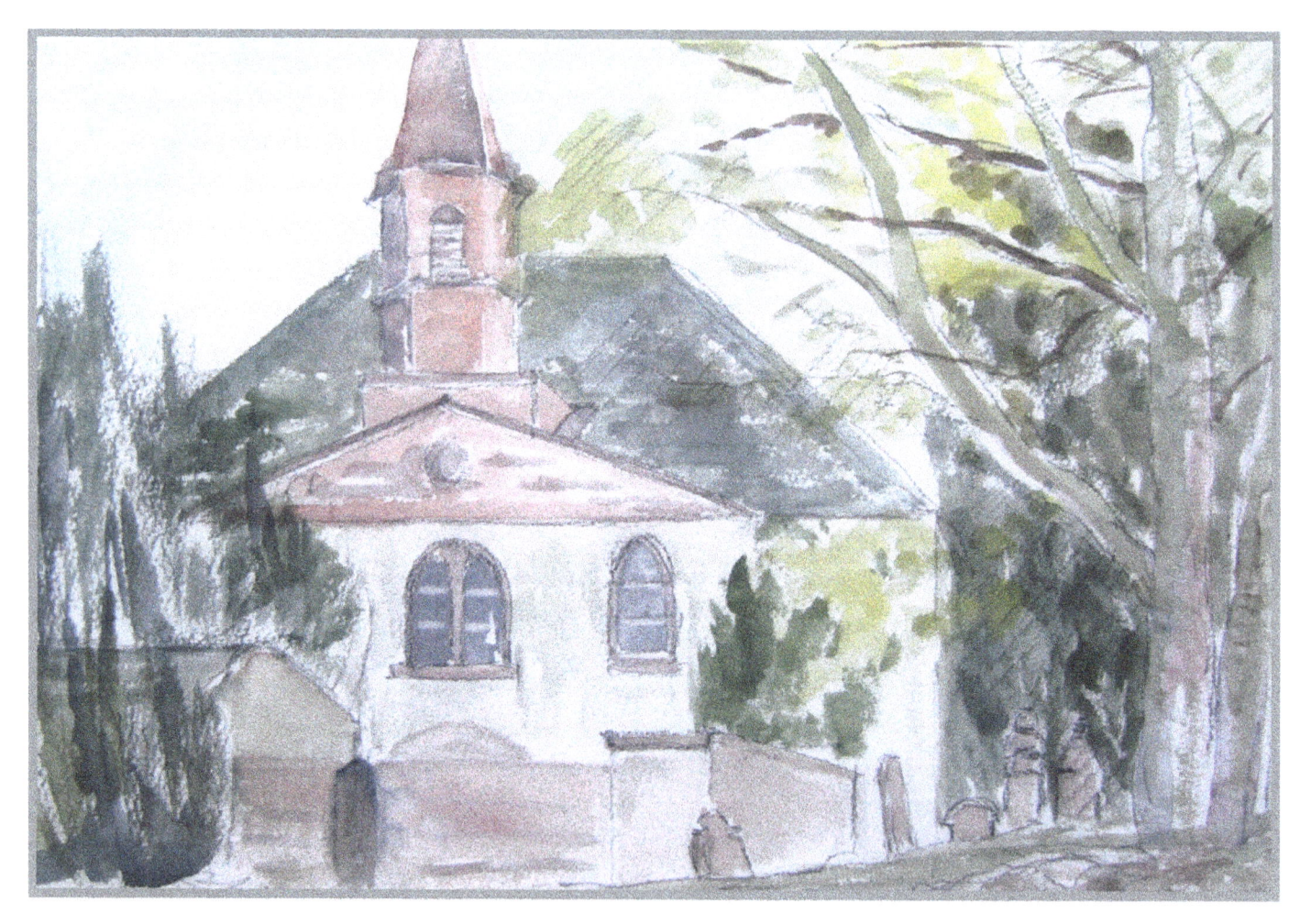

St Clements Church
By Jane Robertson
2017 Watercolour 16" x 12"

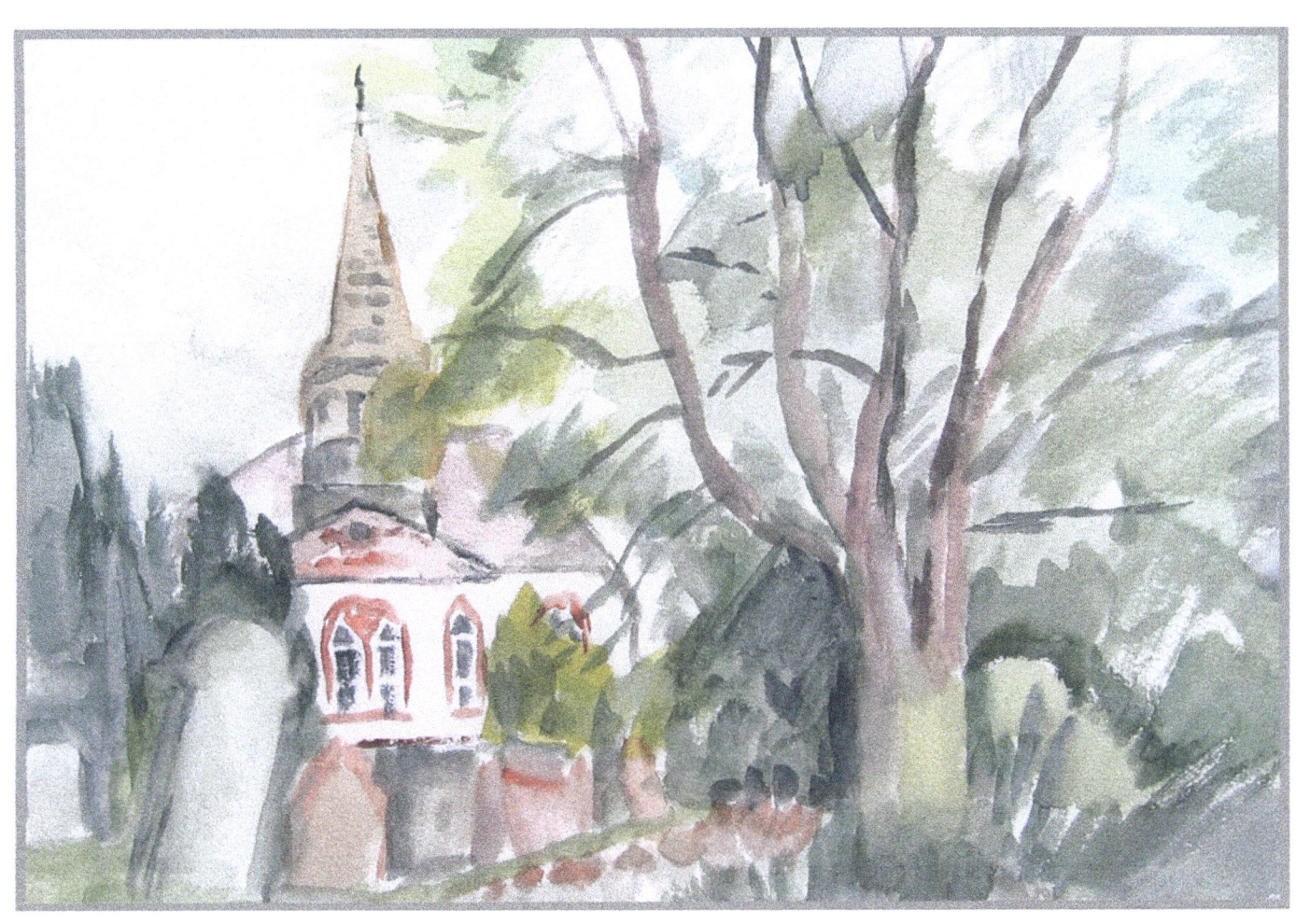

St Clements Church
By John Robertson
2017 Watercolour 20" x 16"

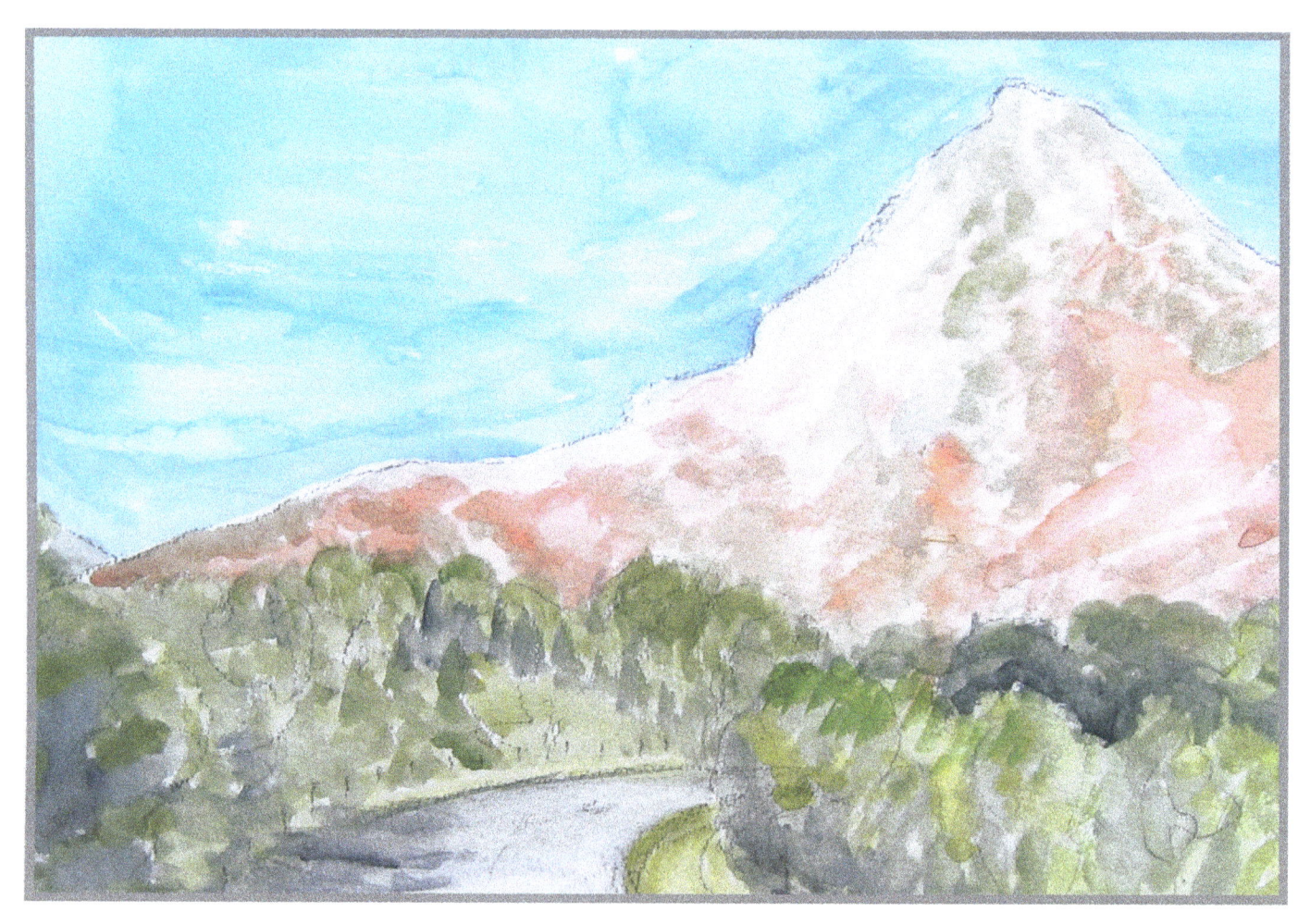

Glen Shiel
By Jane Robertson
July 2015 Watercolour 16" x 12"

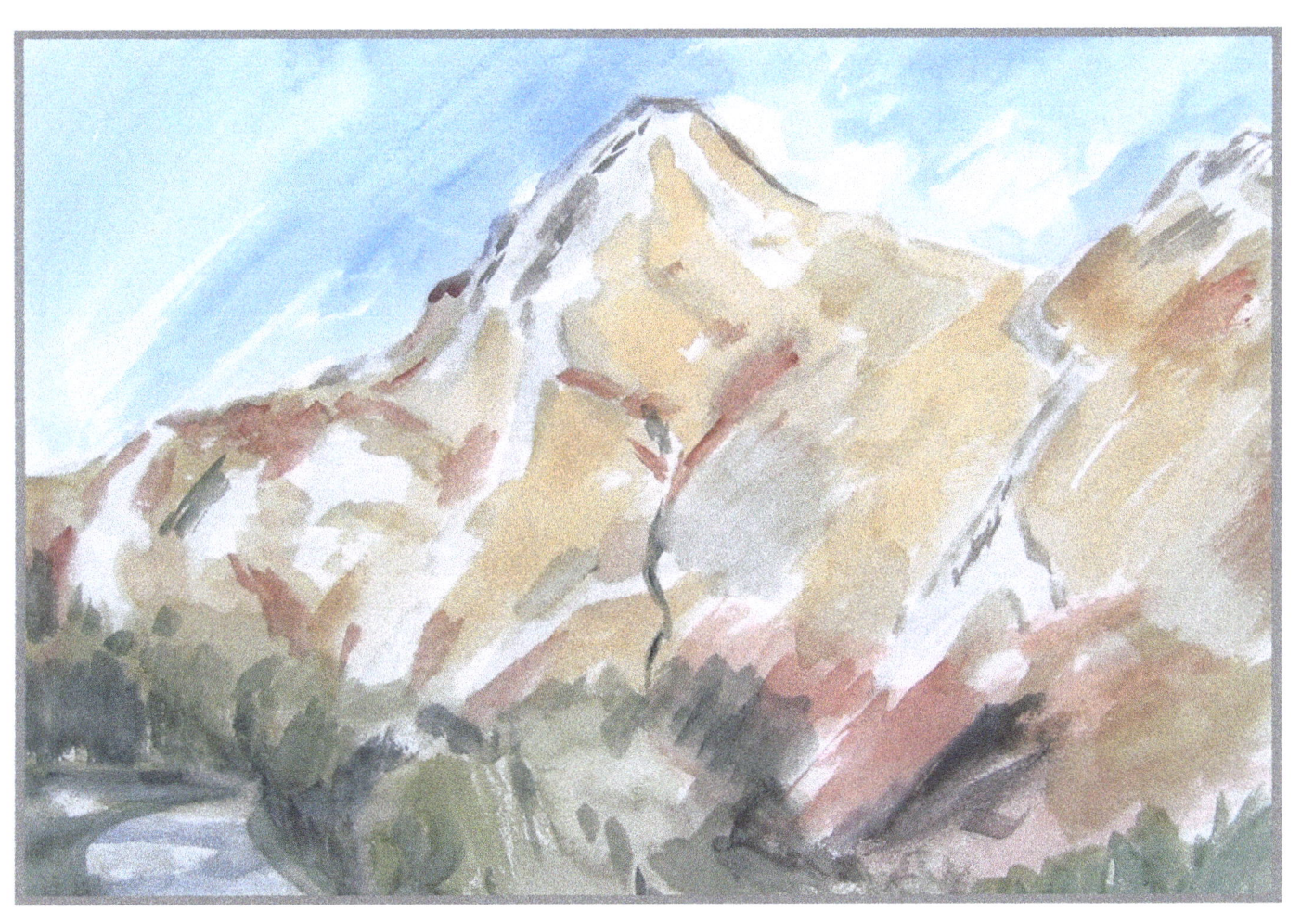

Glen Shiel
By John Robertson
July 2015 Watercolour 20" x 16"

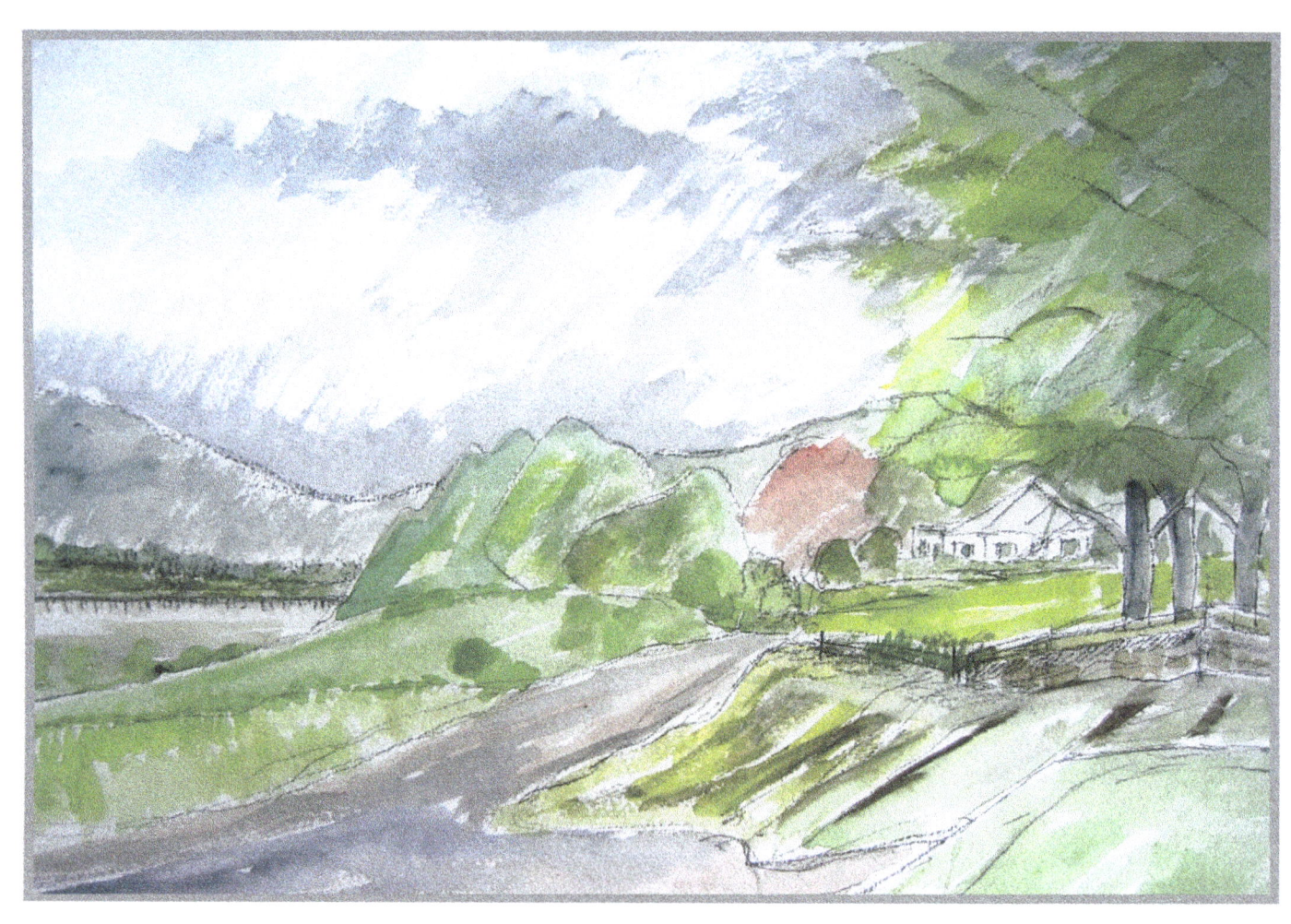

Black Isle
By Jane Robertson
04.07.2013 Watercolour 16" x 12"

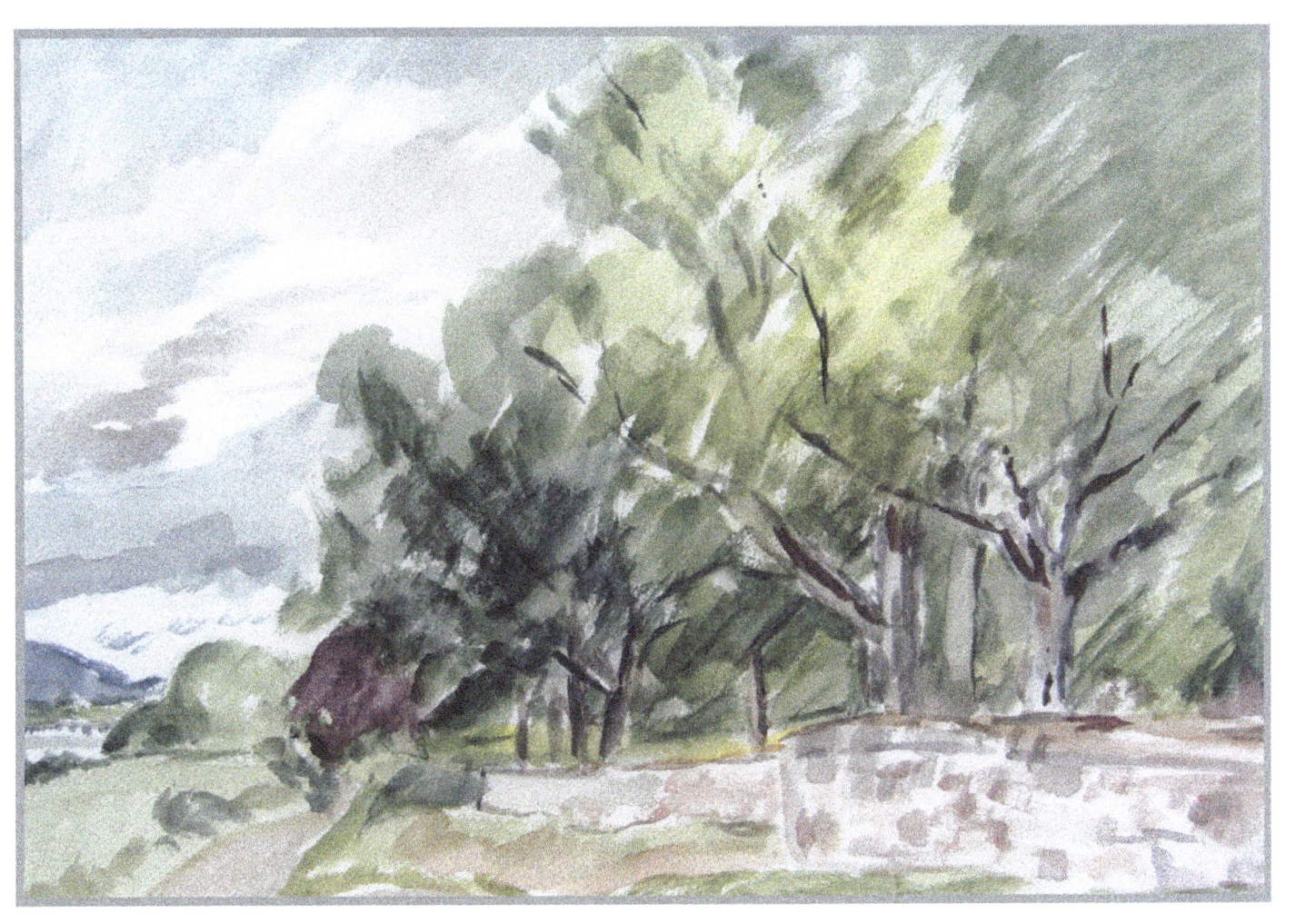

Black Isle
By John Robertson
04.07.2013 Watercolour 20" x 16"

English Landscape
John

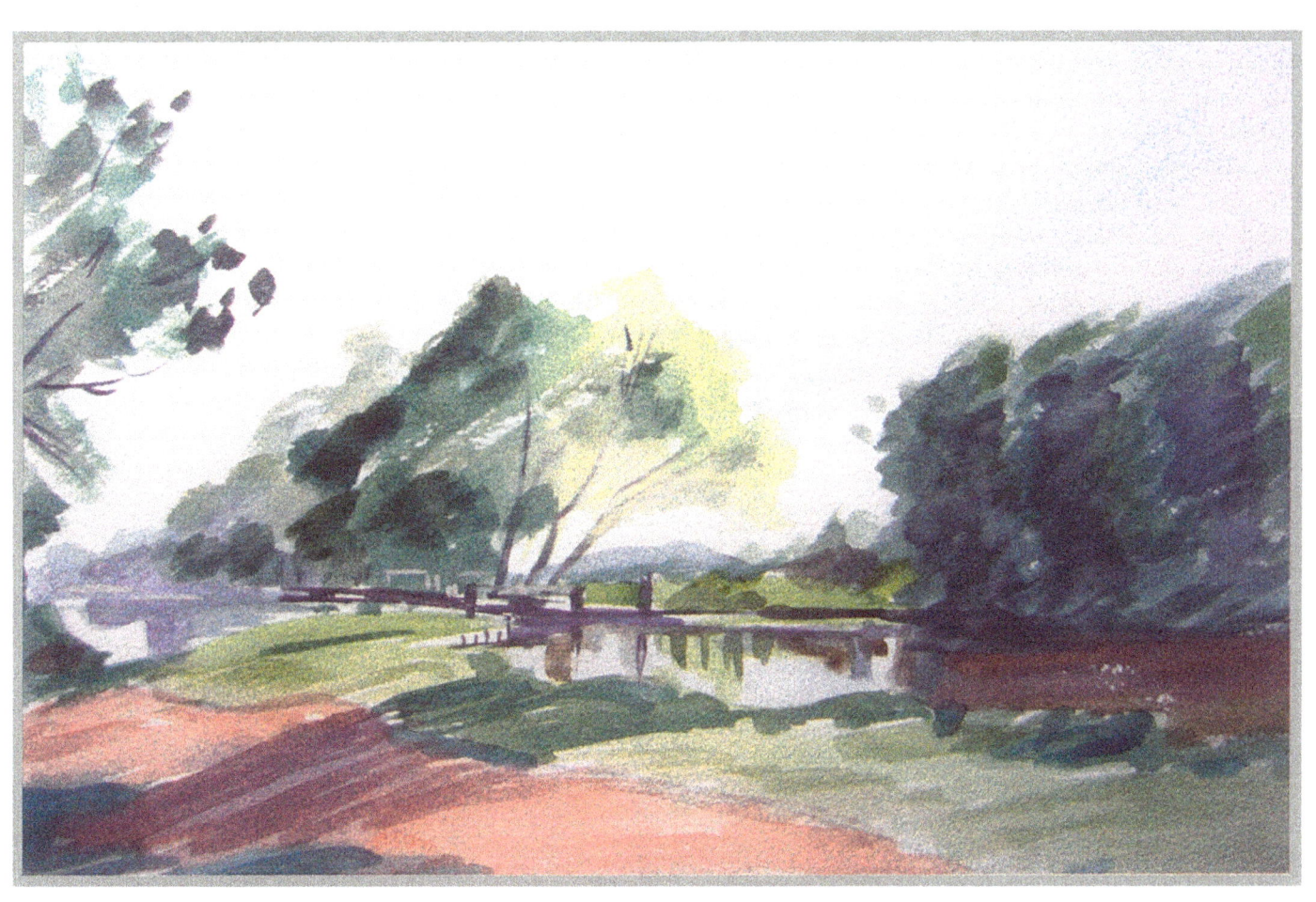

Fradley Junction
By John Robertson
Pre 2007 Watercolour 20" x 16"

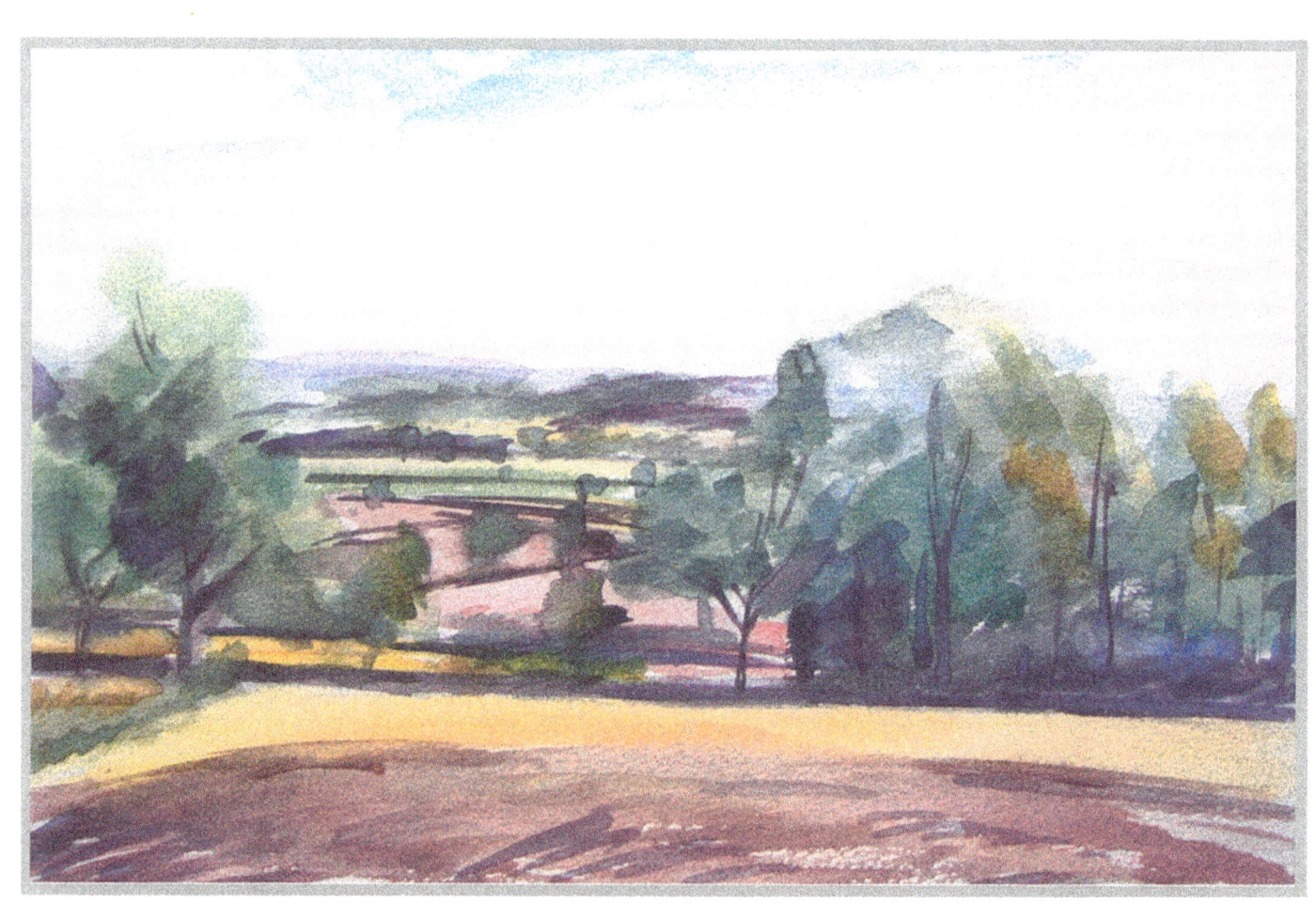

Barton Fields
By John Robertson
Pre 2007 Watercolour 20" x 16"

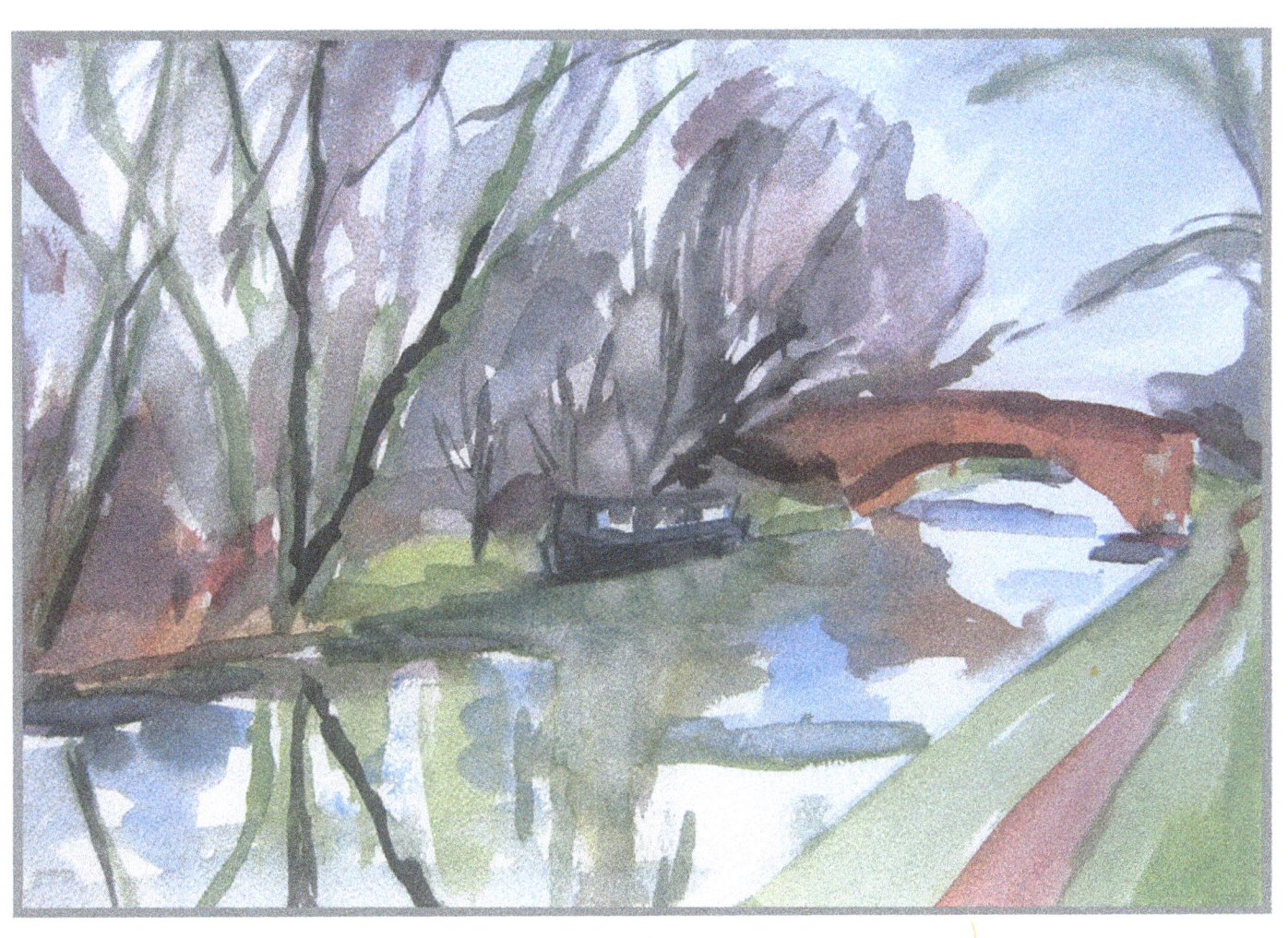

Trent and Mersey
By John Robertson
06.01.2000 Watercolour 20" x 16"

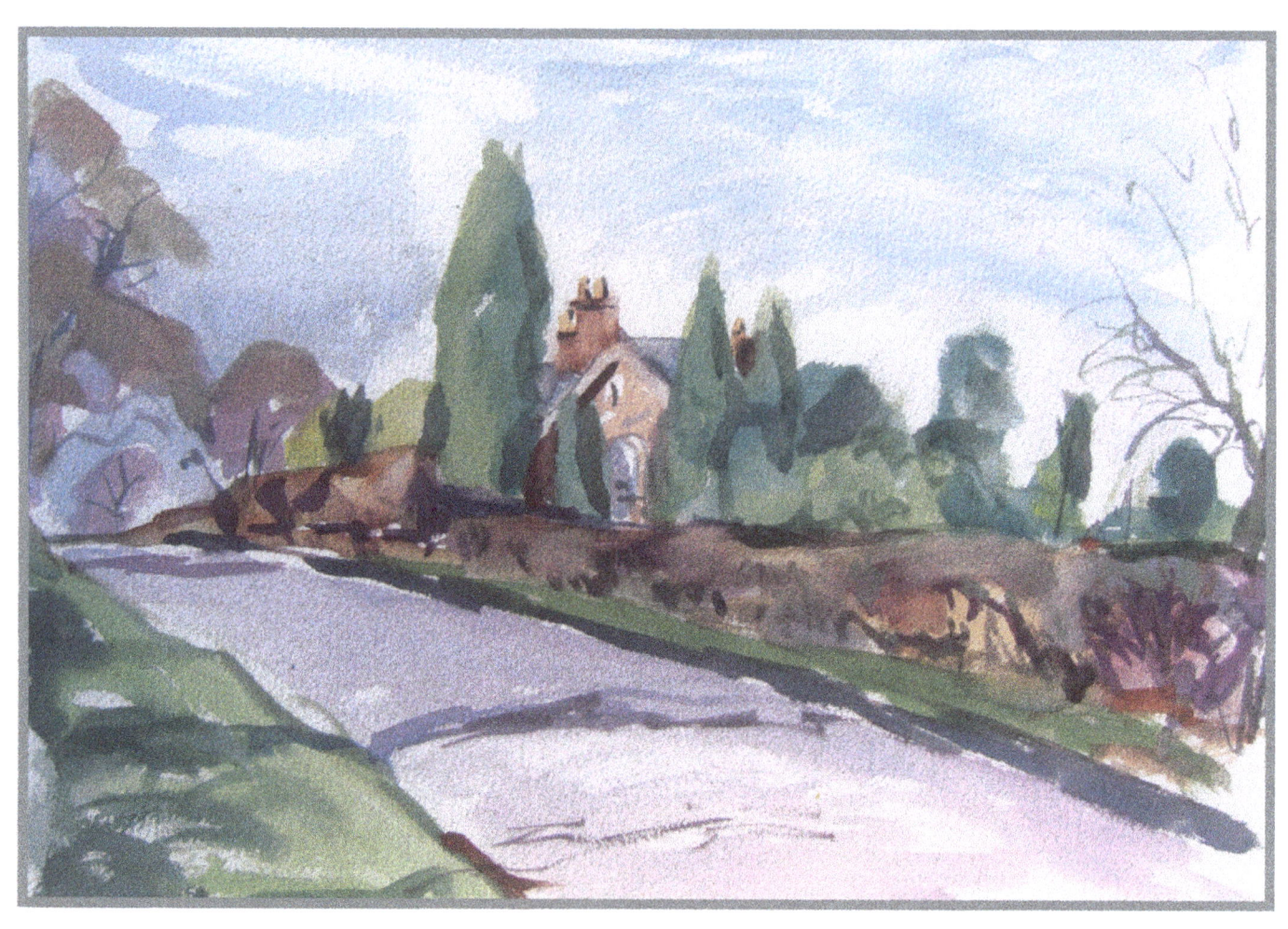

Tatenhill
By John Robertson
02.02.2000 Watercolour 20" x 16"

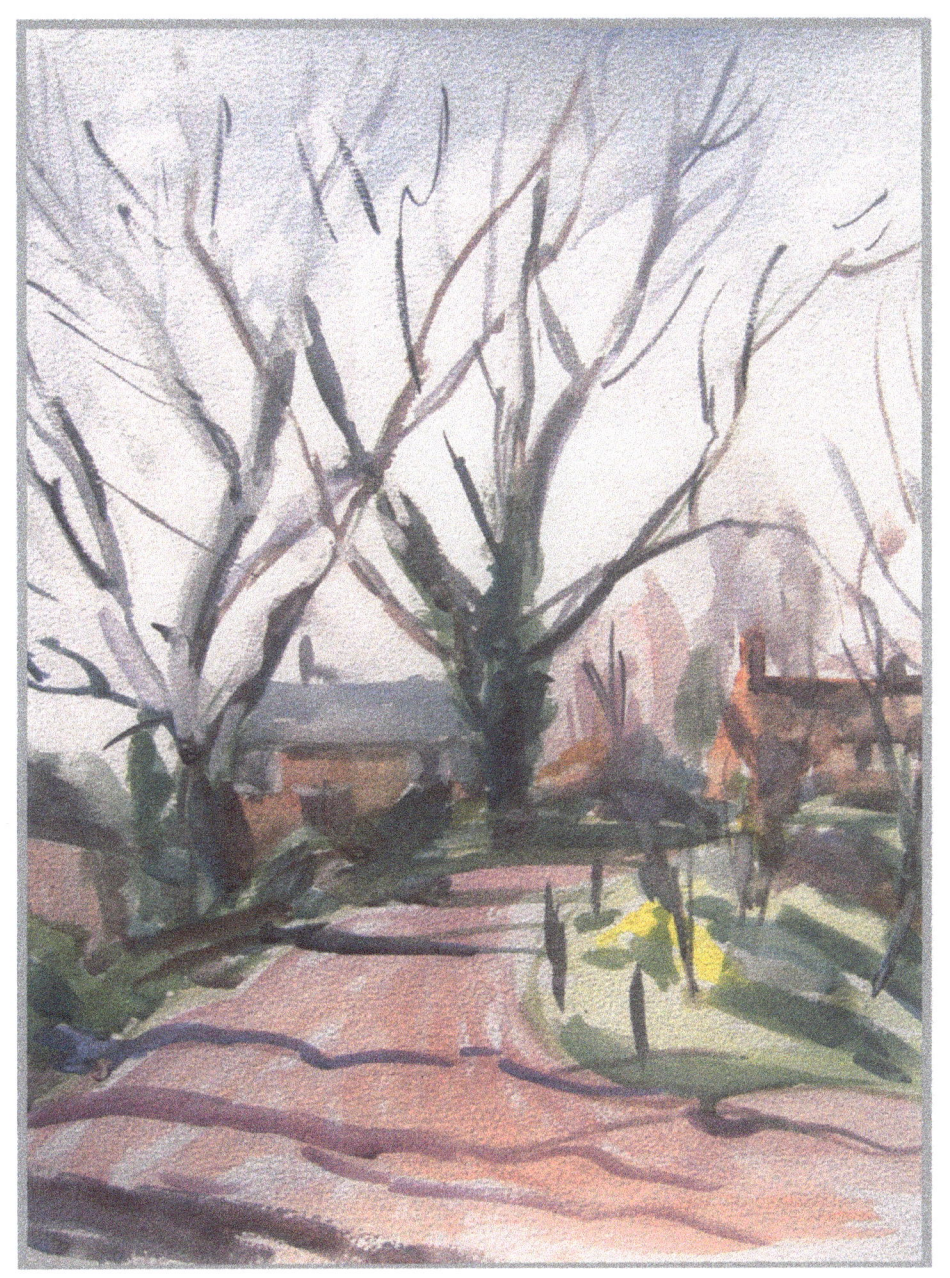

Tatenhill
By John Robertson
22.03.1998 Watercolour 20" x 16"

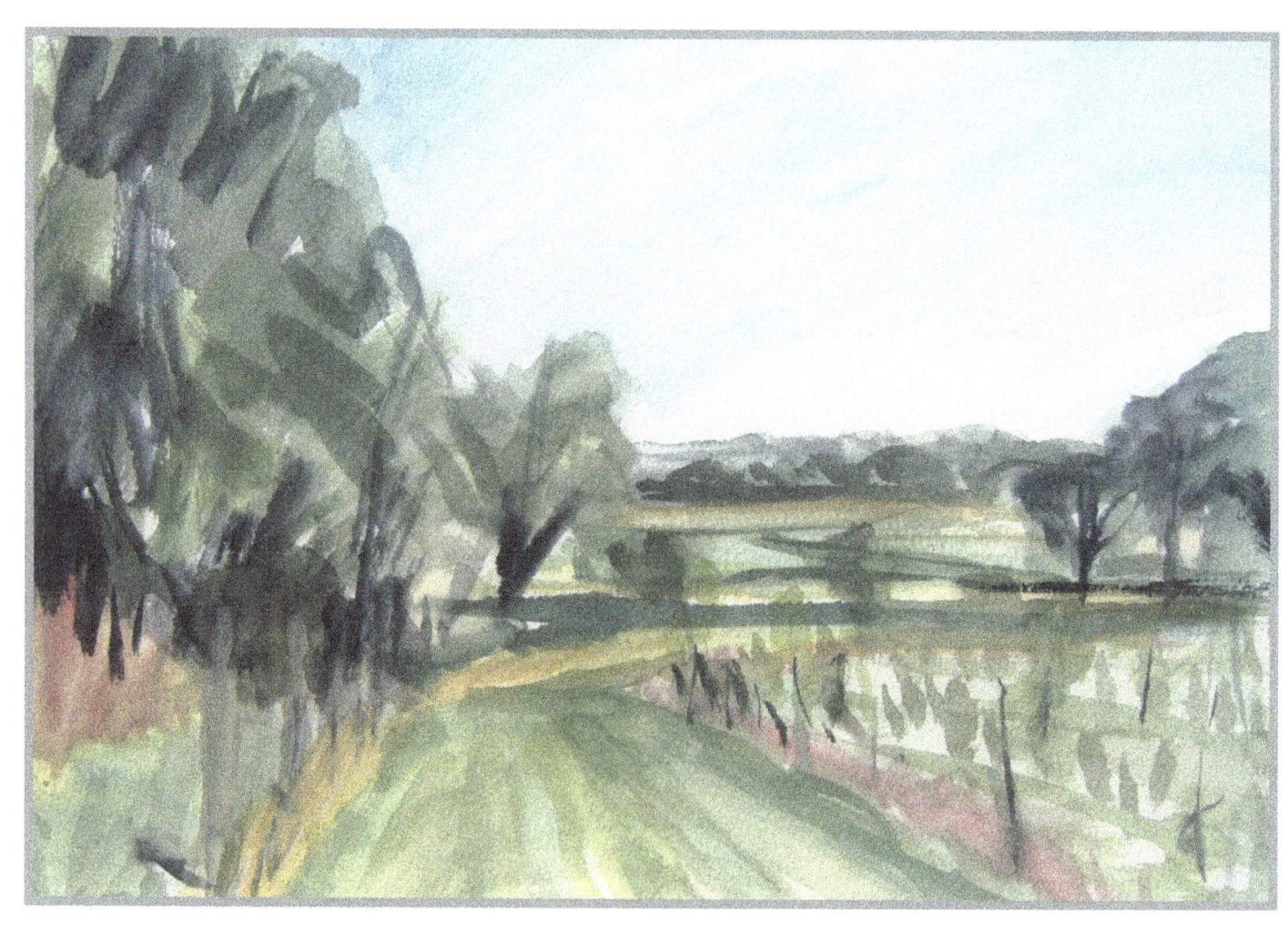

Barton
By John Robertson
07.09.2004 Watercolour 20" x 16"

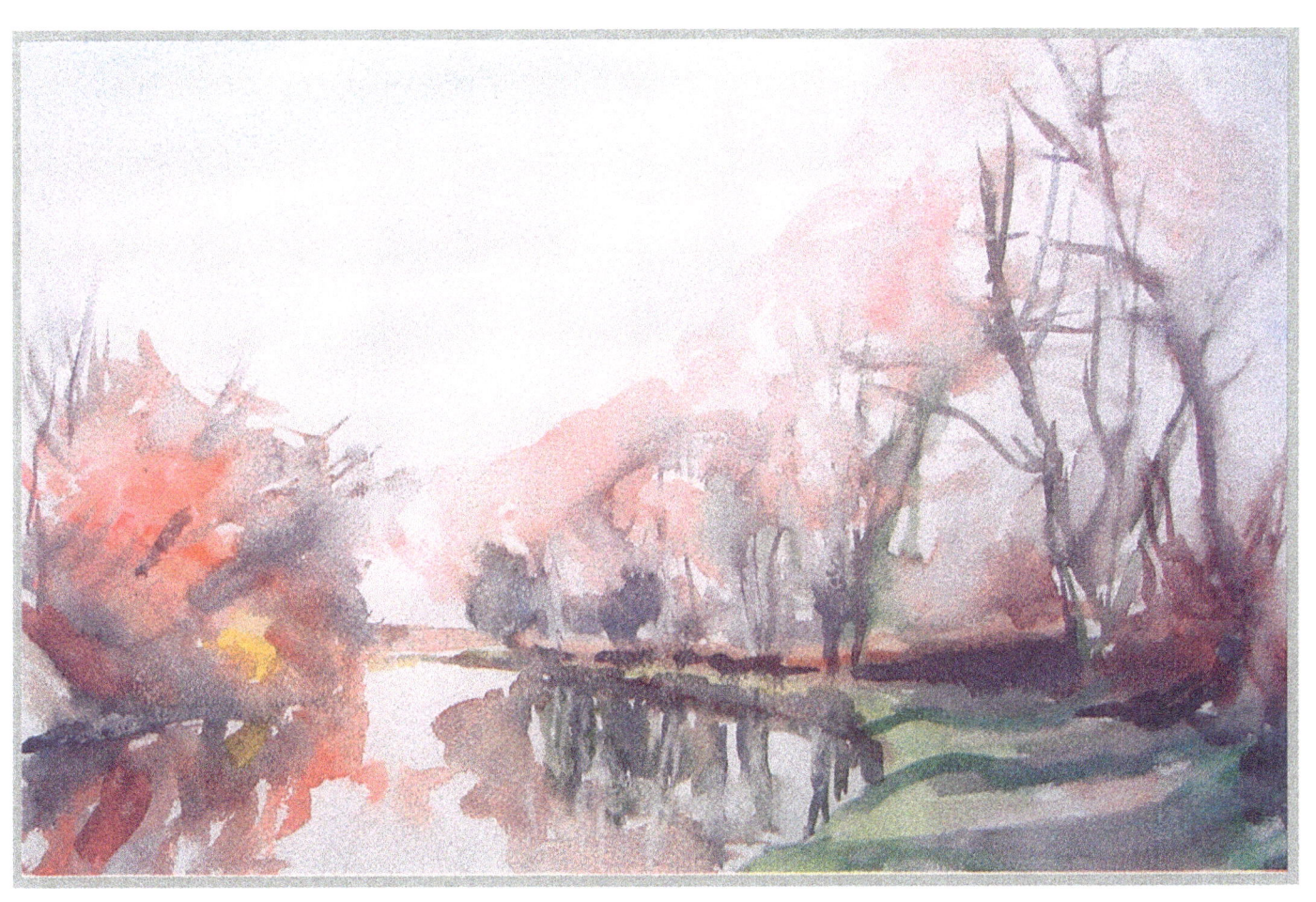

Reflections on the Trent and Mersey
By John Robertson
Pre 2007 Watercolour 20" x 16"

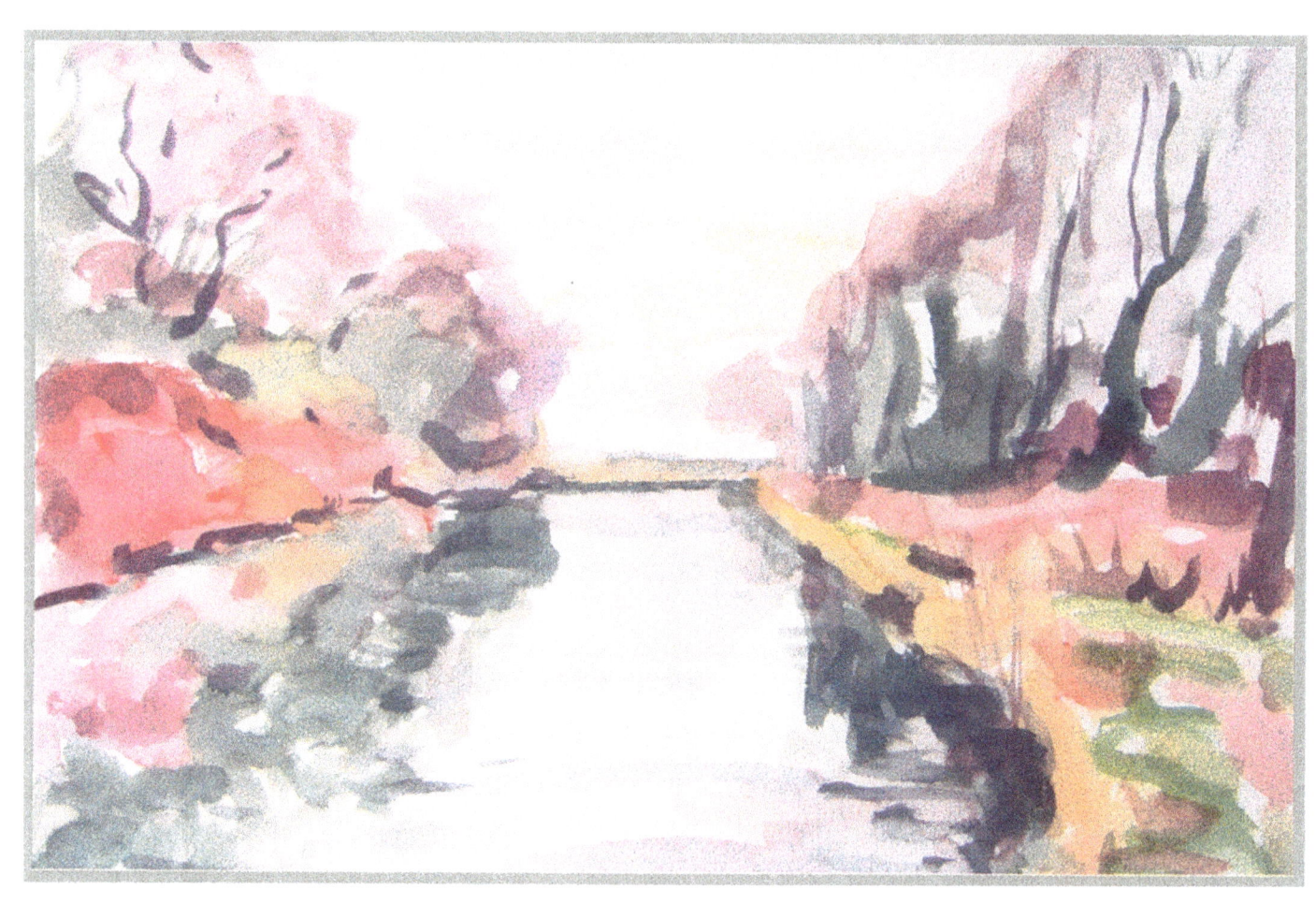

Trent and Mersey Canal II
By John Robertson
Post 2007 Watercolour 20" x 16"

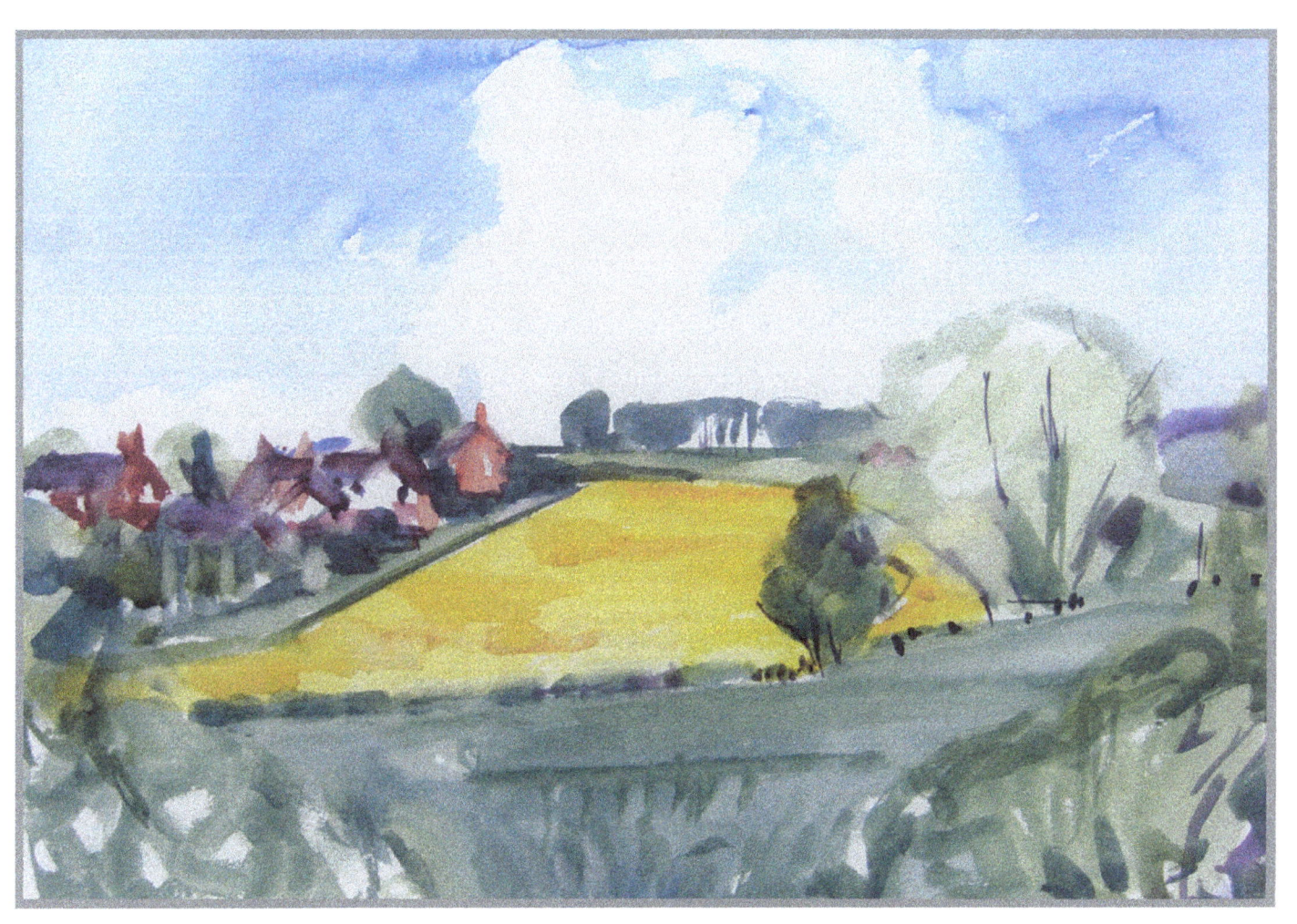

The Top Bell
By John Robertson
2000 Watercolour 20" x 16"

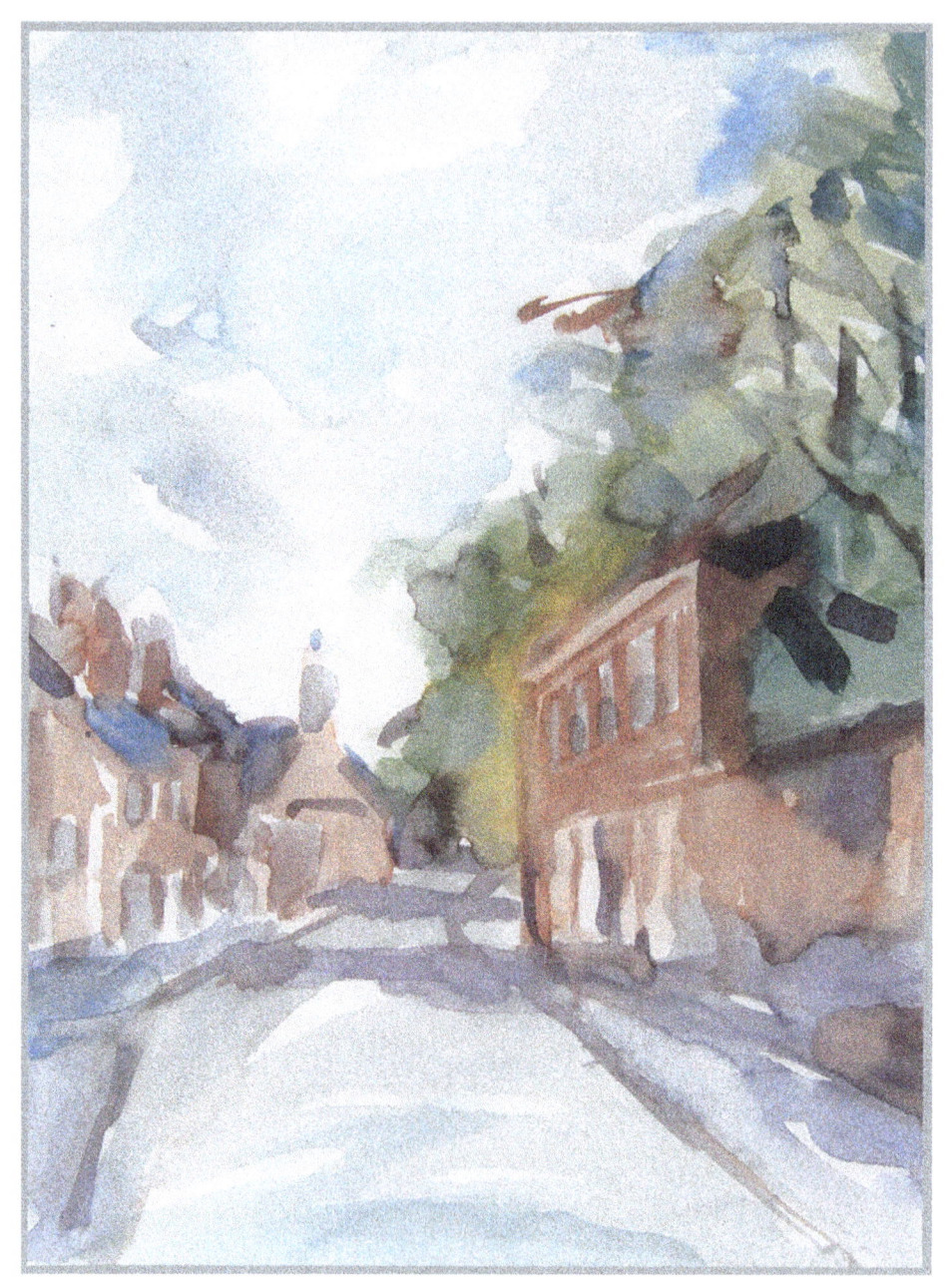

Barton
By John Robertson
12.10.1999 Watercolour 20" x 16"

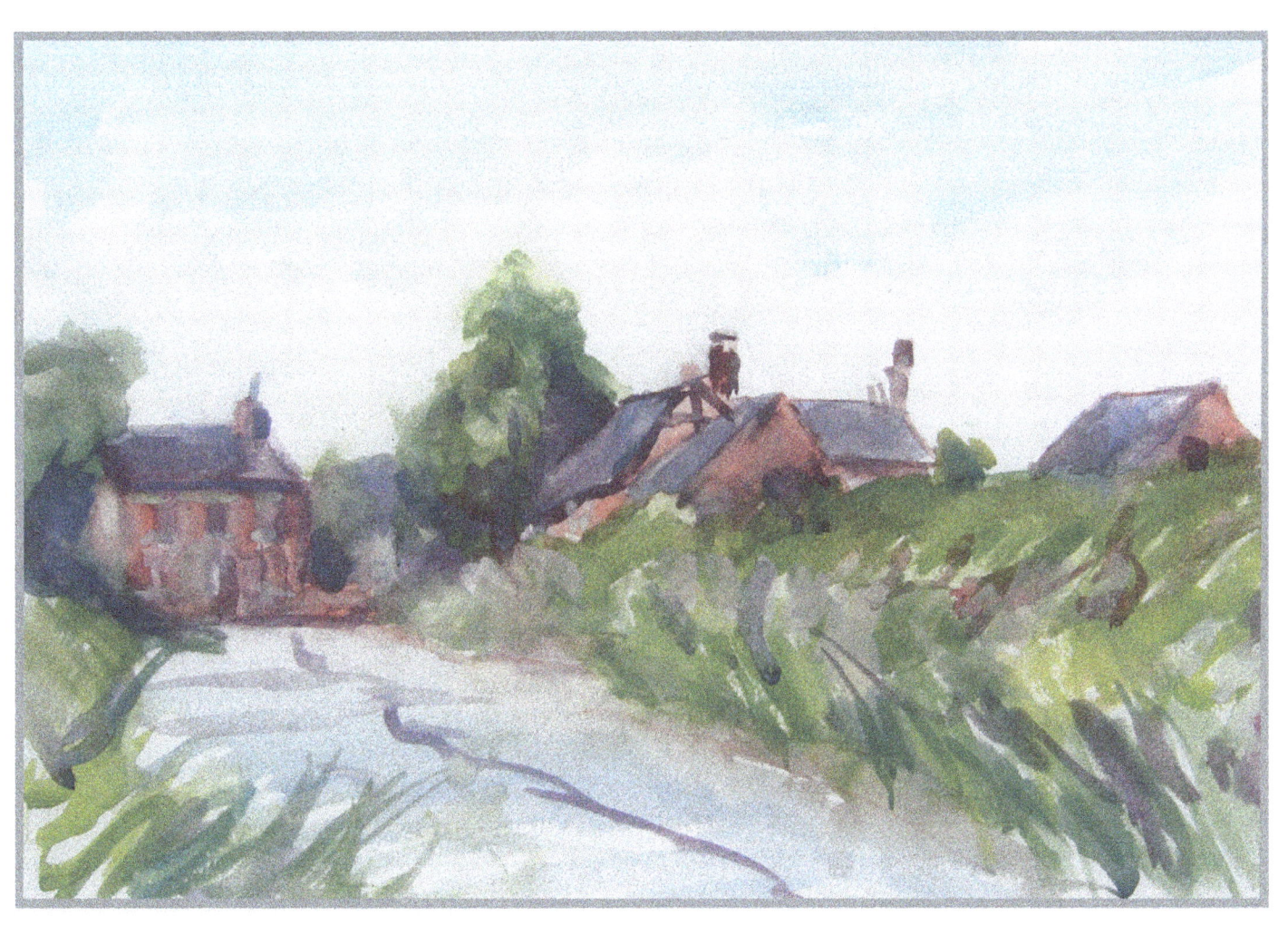

Dog's Head Lane
By John Robertson
15.06.1996 Watercolour 20" x 16"

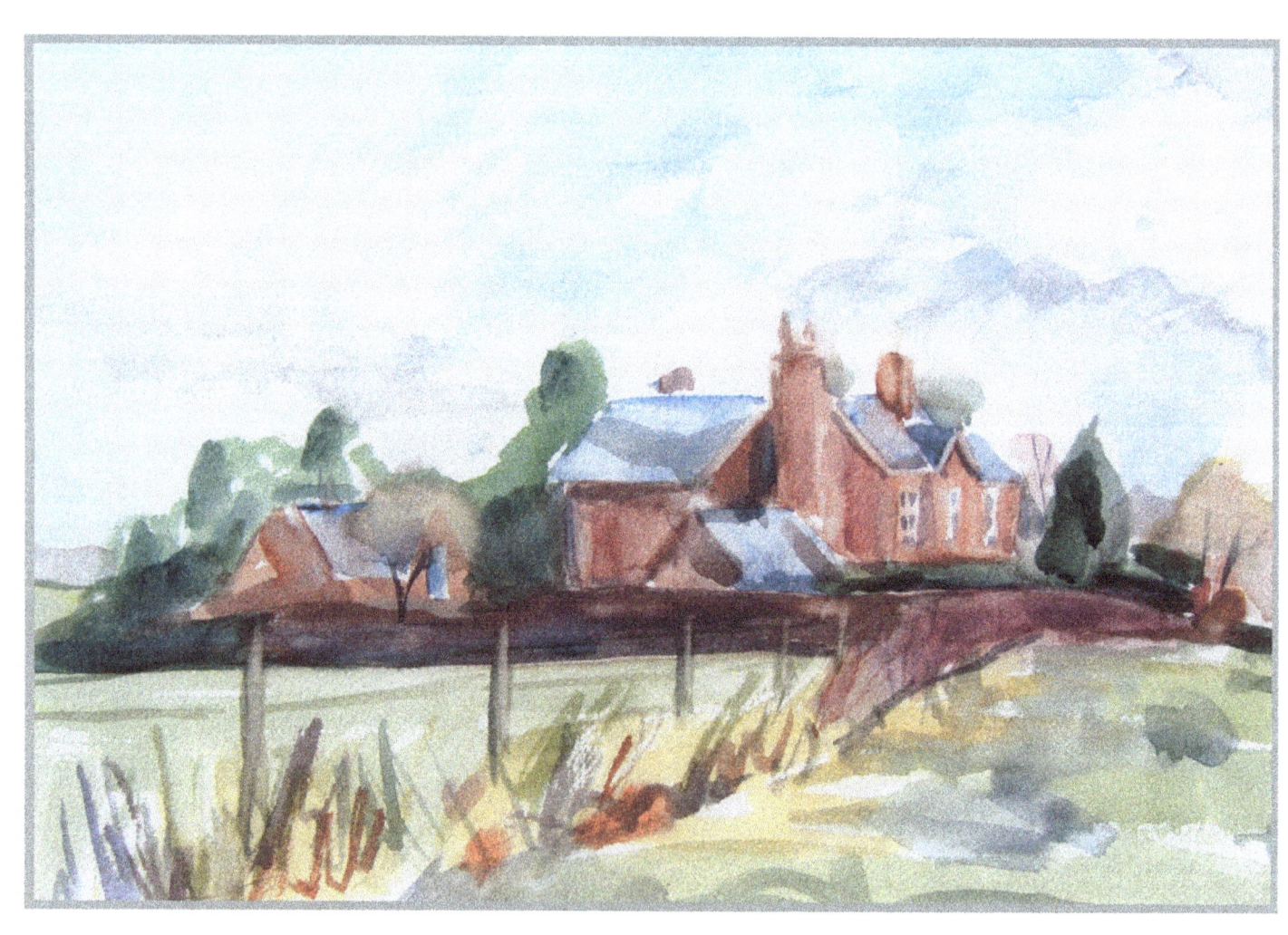

Tatenhilll
By John Robertson
21.02.2000 Watercolour 20" x 16"

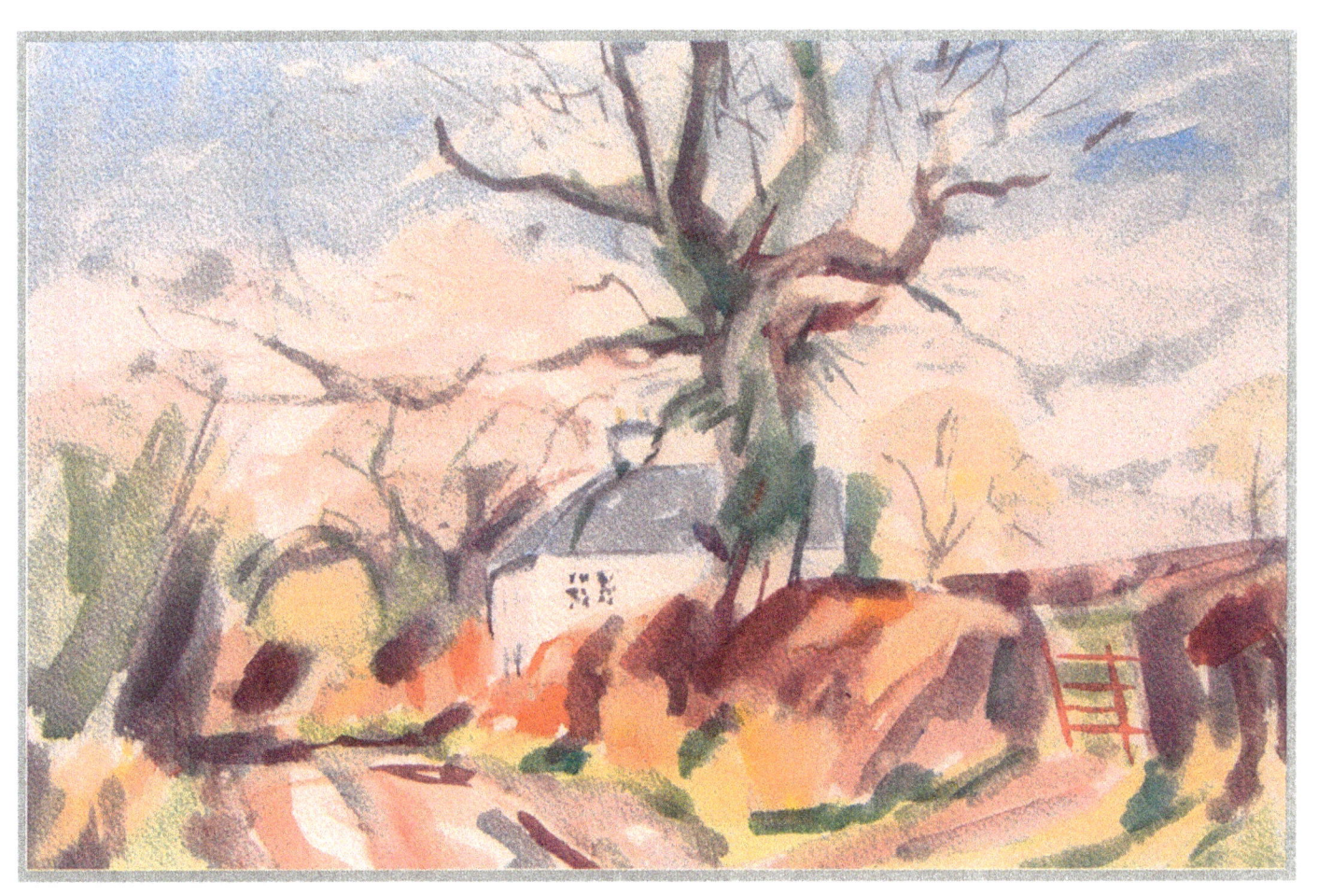

Sich Lane
By John Robertson
Pre 2007 Watercolour 20" x 16"

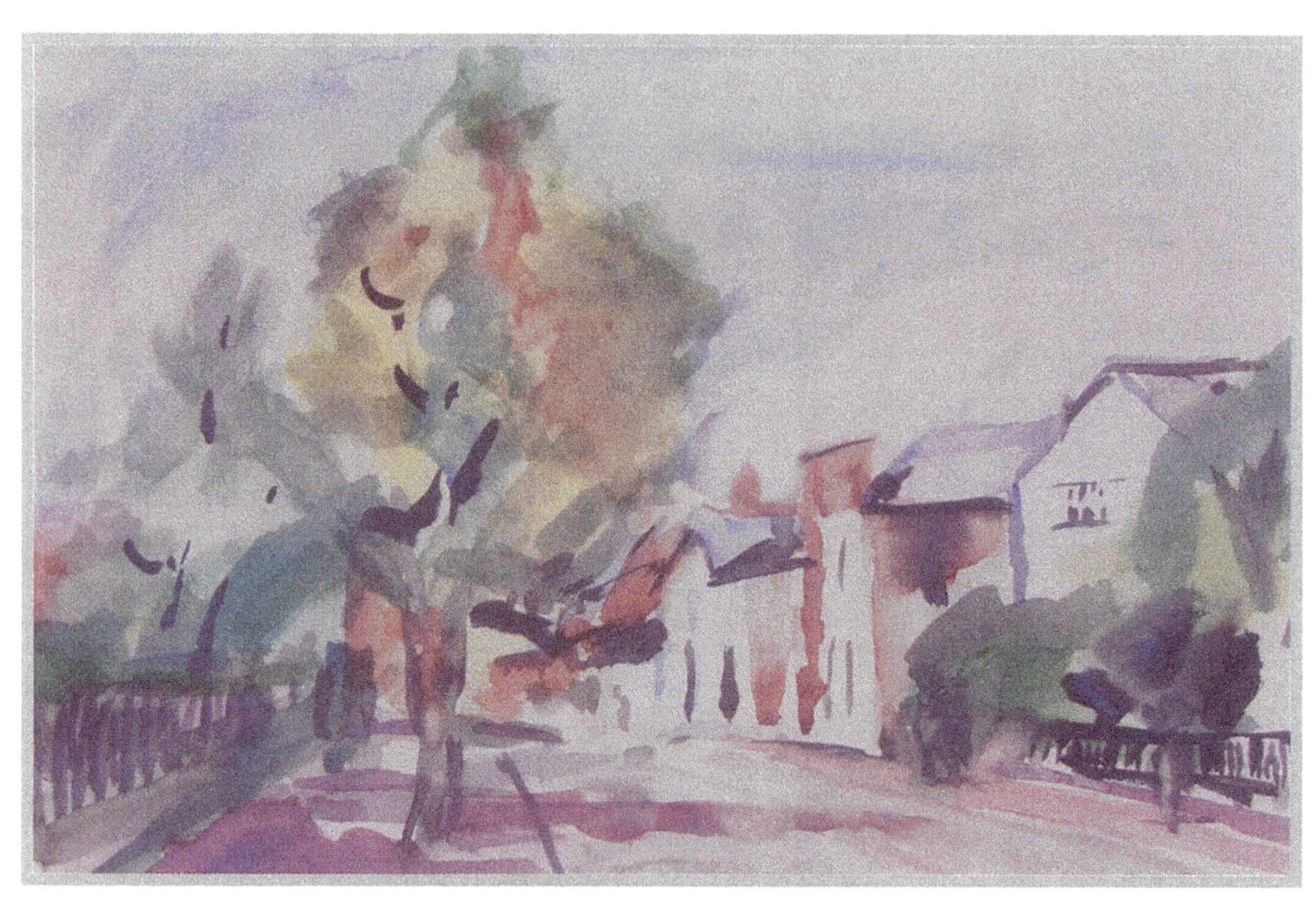

Barton-Under-Needwood
By John Robertson
Pre 2007 Watercolour 20" x 16"

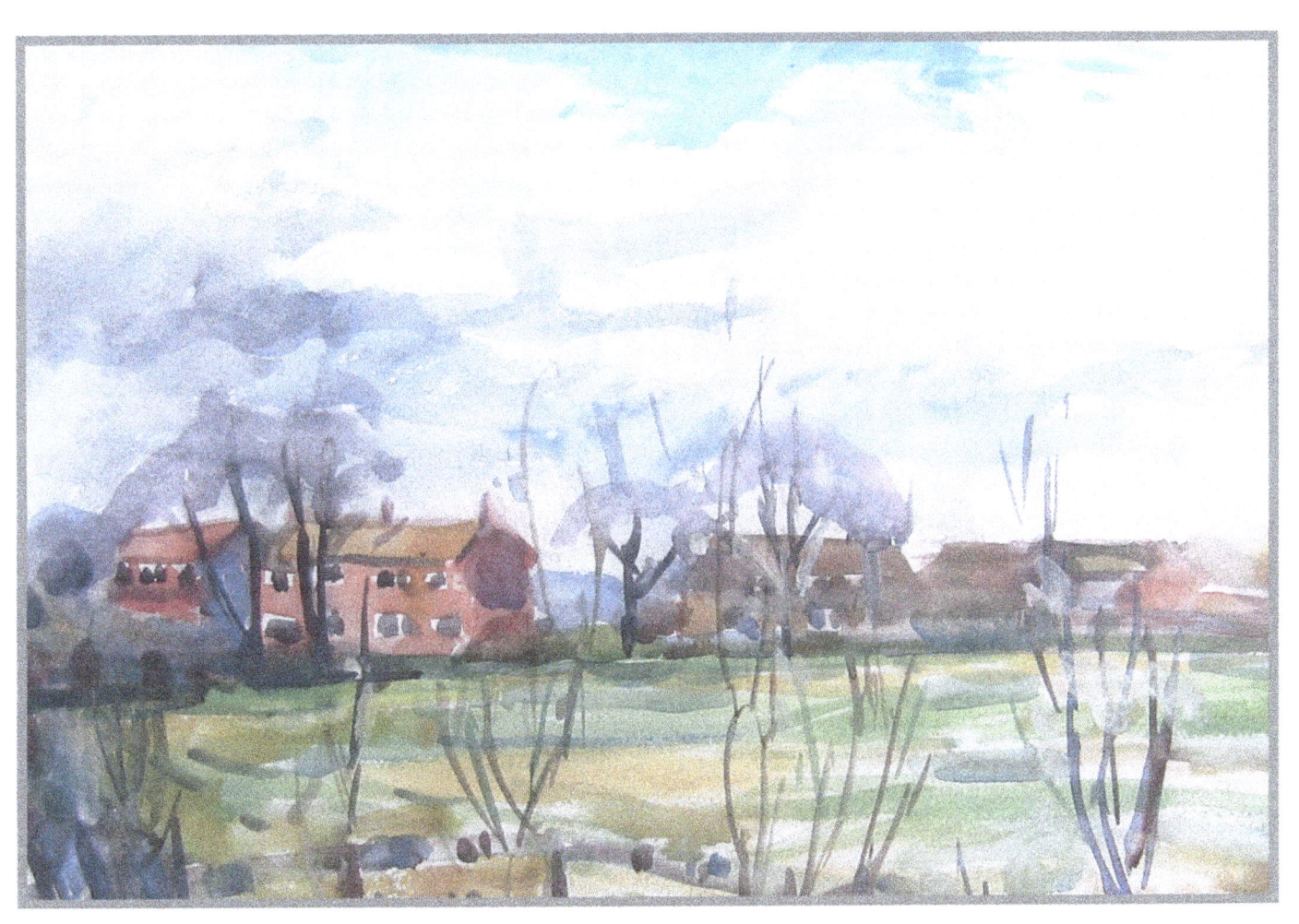

Mill Lane
By John Robertson
28.02.1998 Watercolour 20" x 16"

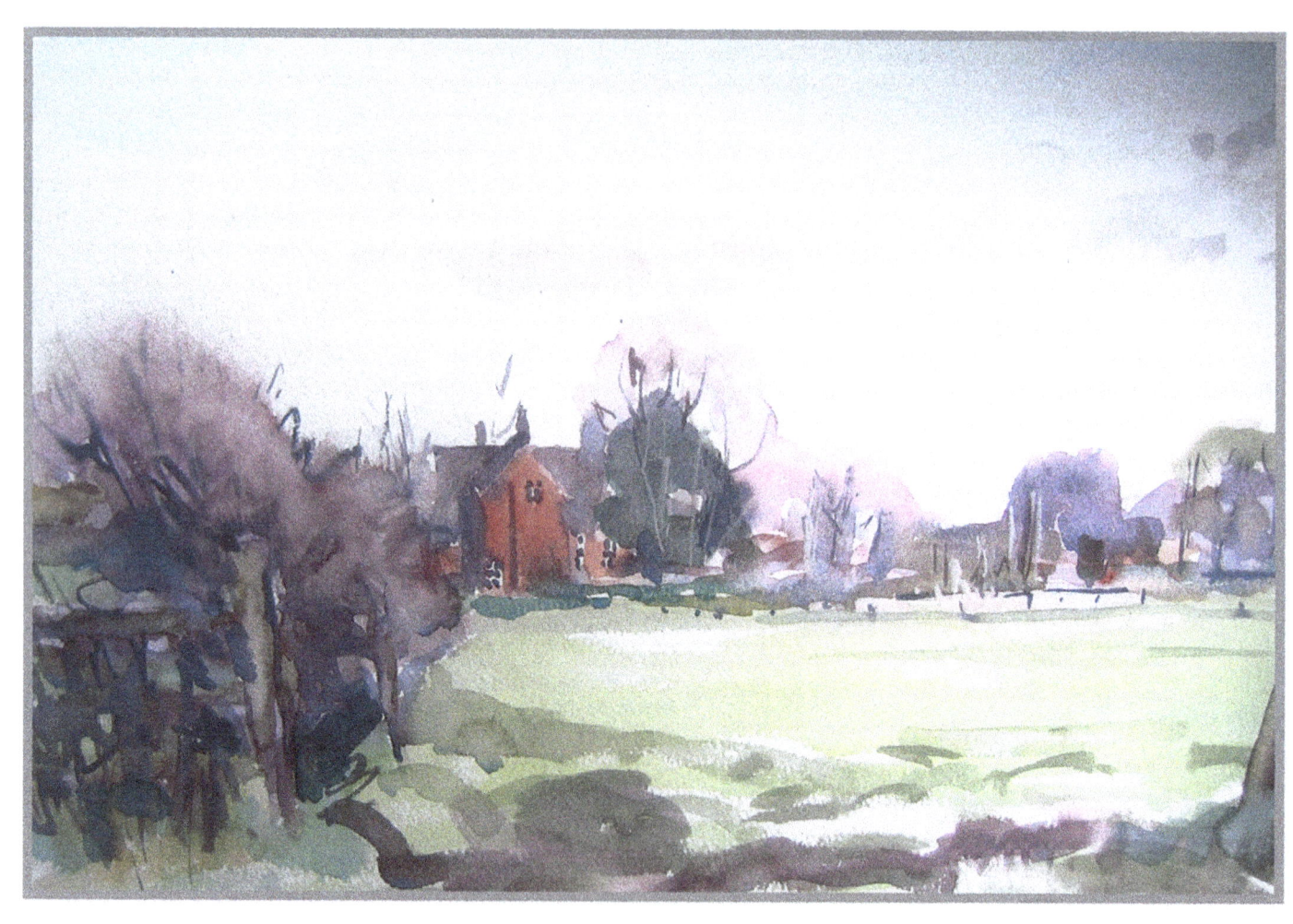

Bar Lane
By John Robertson
28.01.1999 Watercolour 20" x 16"

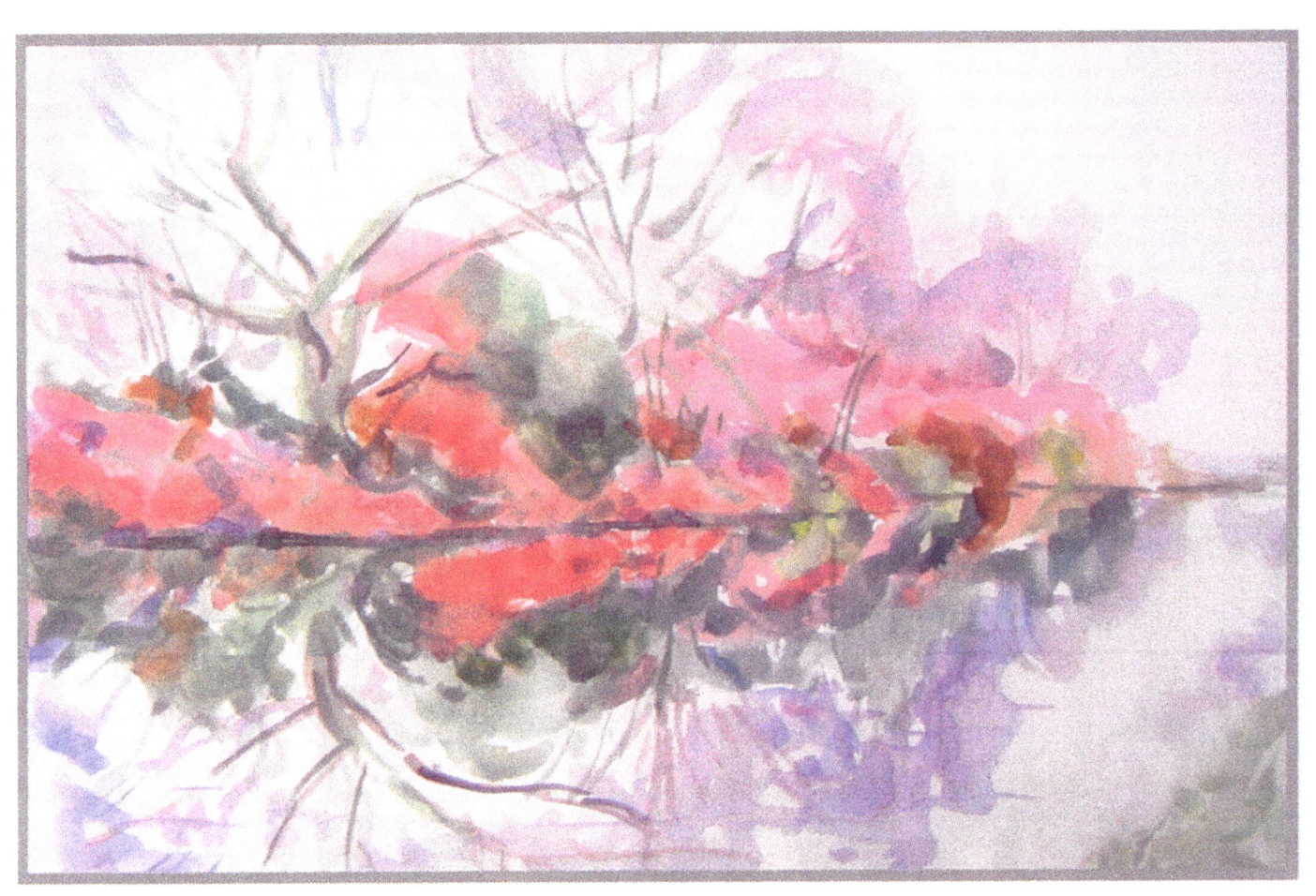

The Canal at Barton
By John Robertson
Pre 2007 Watercolour 20" x 16"

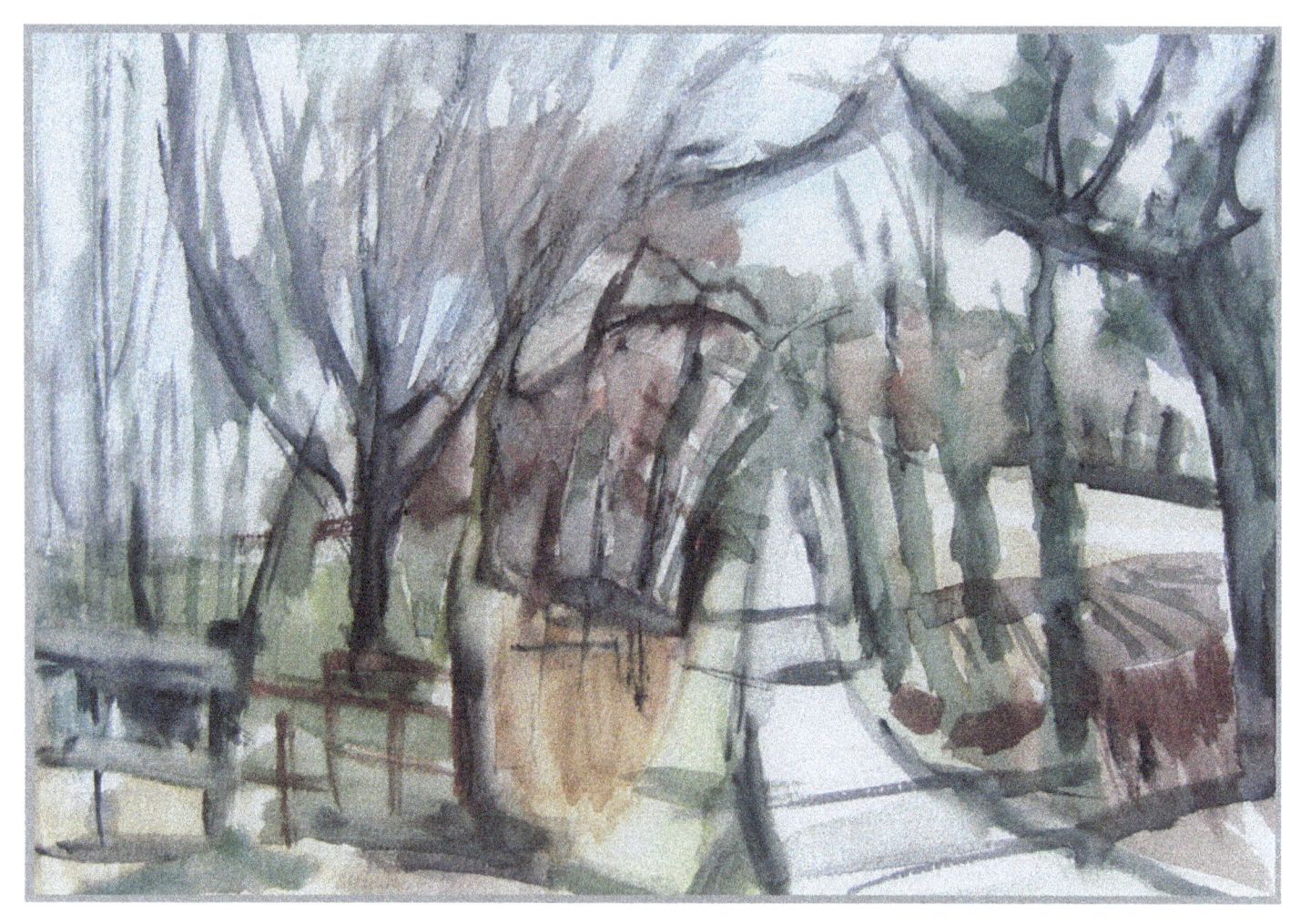

Scotch Hills
By John Robertson
28.02.2004 Watercolour 20" x 16"

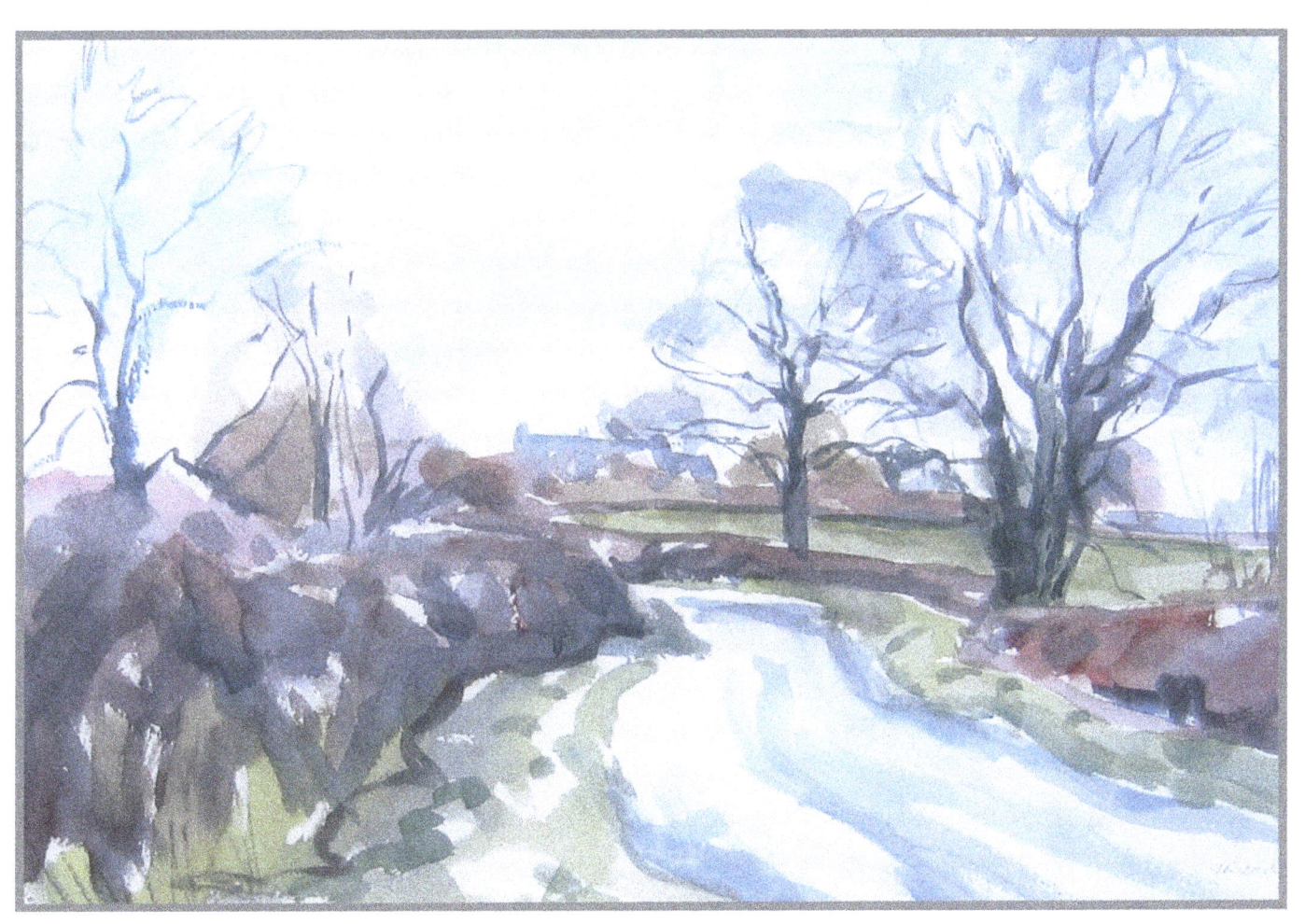

First Snow
By John Robertson
17.02.2000 Watercolour 20" x 16"

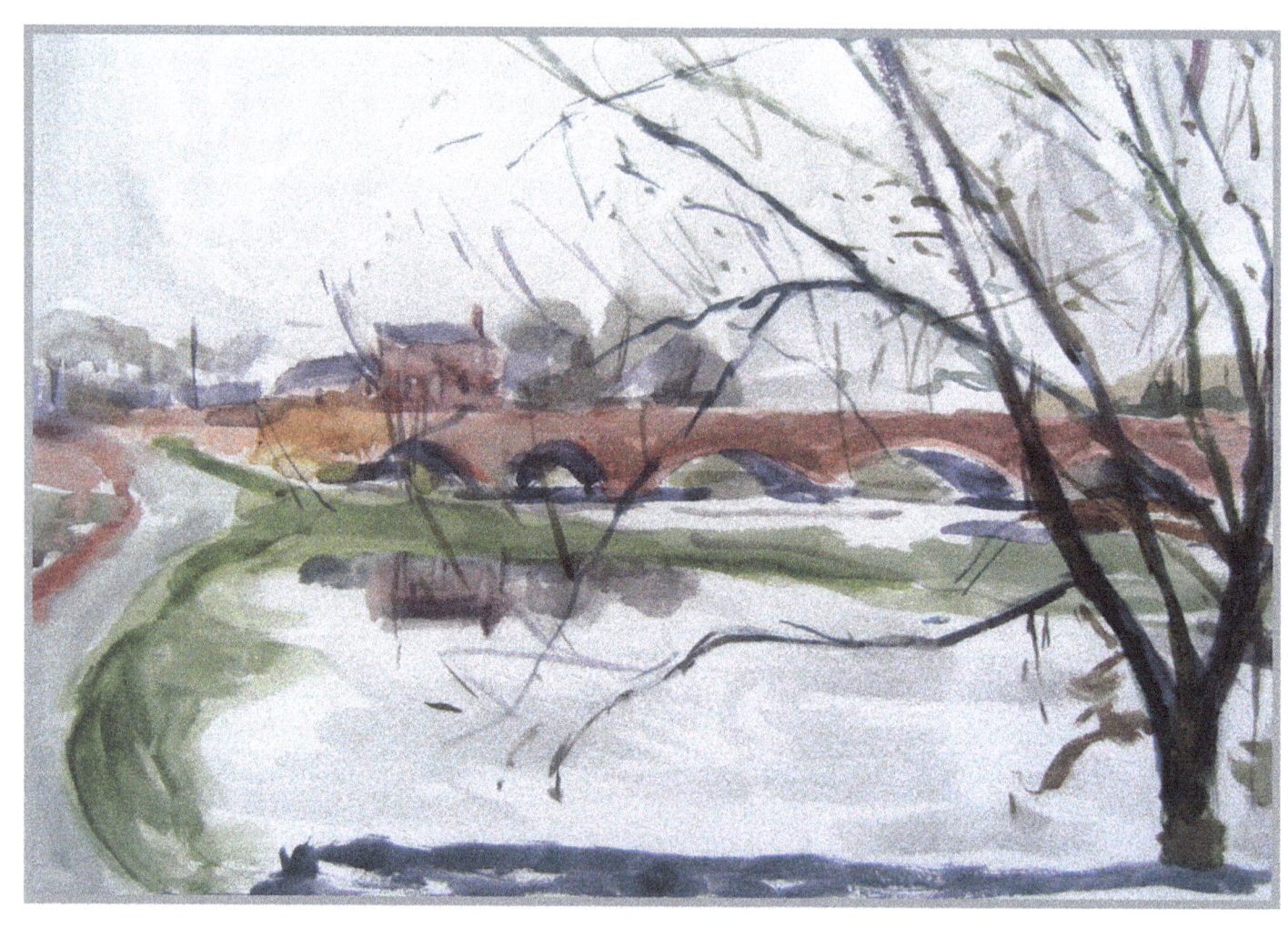

The Flood, Burton
By John Robertson
01.01.2003 Watercolour 20" x 16"

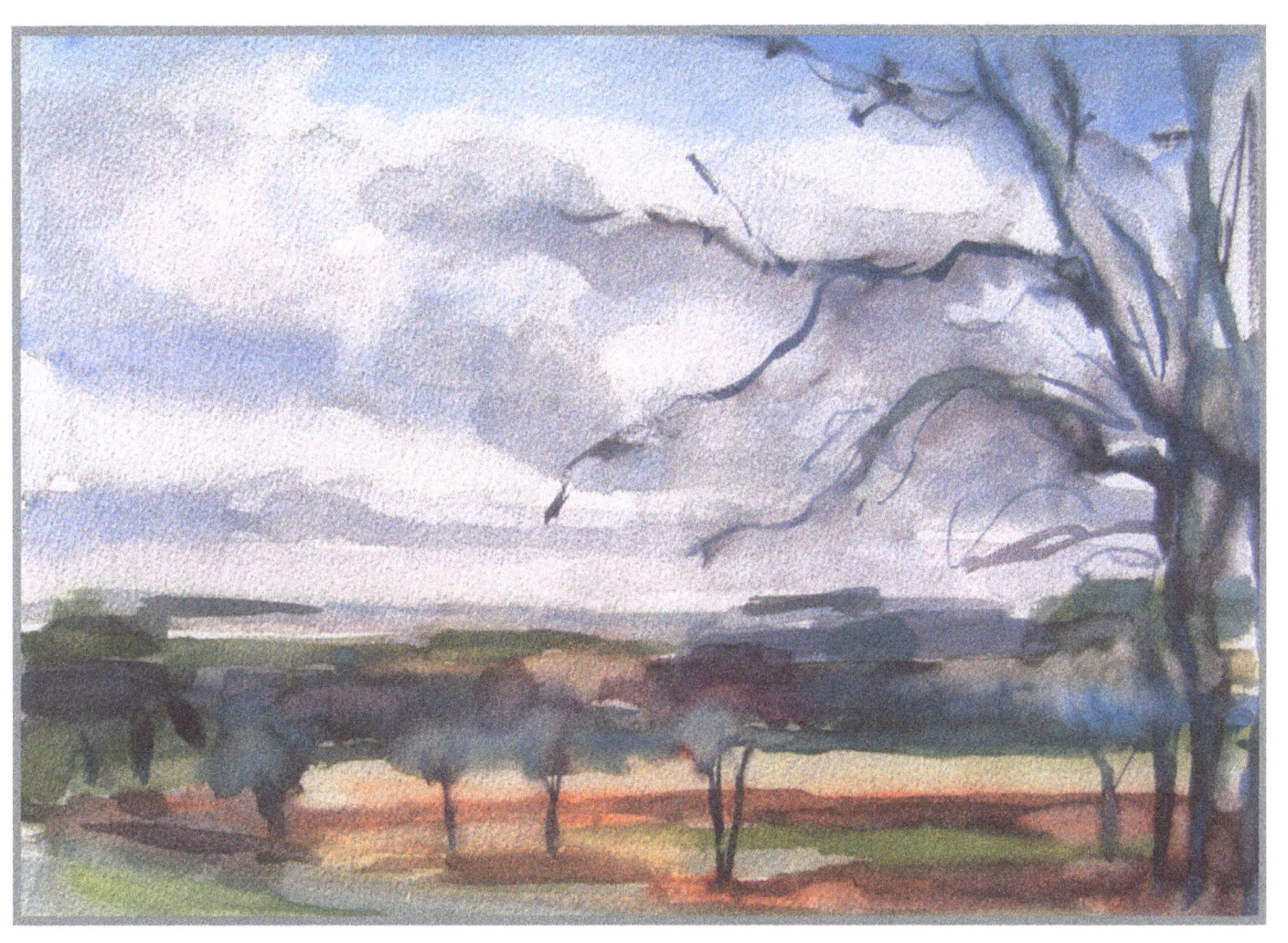

Tatenhill
By John Robertson
10.02.2000 Watercolour 20" x 16"

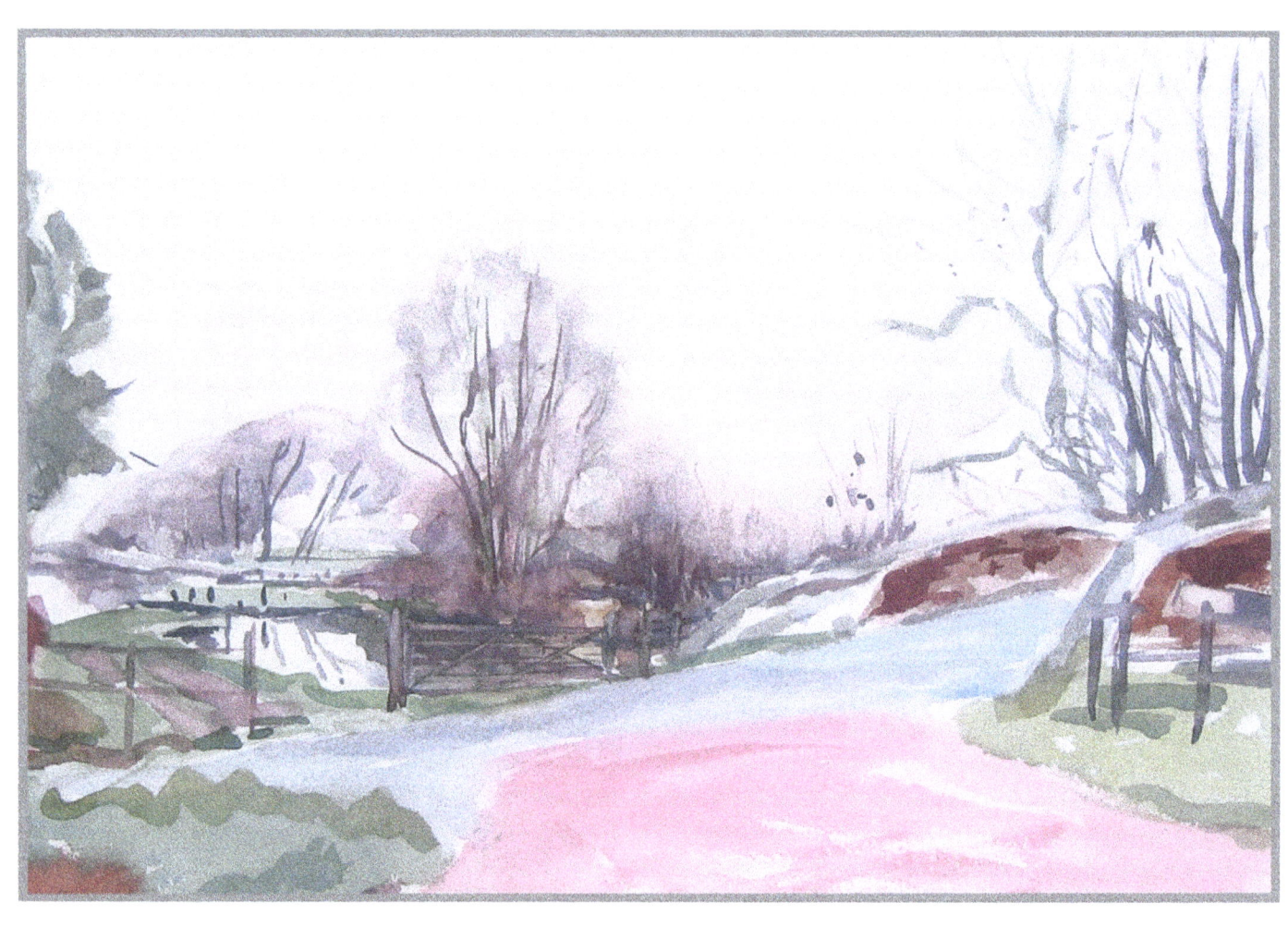

Fradley Junction
By John Robertson
29.01.1999 Watercolour 20" x 16"

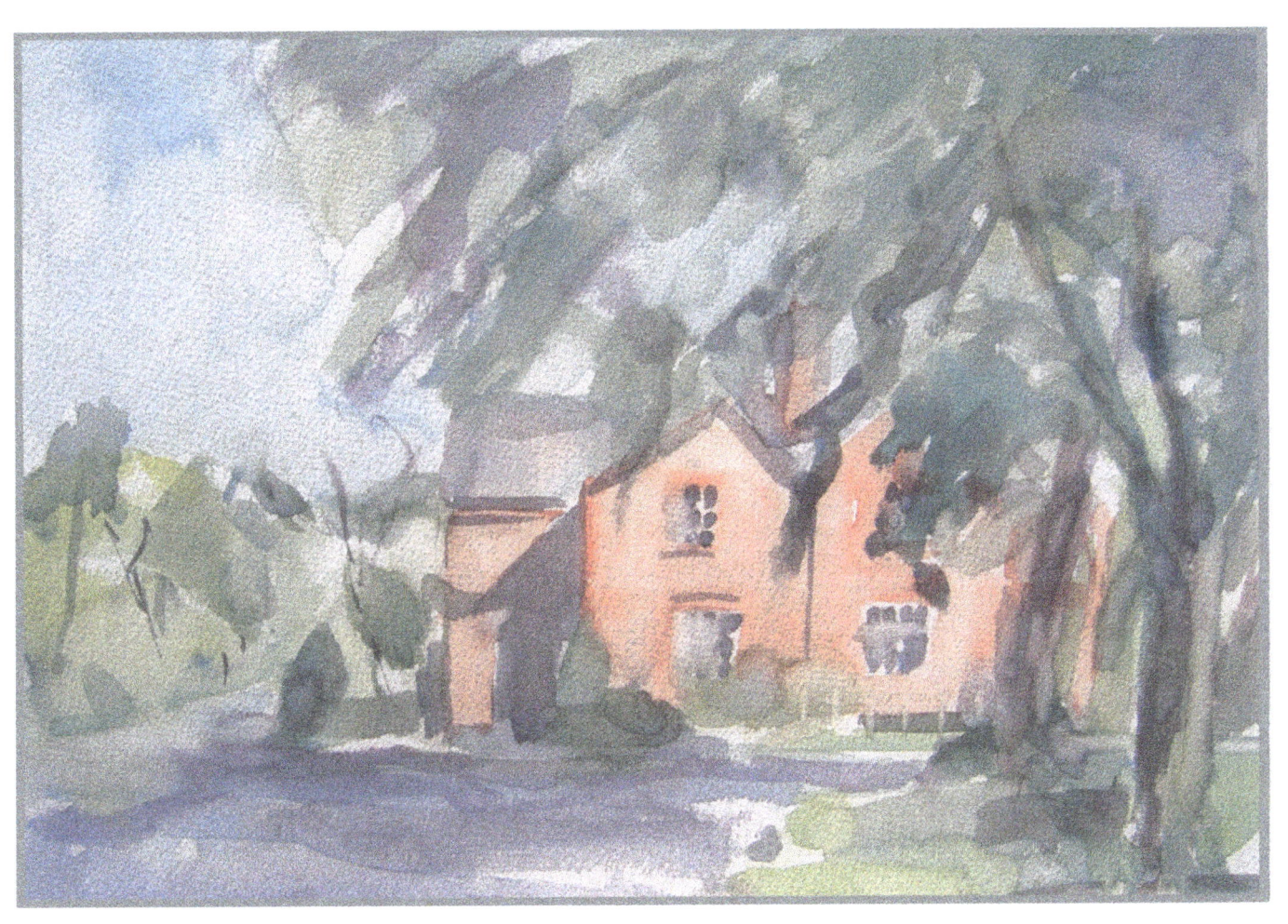

Hoar Cross
By John Robertson
09.09.1999 Watercolour 20" x 16"

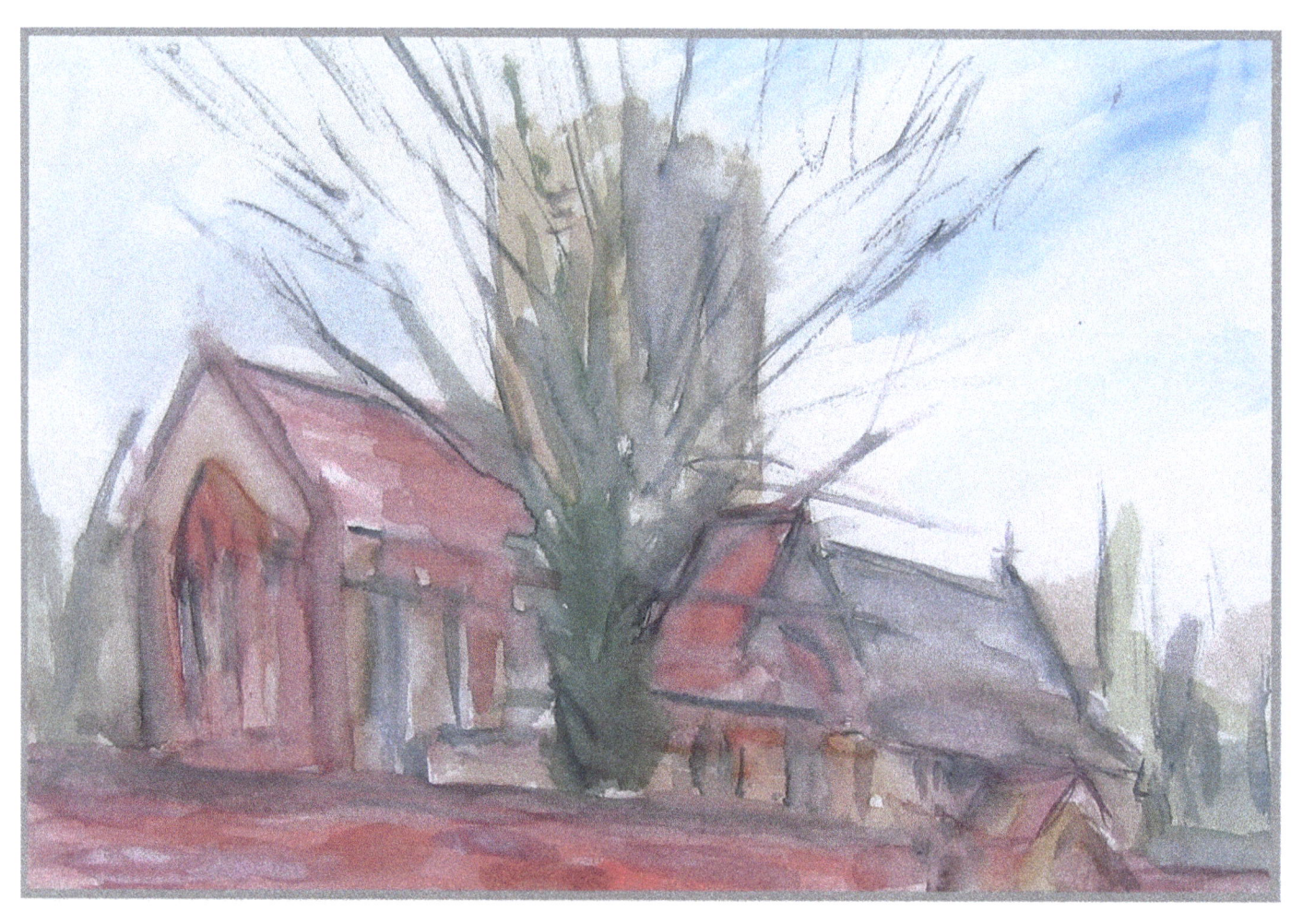

Hoar Cross Church
By John Robertson
24.01.2005 Watercolour 20" x 16"

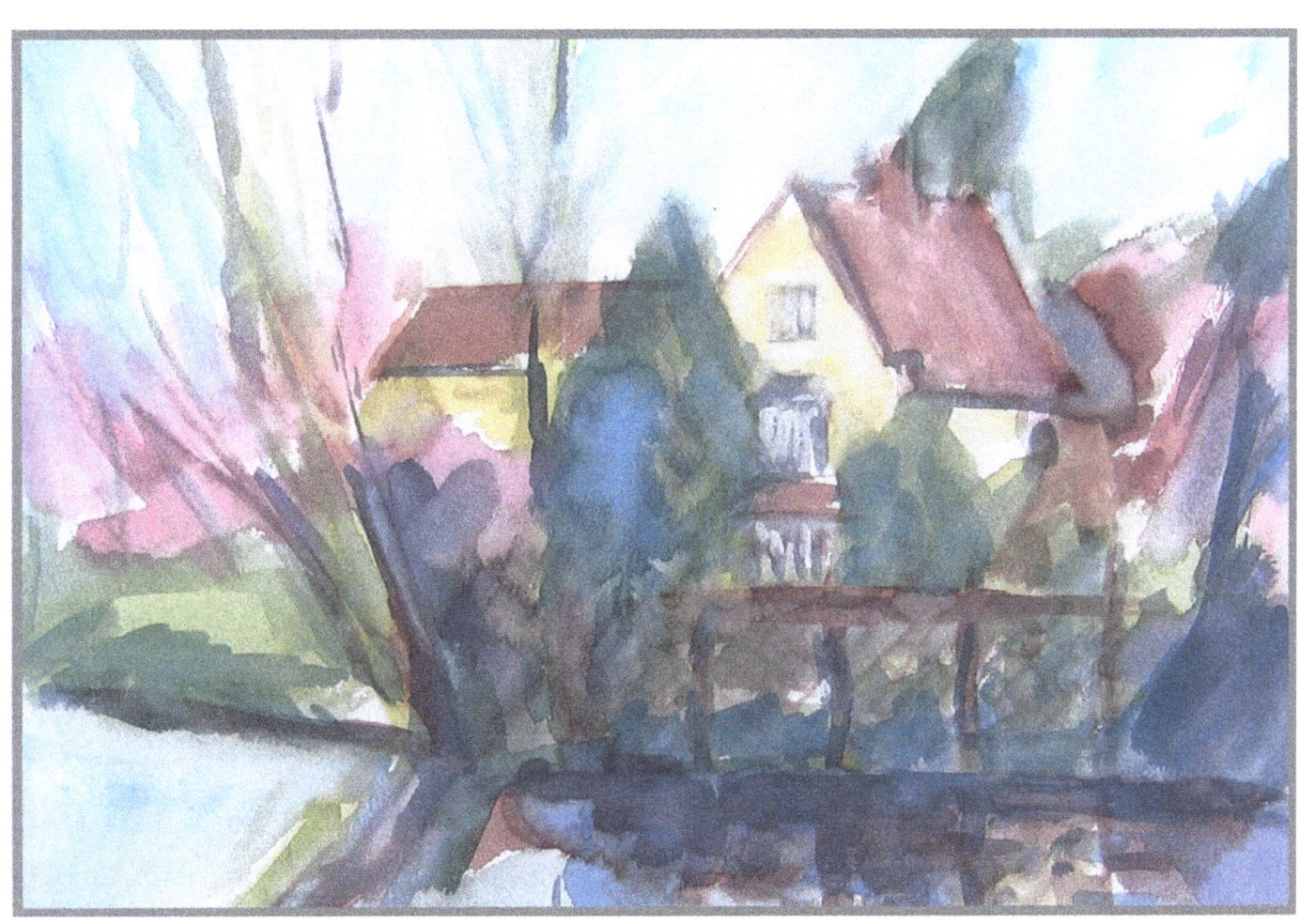

Upper Swarbourn
By John Robertson
21.01.2000 Watercolour 20" x 16"

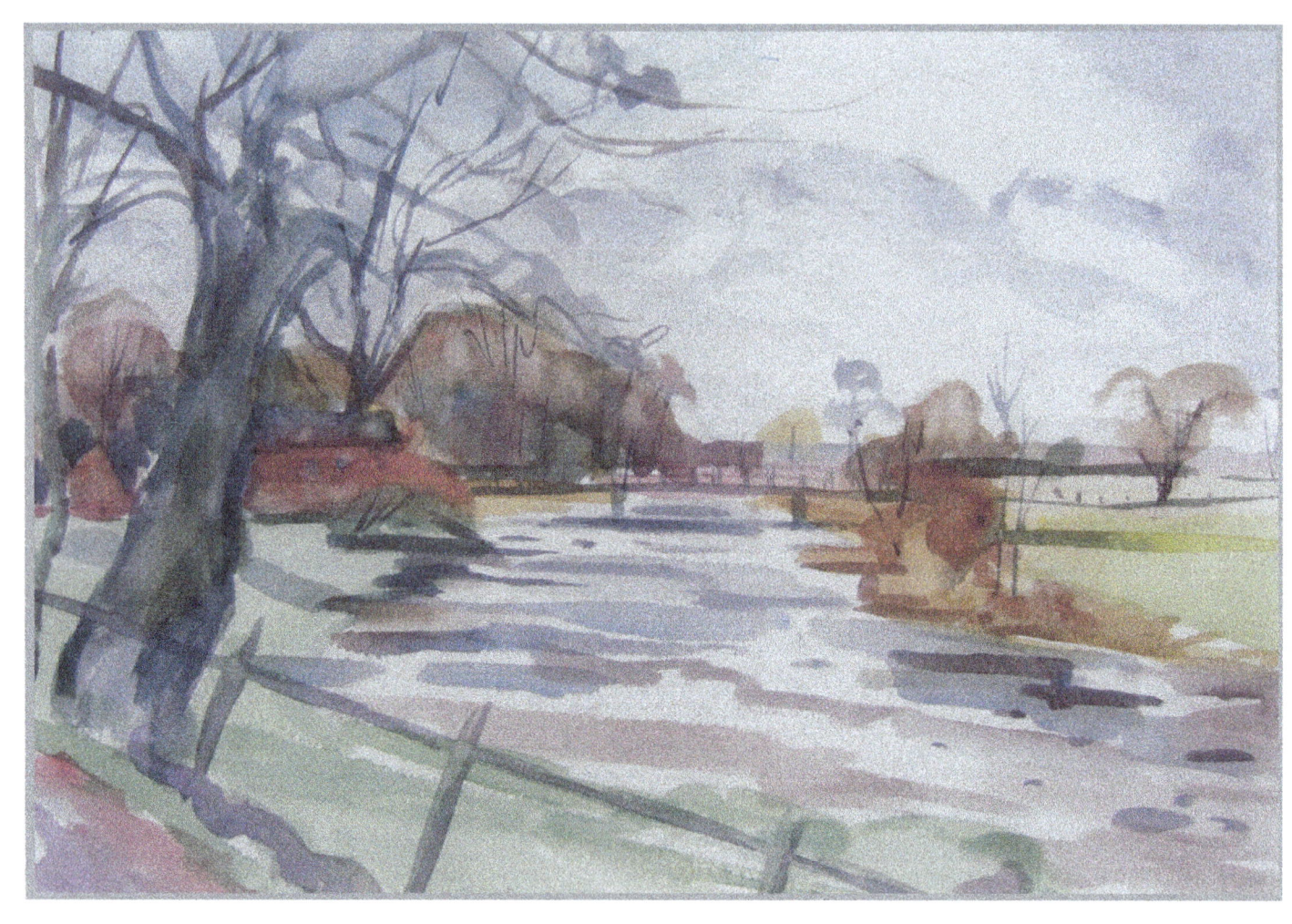

King's Bromley
By John Robertson
08.02.2000 Watercolour 20" x 16"

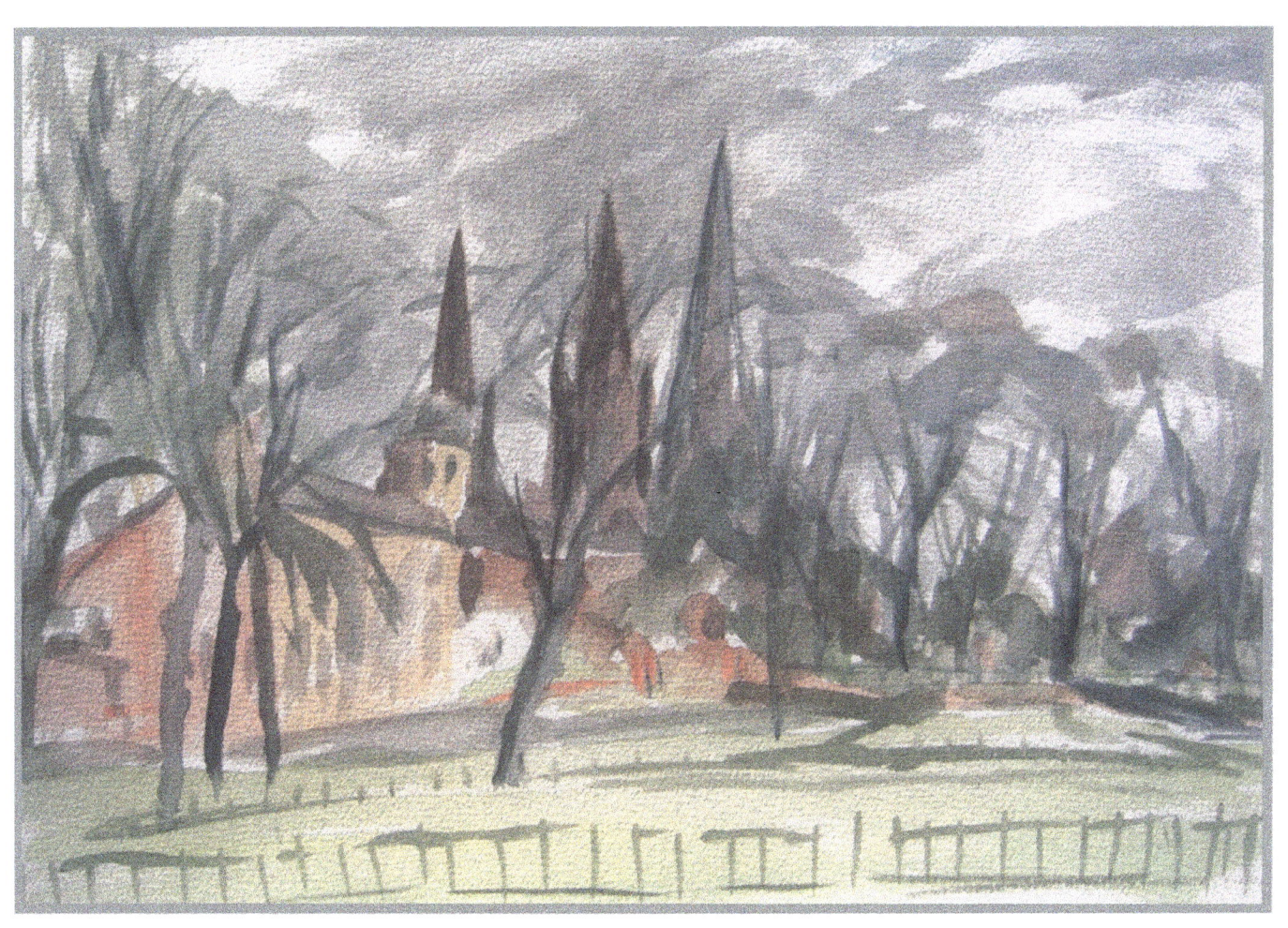

Lichfield
By John Robertson
16.04.2006 Watercolour 20" x 16"

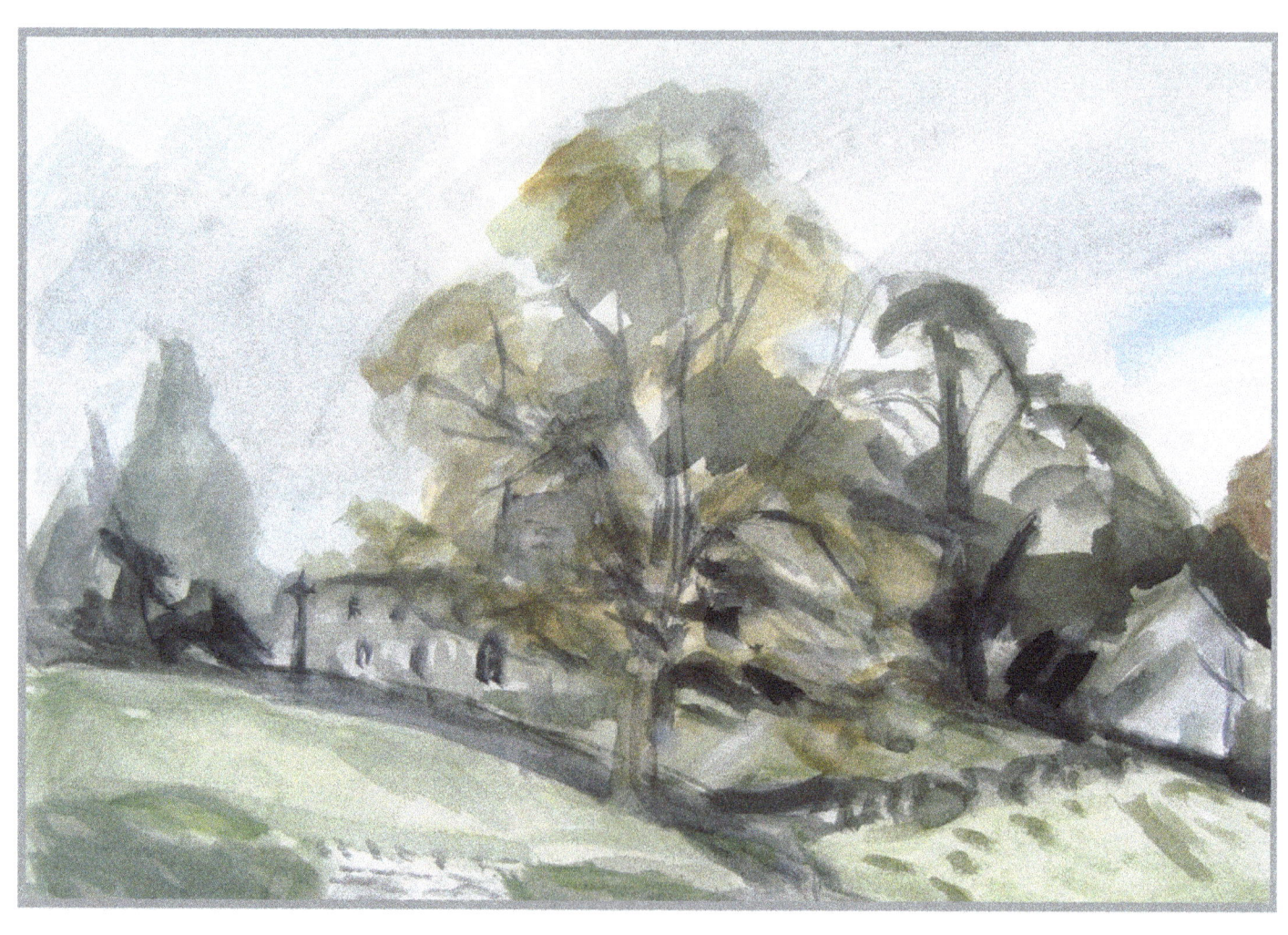

Tissington
By John Robertson
07.10.2004 Watercolour 20" x 16"

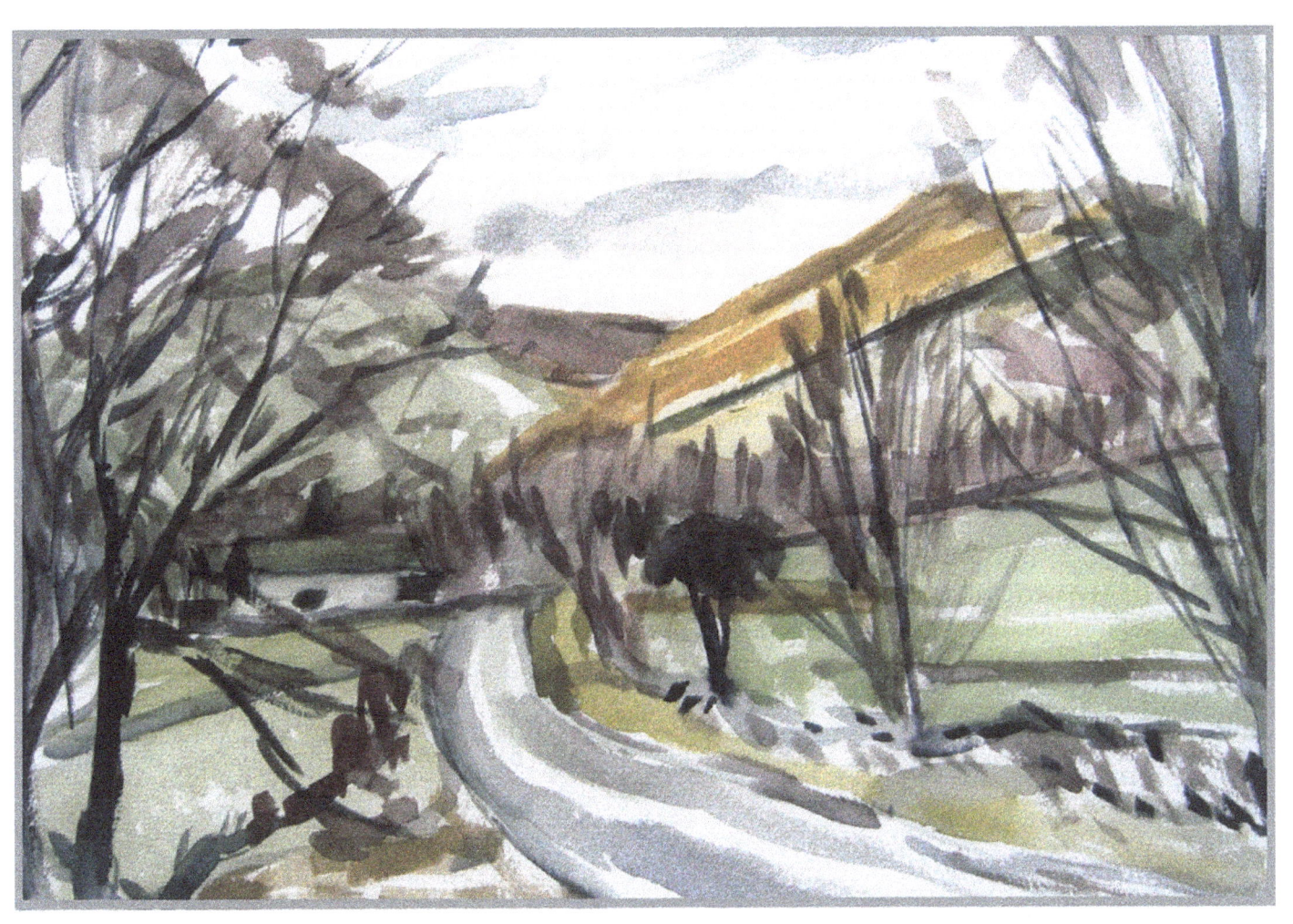

High Peaks
By John Robertson
15.04.2006 Watercolour 20" x 16"

Scottish Landscape
John

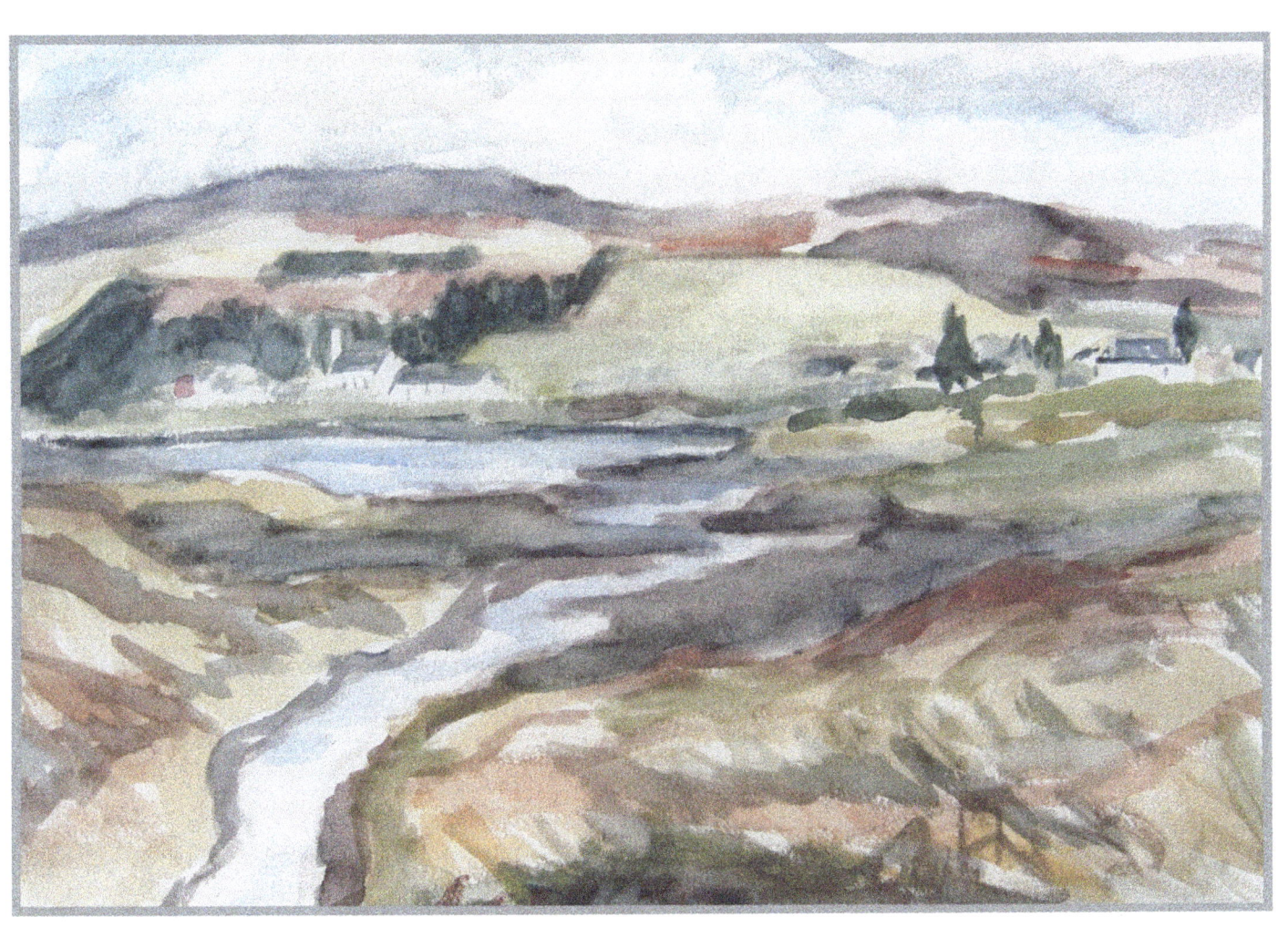

Dunvegan
By John Robertson
2010 Watercolour 20" x 16"

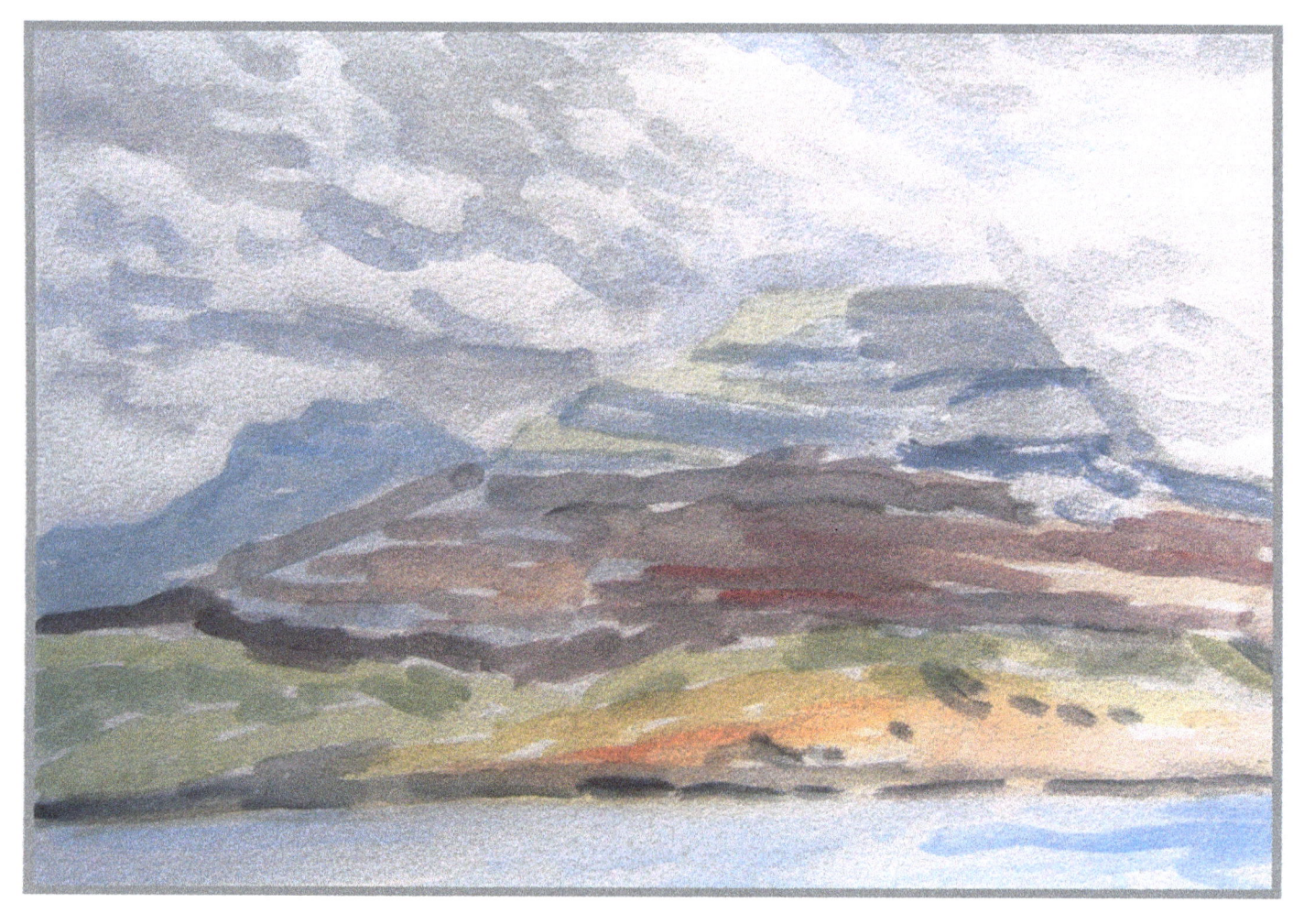

Macleod's Tables
By John Robertson
22.10.2003 Watercolour 20" x 16"

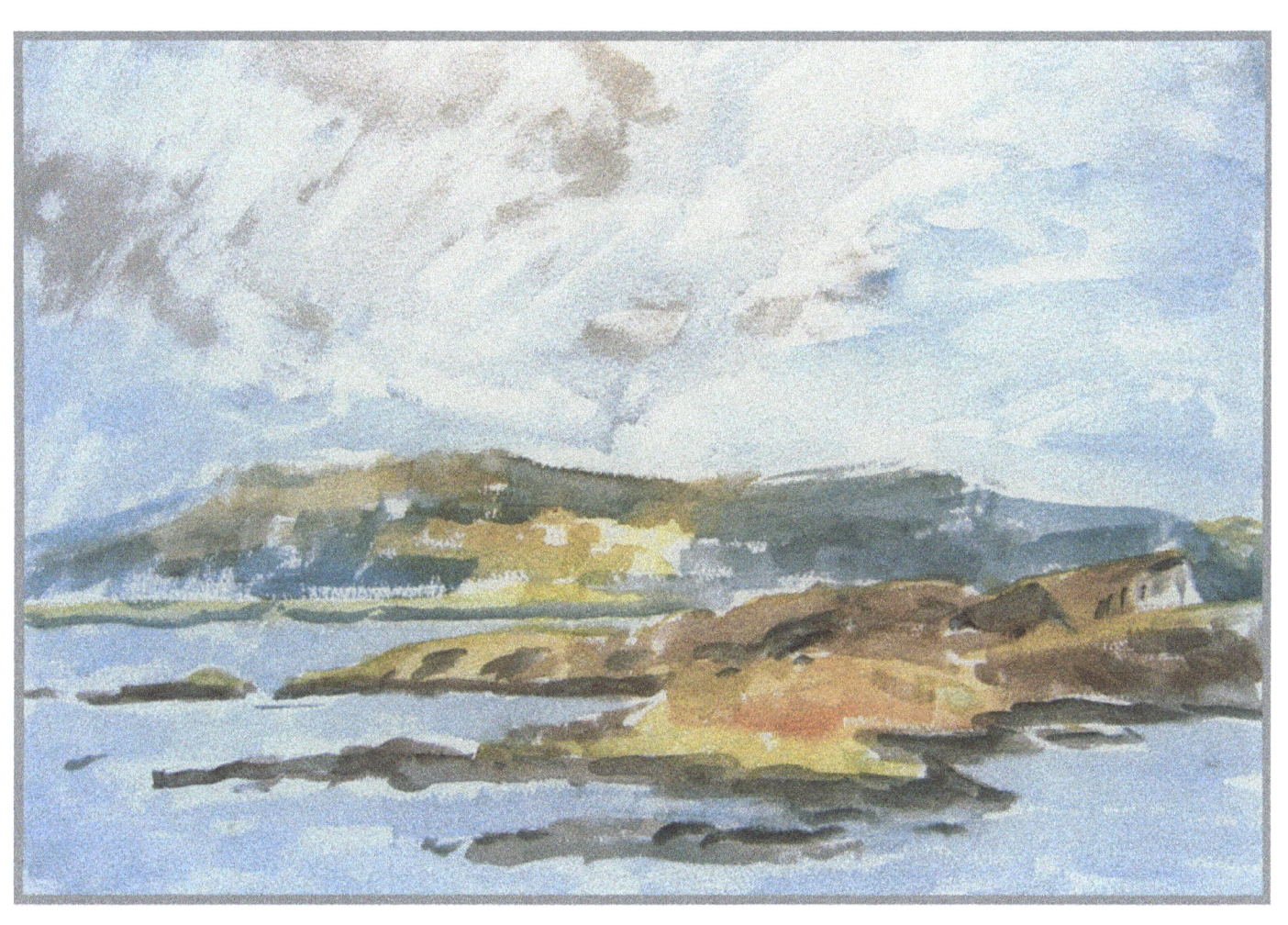

Loch Dunvegan
By John Robertson
16.02.2012 Watercolour 20" x 16"

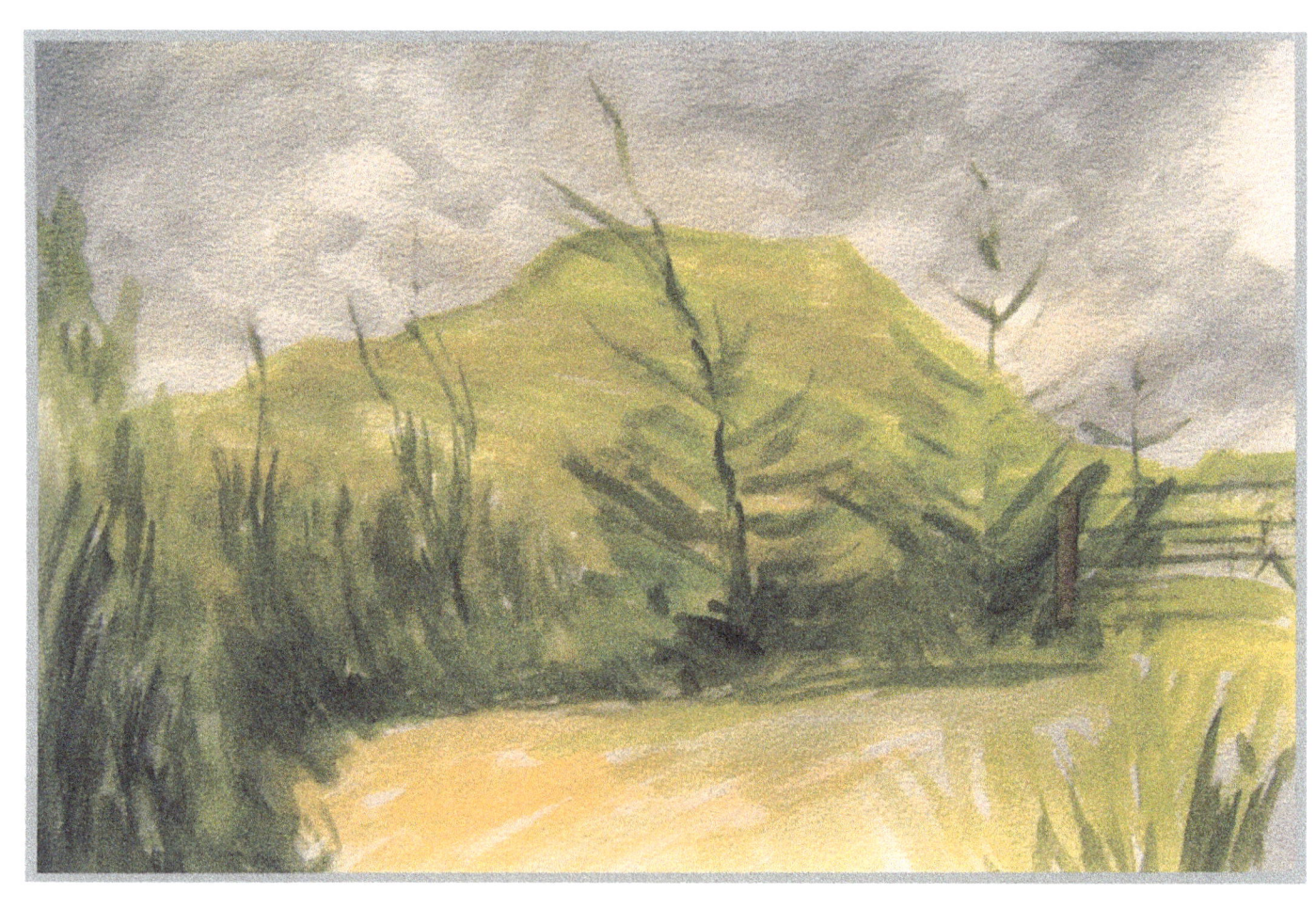

MacLeods Table from Green Gates
By John Robertson
2007 Watercolour 20" x 16"

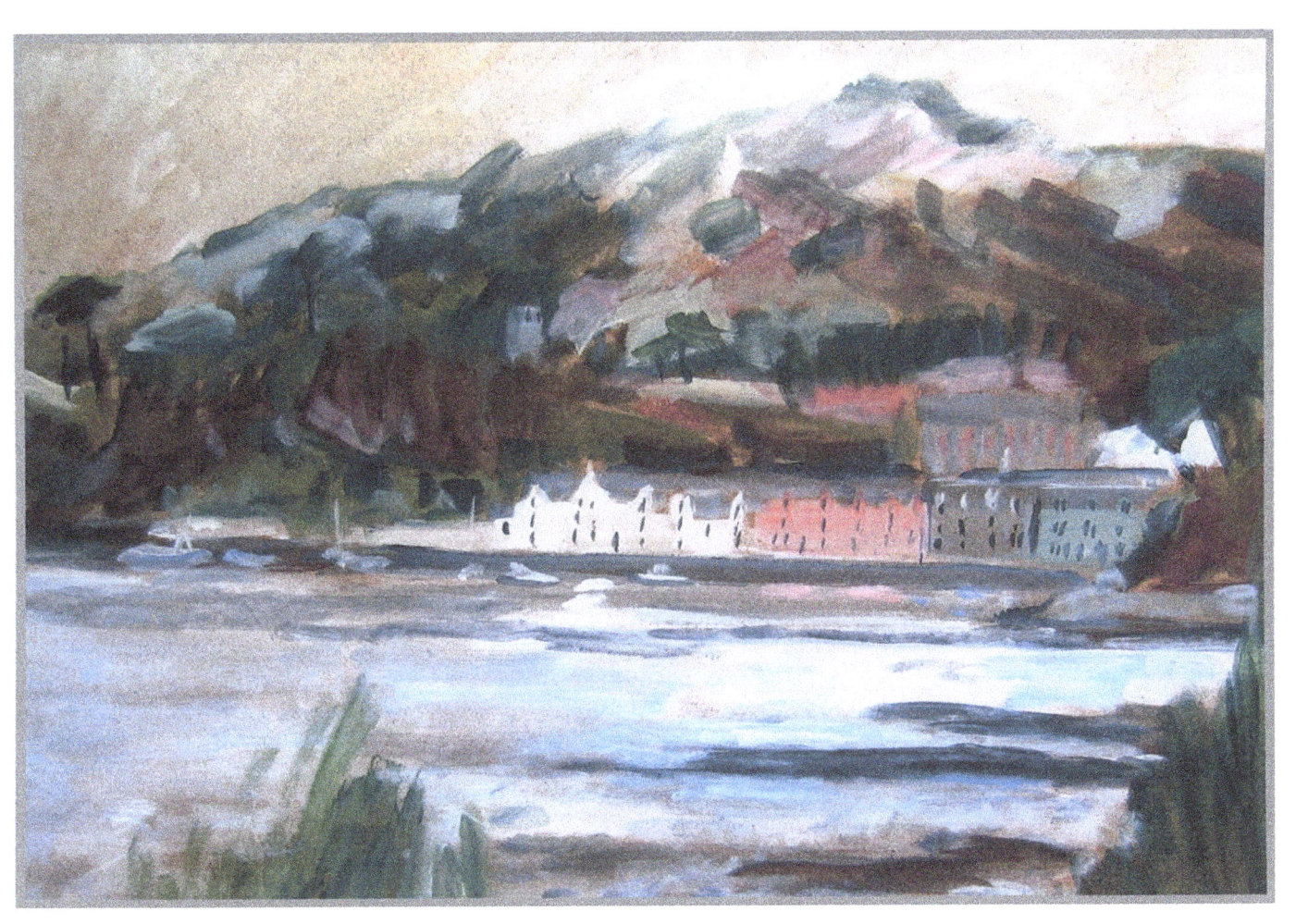

Portree Harbour
By John Robertson
29.01.2011 Acrylic 20" x 16"

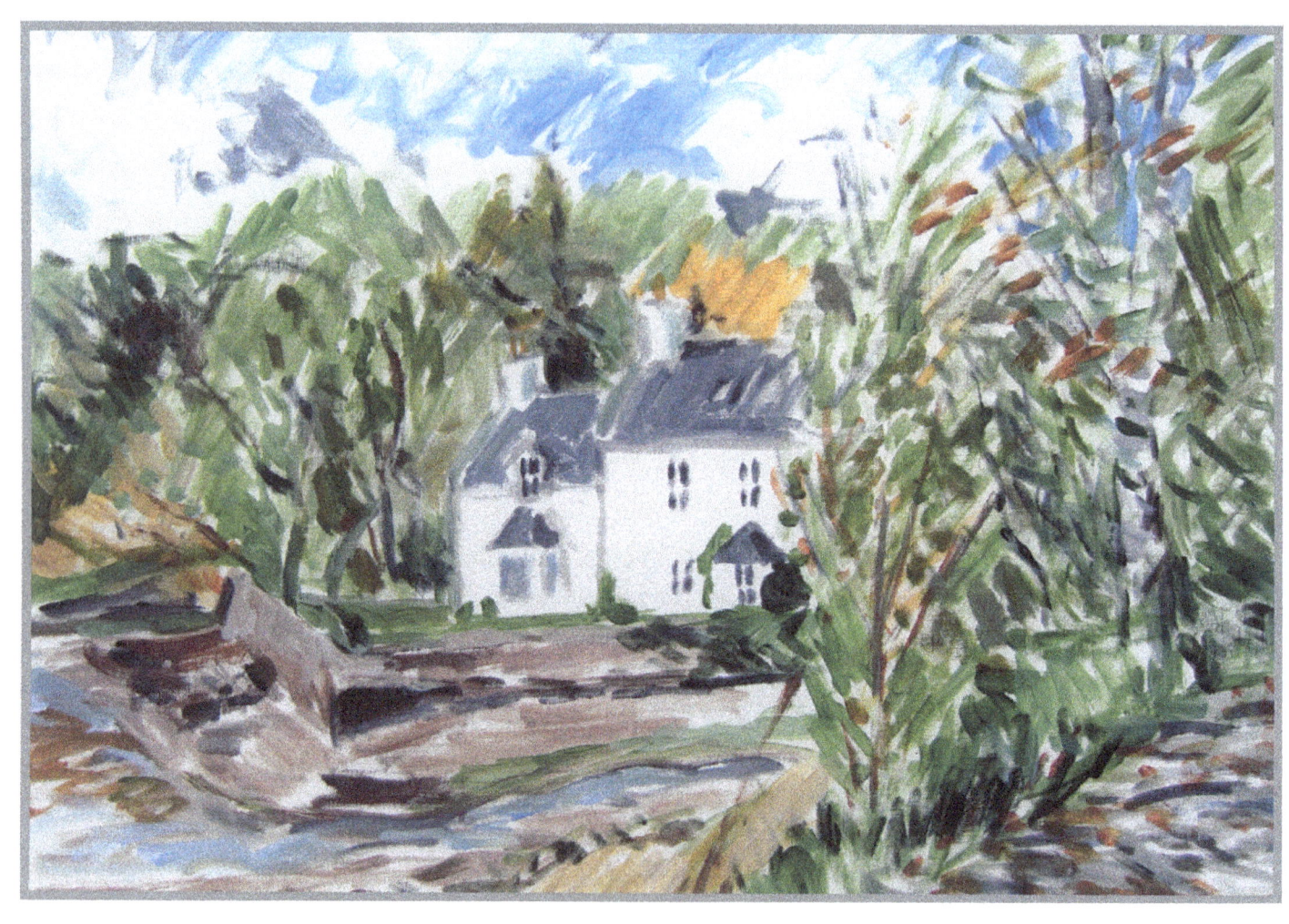

Portree
By John Robertson
20.09.2011 Acrylic 20" x 16"

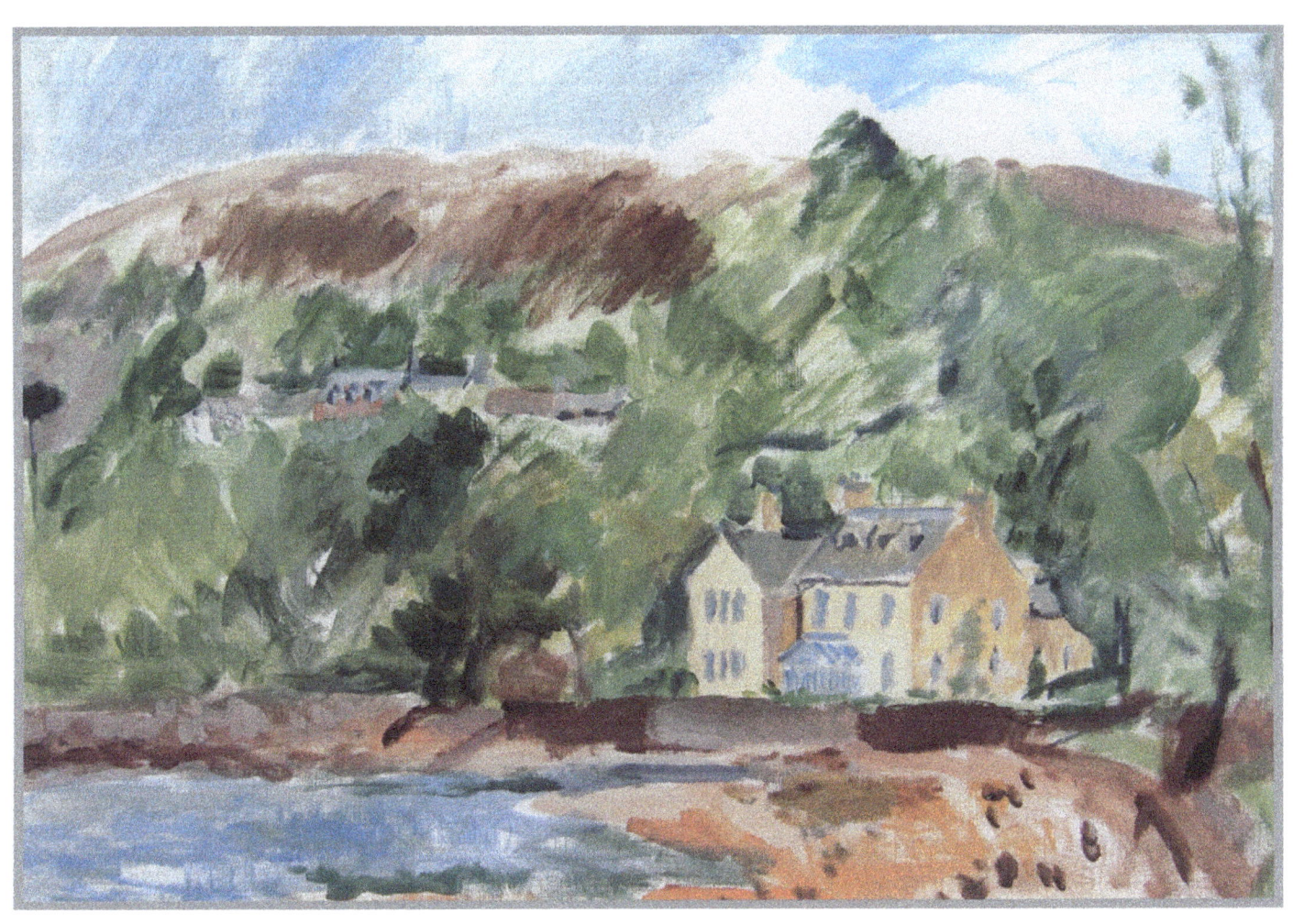

Portree
By John Robertson
2010 Acrylic 20" x 16"

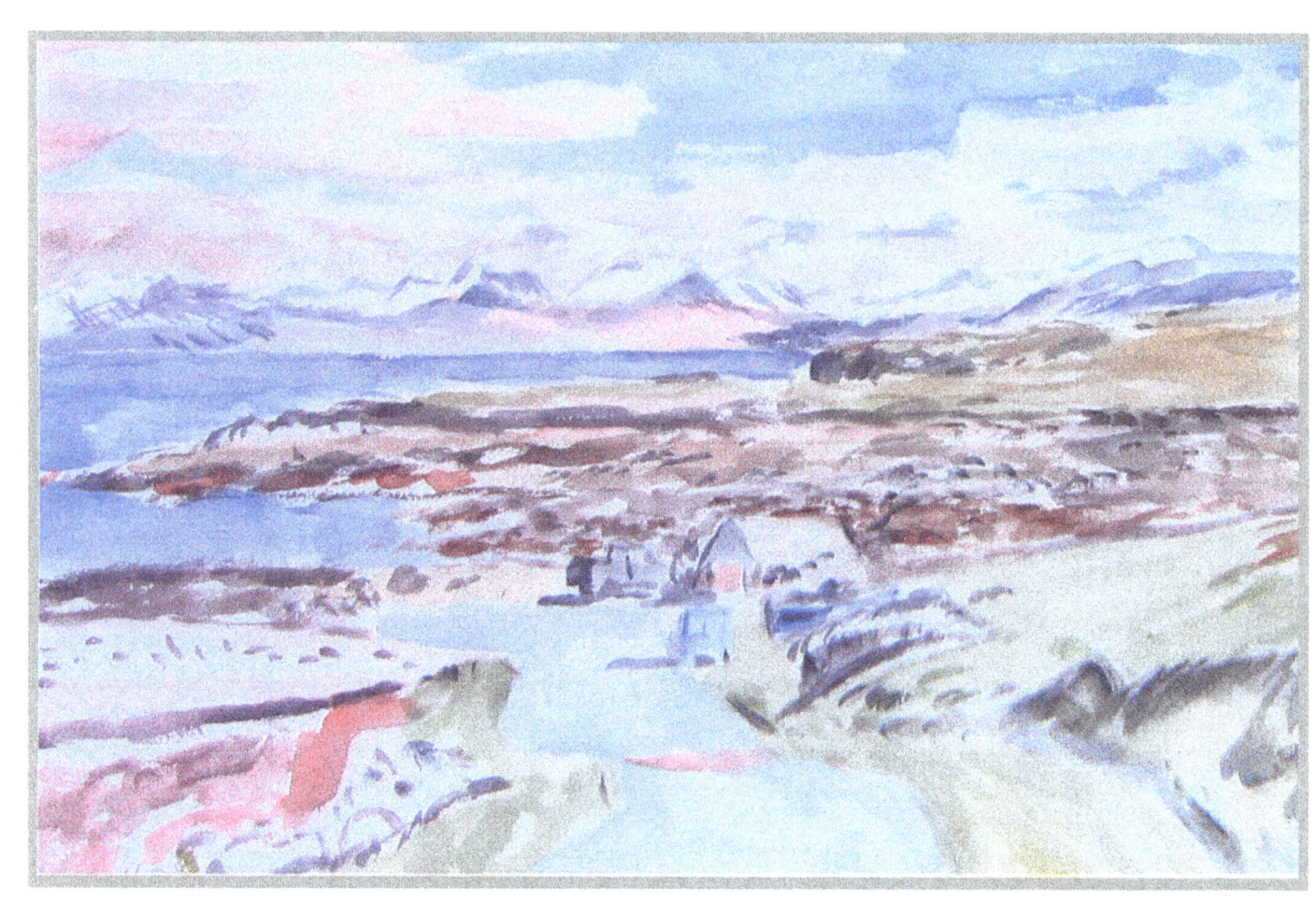

The Harbour at Staffin
By John Robertson
2013 Watercolour 20" x 16"

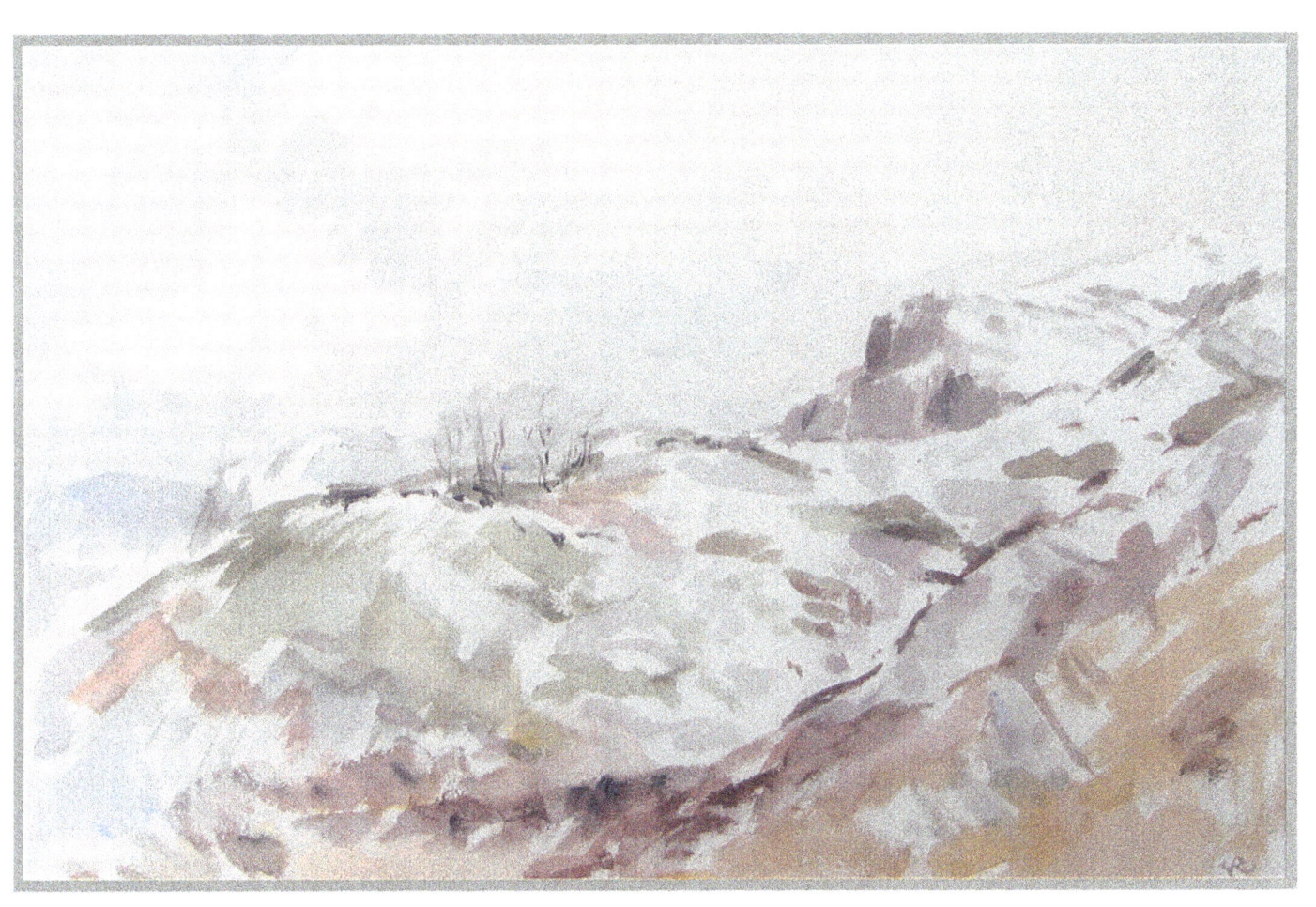

Reflections on Snow
By John Robertson
2007 Watercolour 20" x 16"

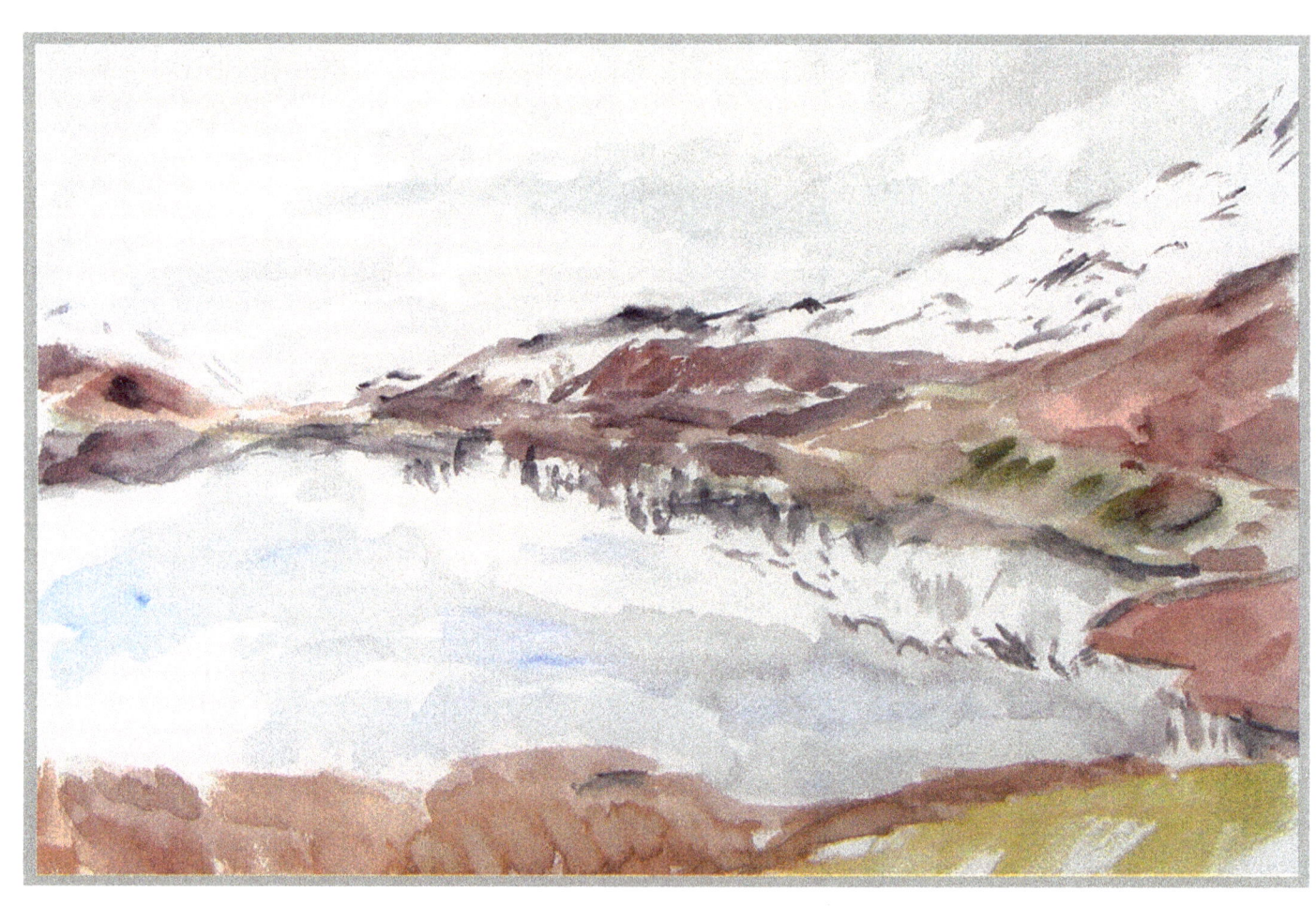

Reflections
By John Robertson
2007 Watercolour 20" x 16"

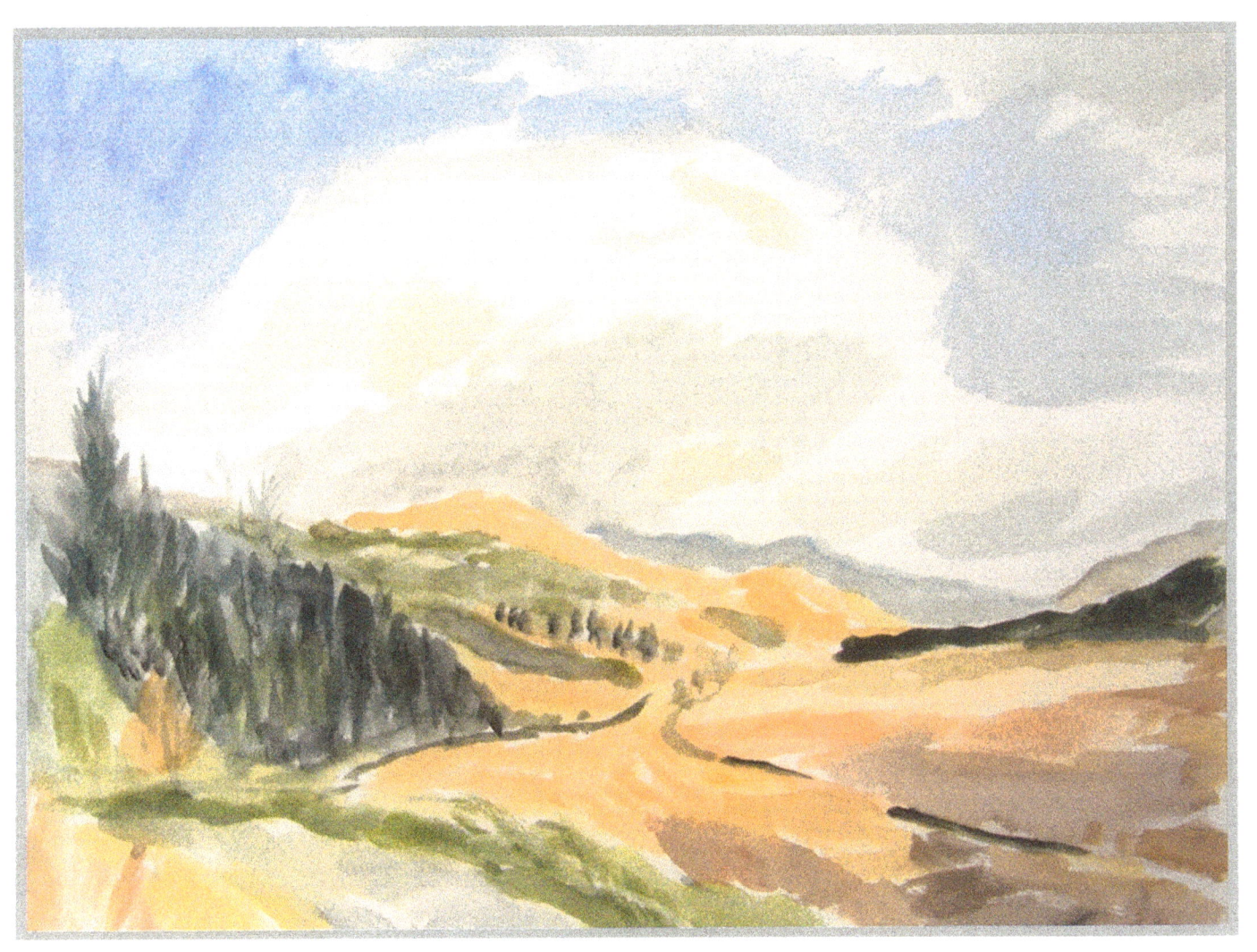

Approaching Achnasheen
By John Robertson
2014 Watercolour 20" x 16"

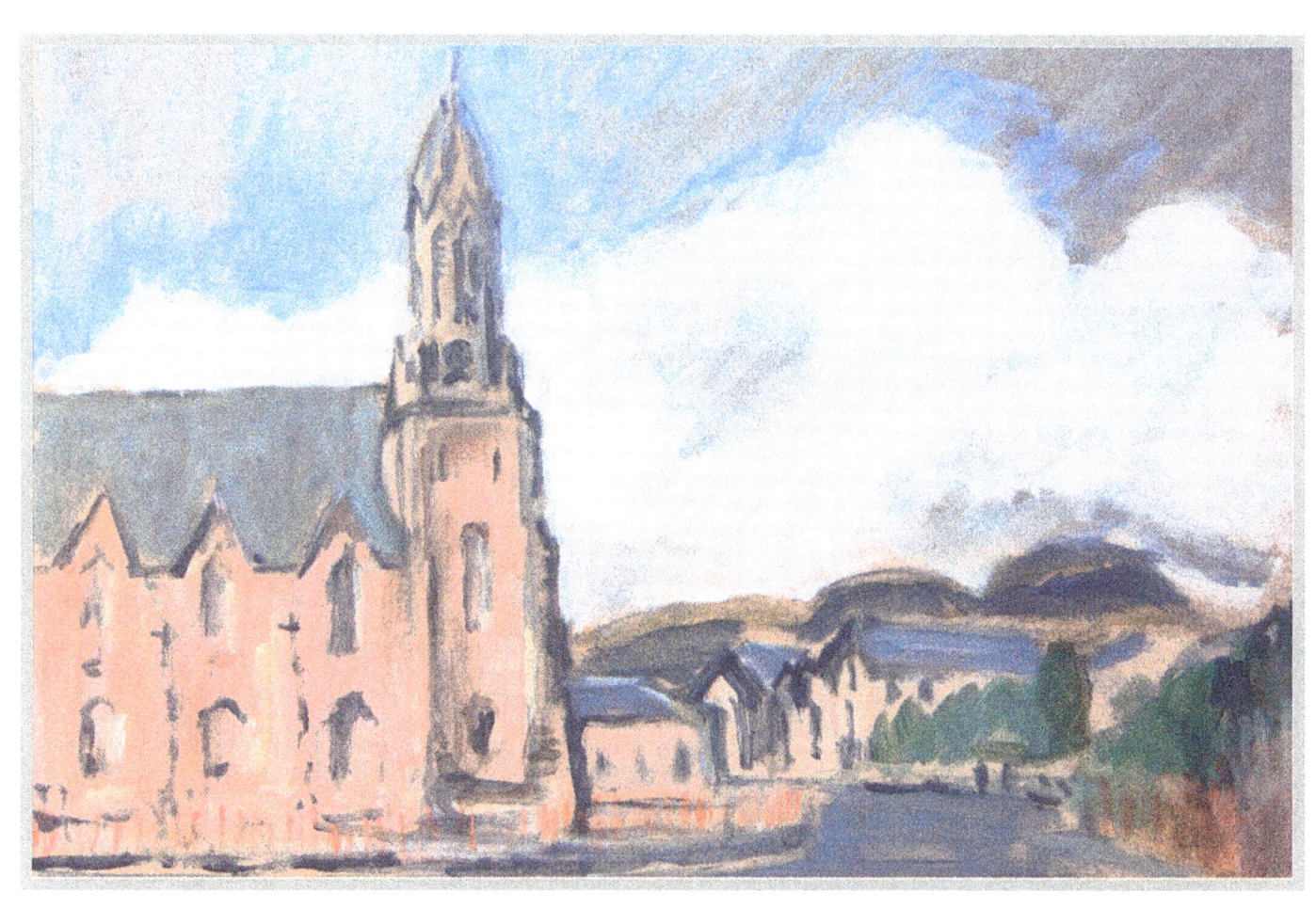

Dingwall
By John Robertson
2007 Acrylic 20" x 16"

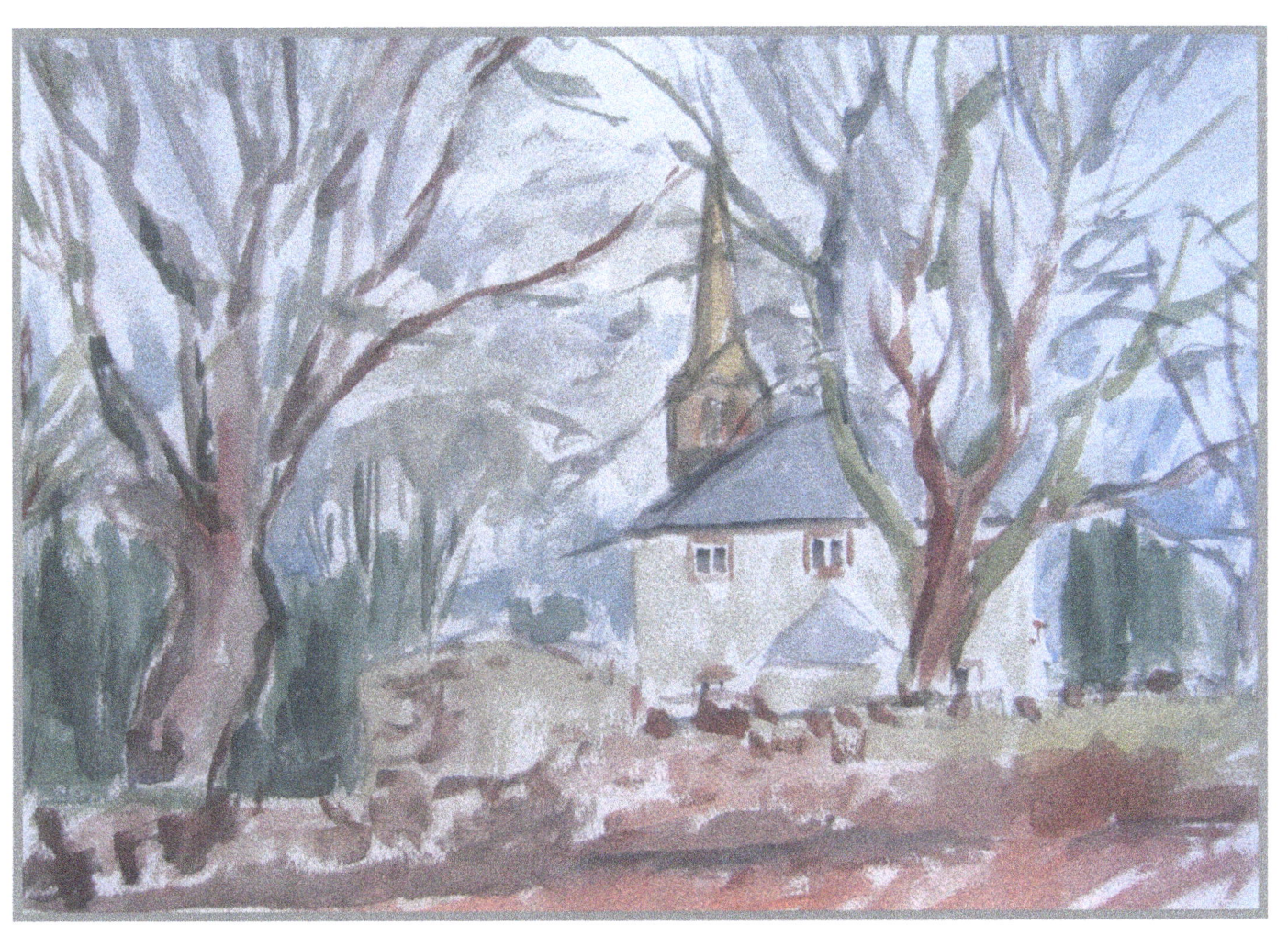

St Clements
By John Robertson
2011 Watercolour 20" x 16"

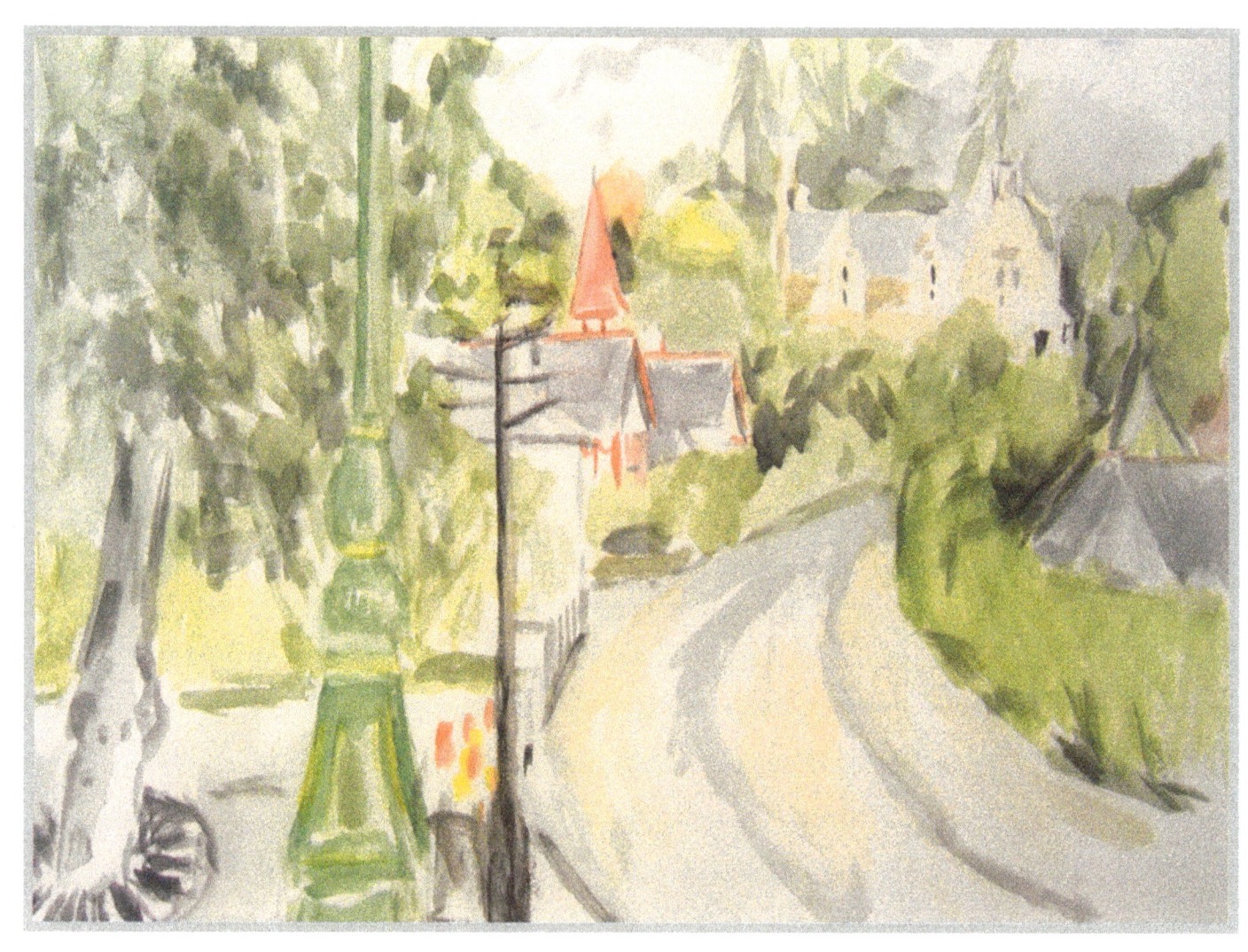

Strathpeffer
By John Robertson
2014 Watercolour 20" x 16"

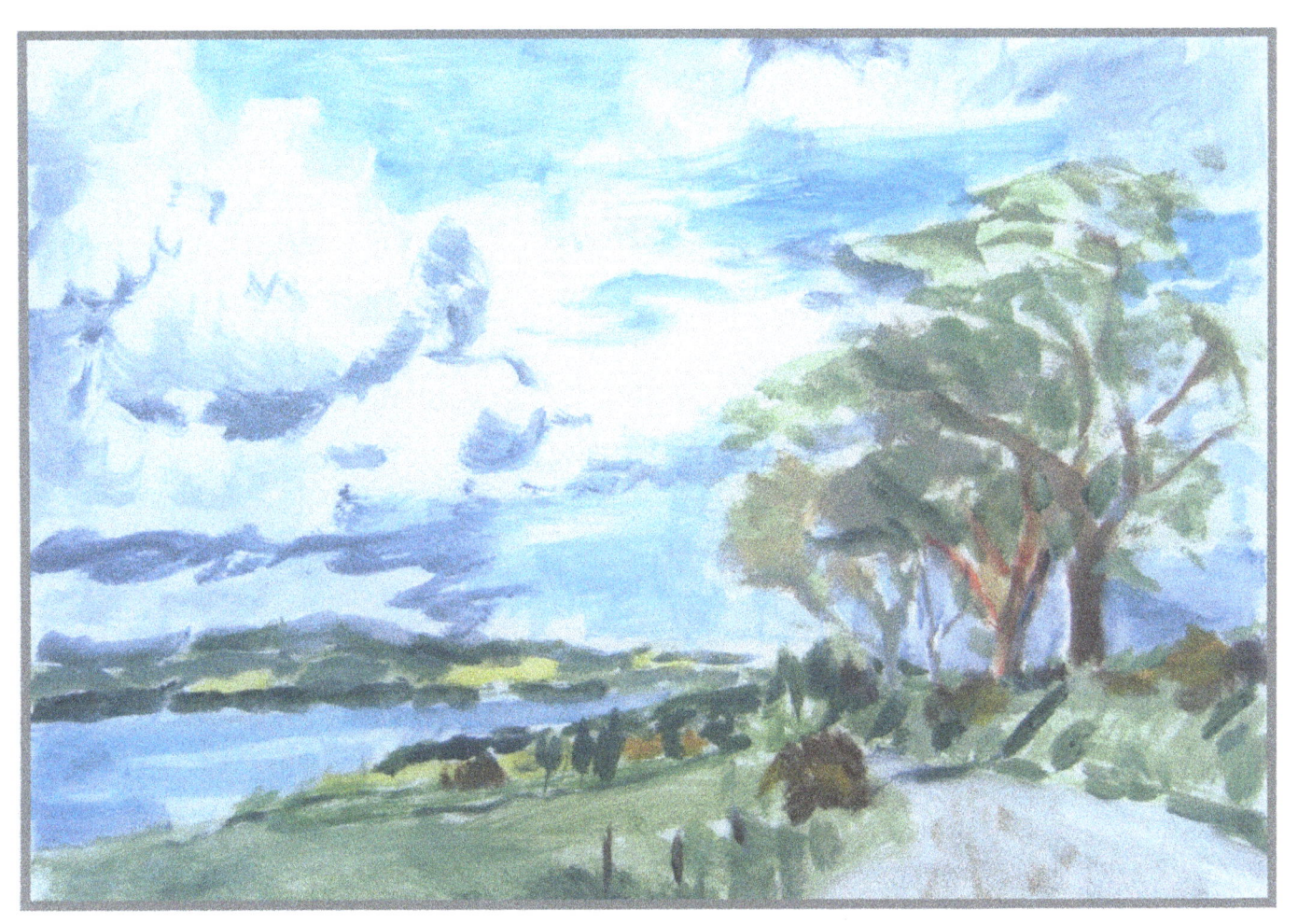

Black Isle
By John Robertson
2010 Acrylic 20" x 16"

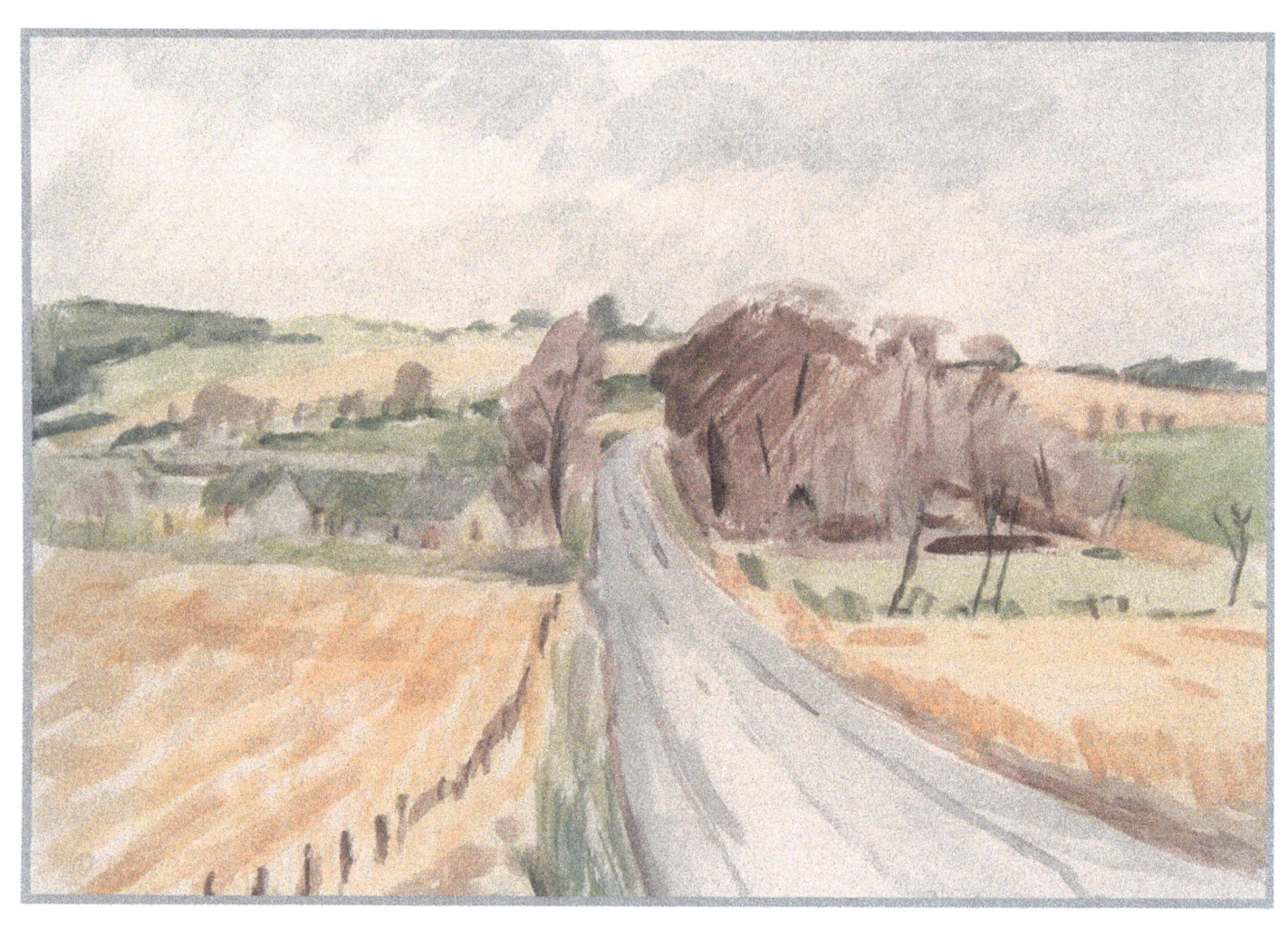

Road to Balmenie
By John Robertson
15.12.2013 Watercolour 20" x 16"

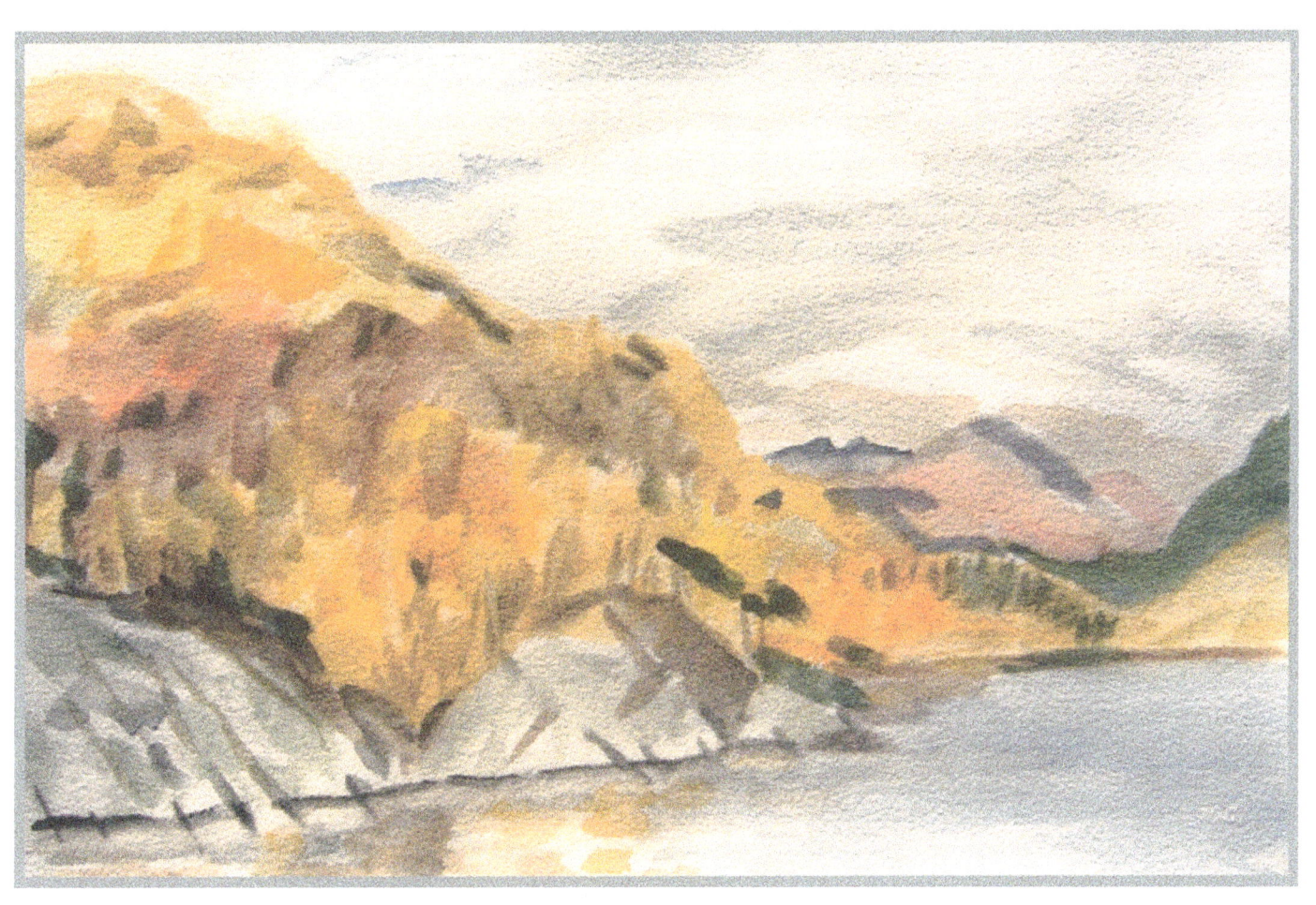

Loch Creran
By John Robertson
2007 Watercolour 20" x 16"

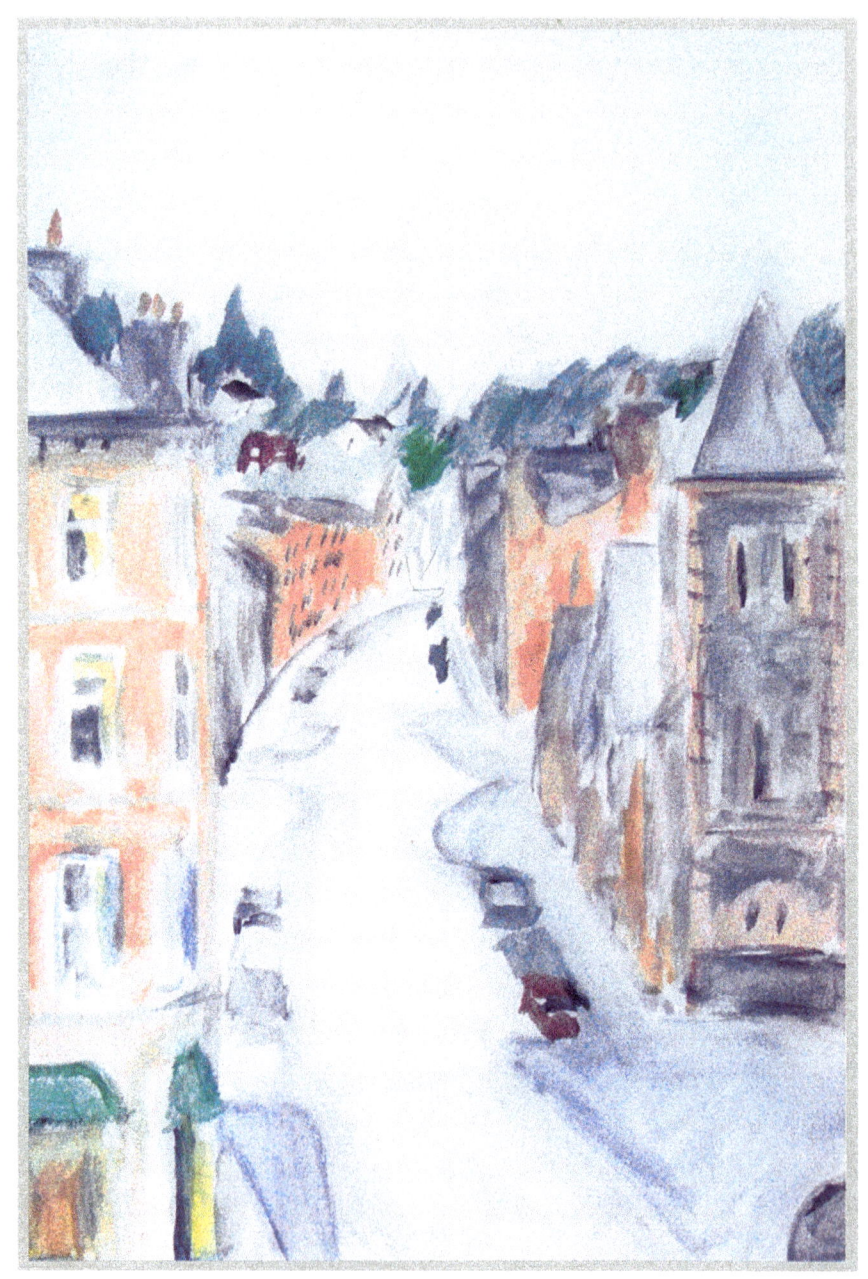

From Room 301
By John Robertson
2007 Watercolour 20" x 16"

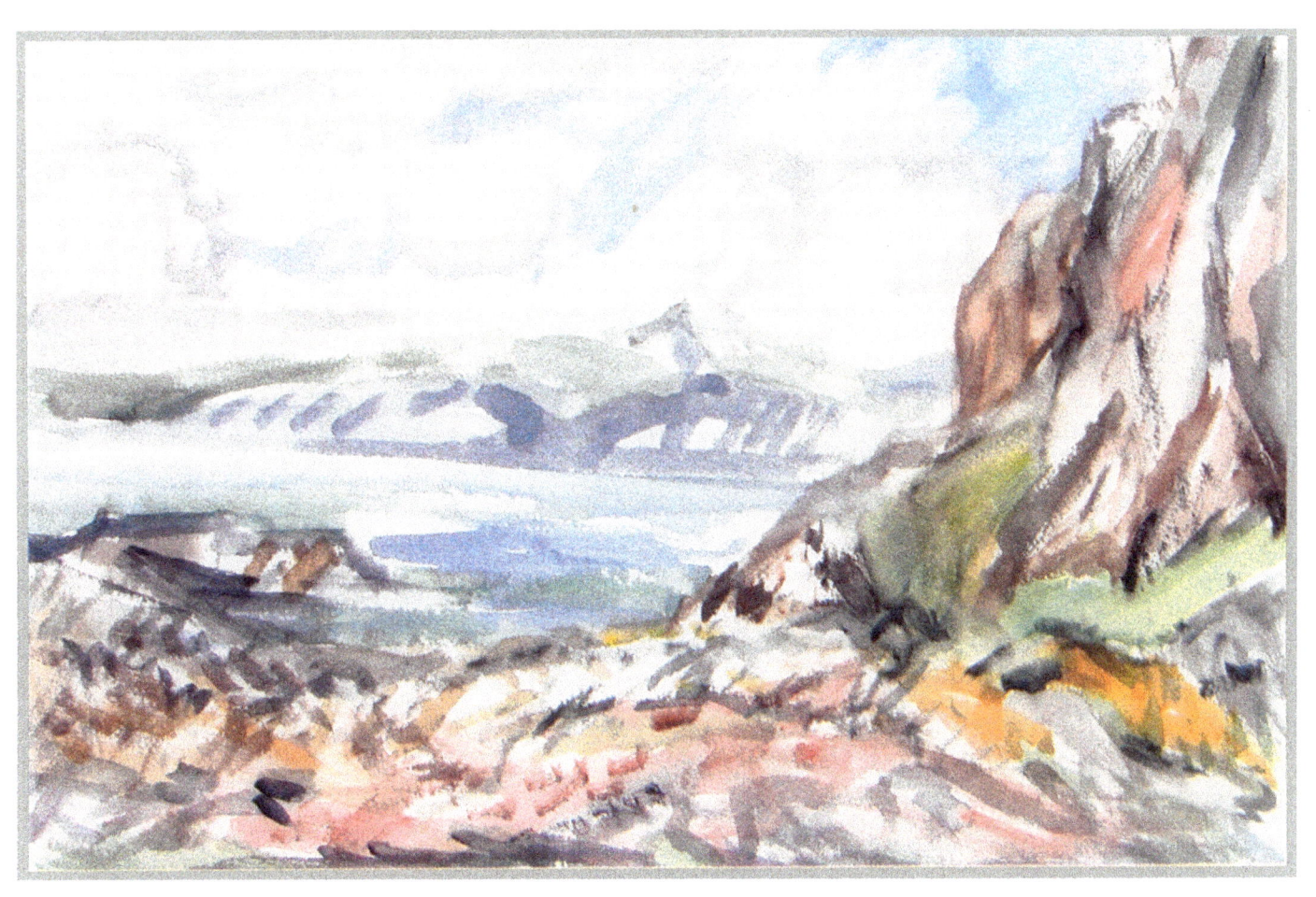

Mull from Seil
By John Robertson
2007 Watercolour 20" x 16"

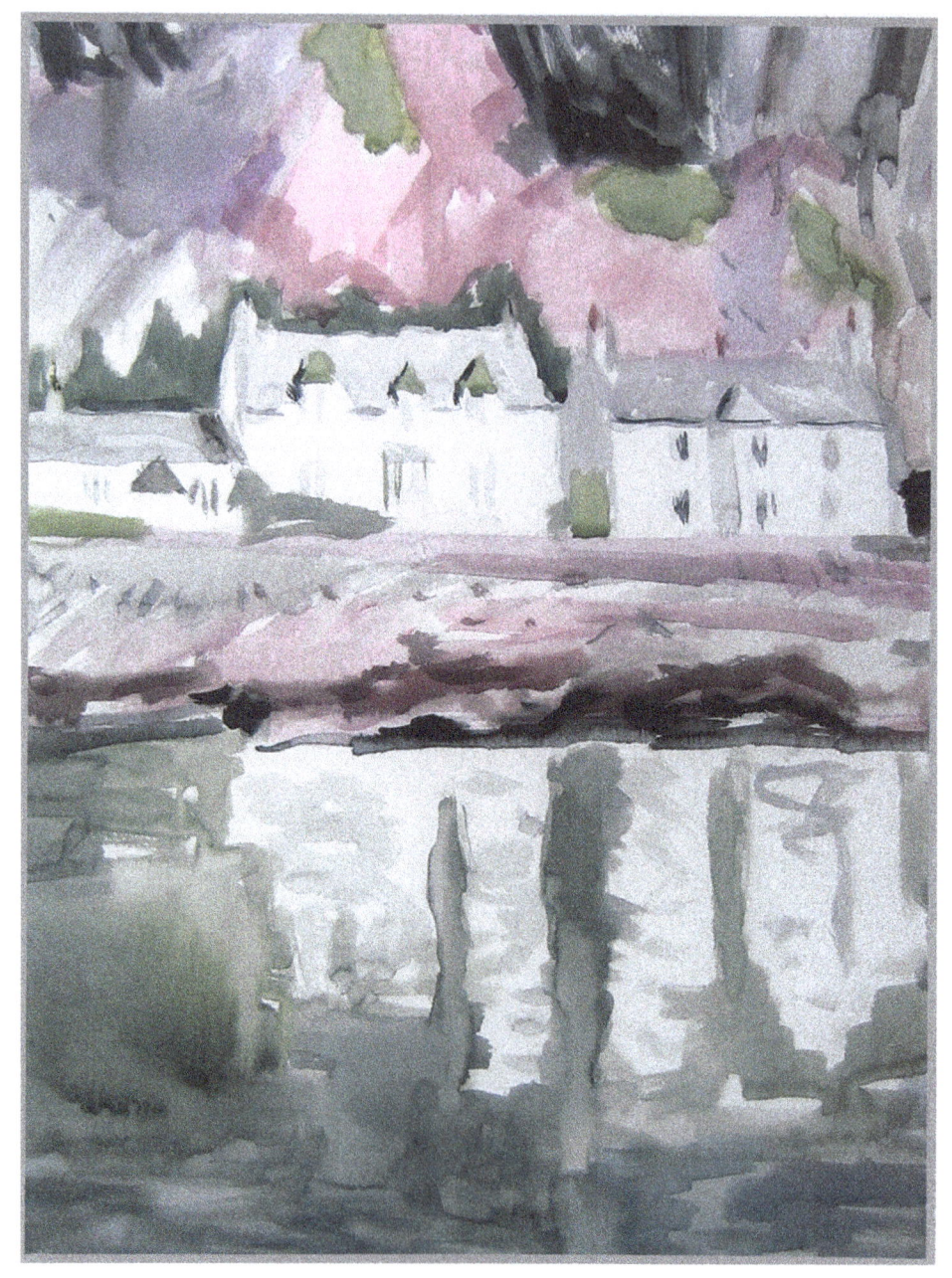

Ellenabeich
By John Robertson
2004 Watercolour 30" x 22"

English Landscape
Jane

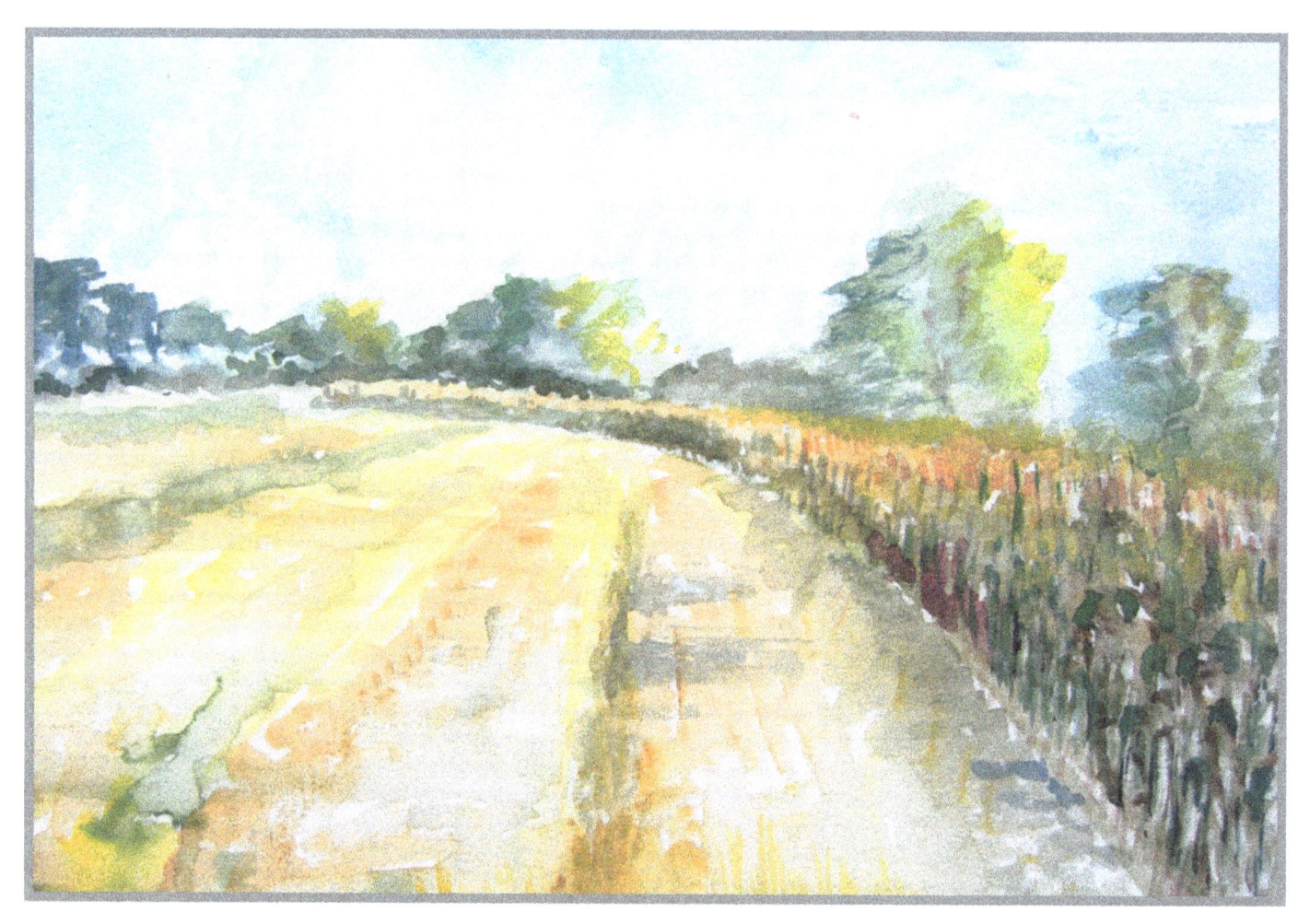

Wychnor
By Jane Robertson
2004 Watercolour 16" x 12"

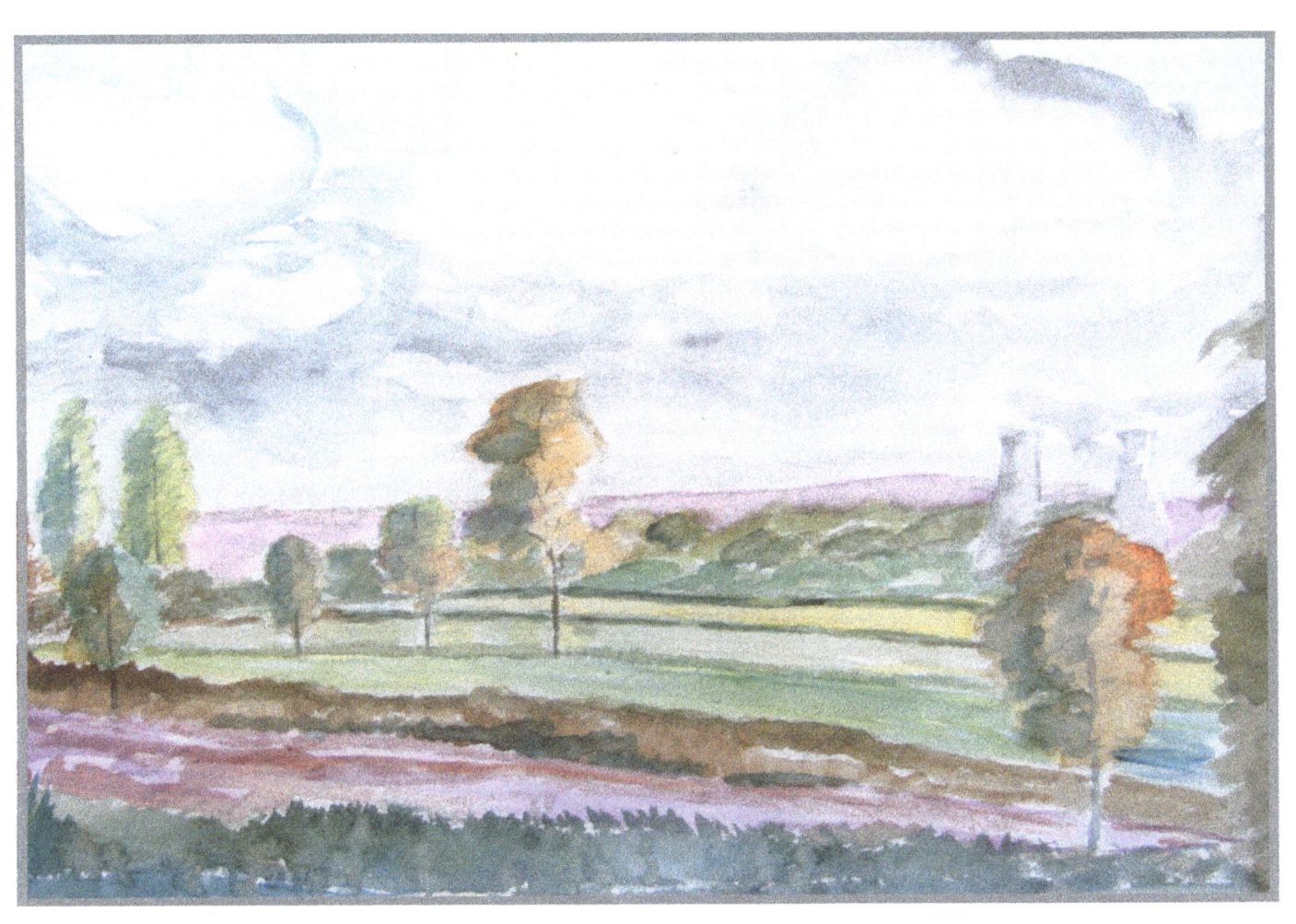

Tatenhill
By Jane Robertson
2004 Watercolour 16" x 12"

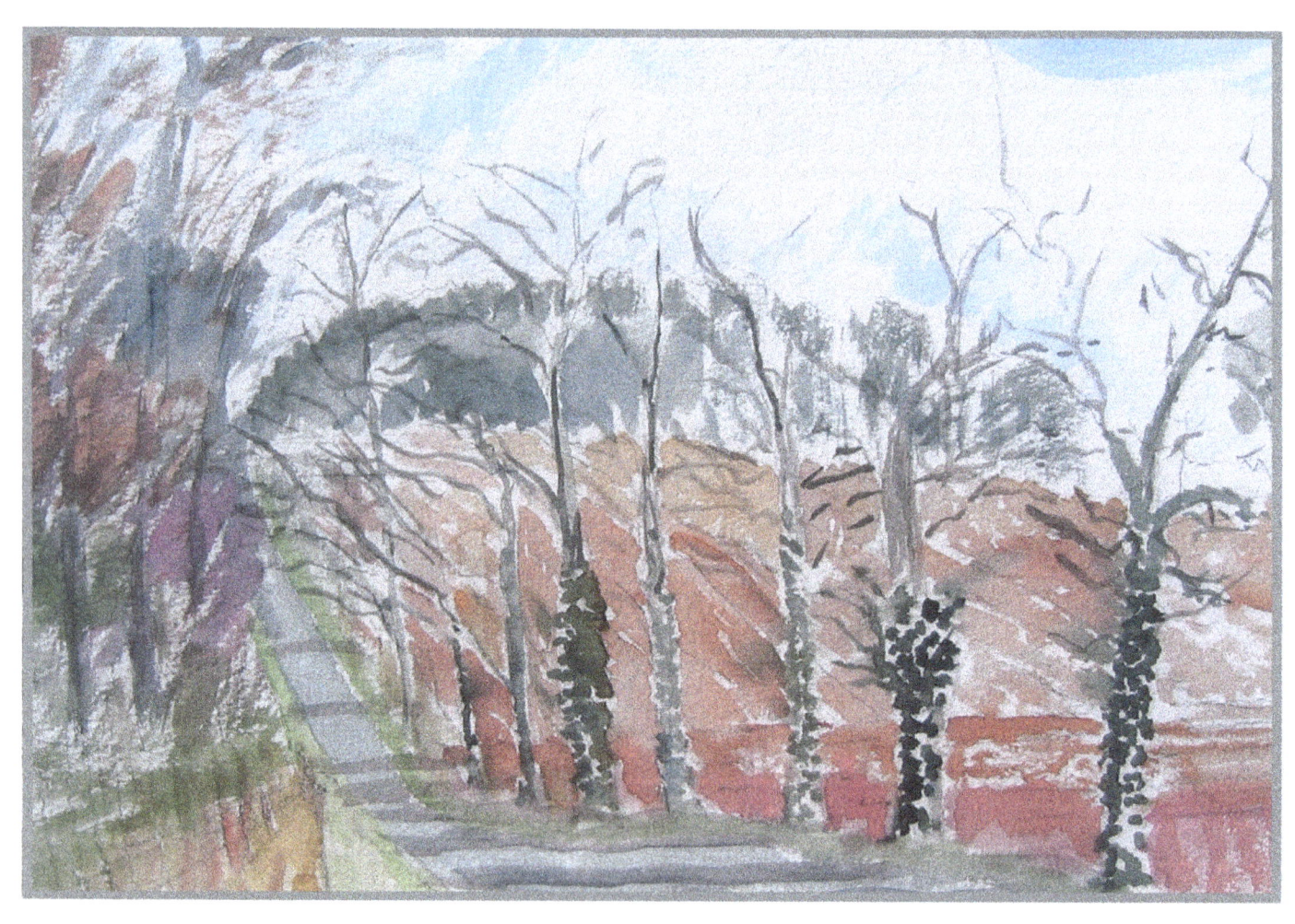

Scotch Hills Barton
By Jane Robertson
2004 Watercolour 16" x 12"

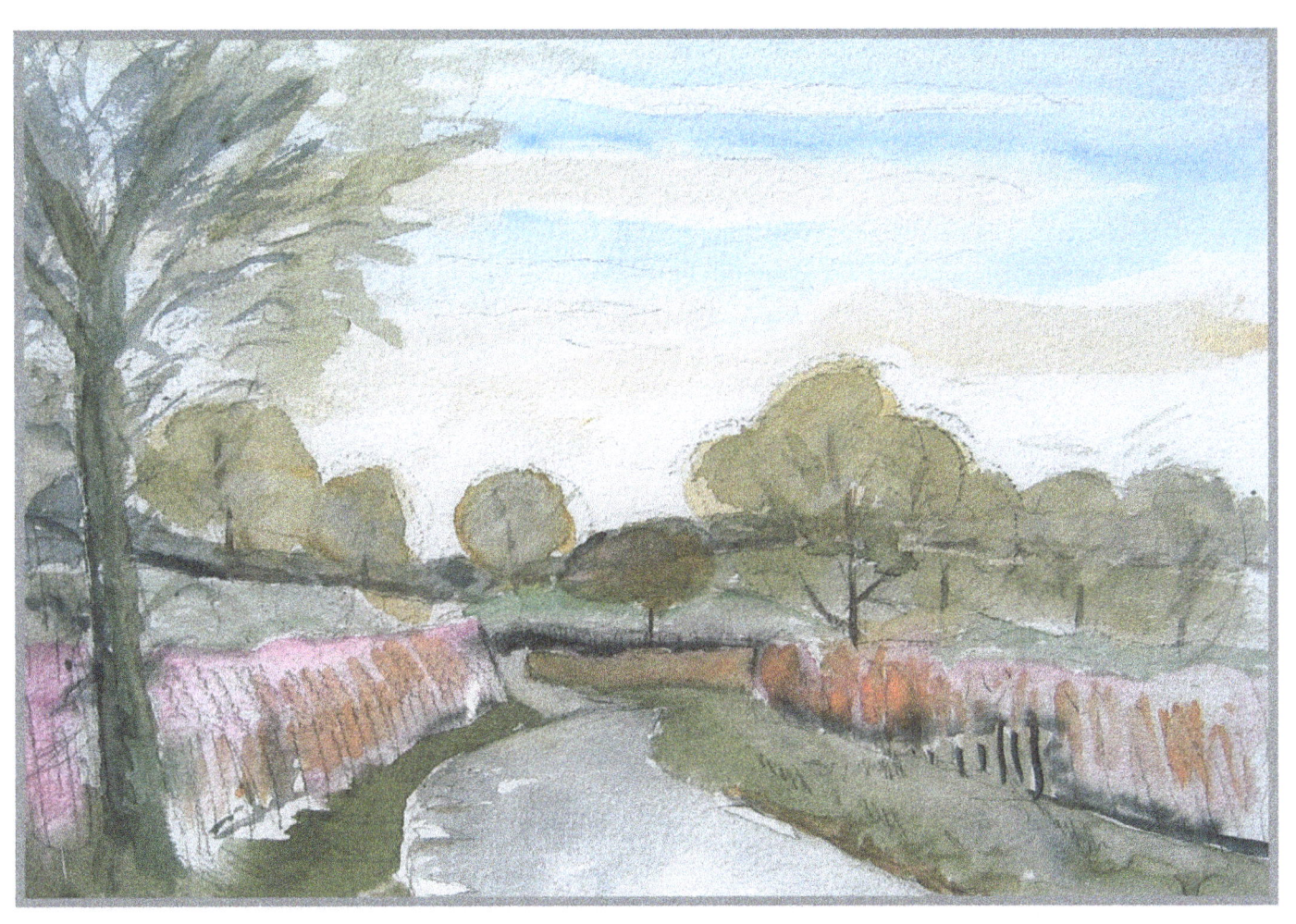

Bar Lane Barton
By Jane Robertson
2005 Watercolour 16" x 12"

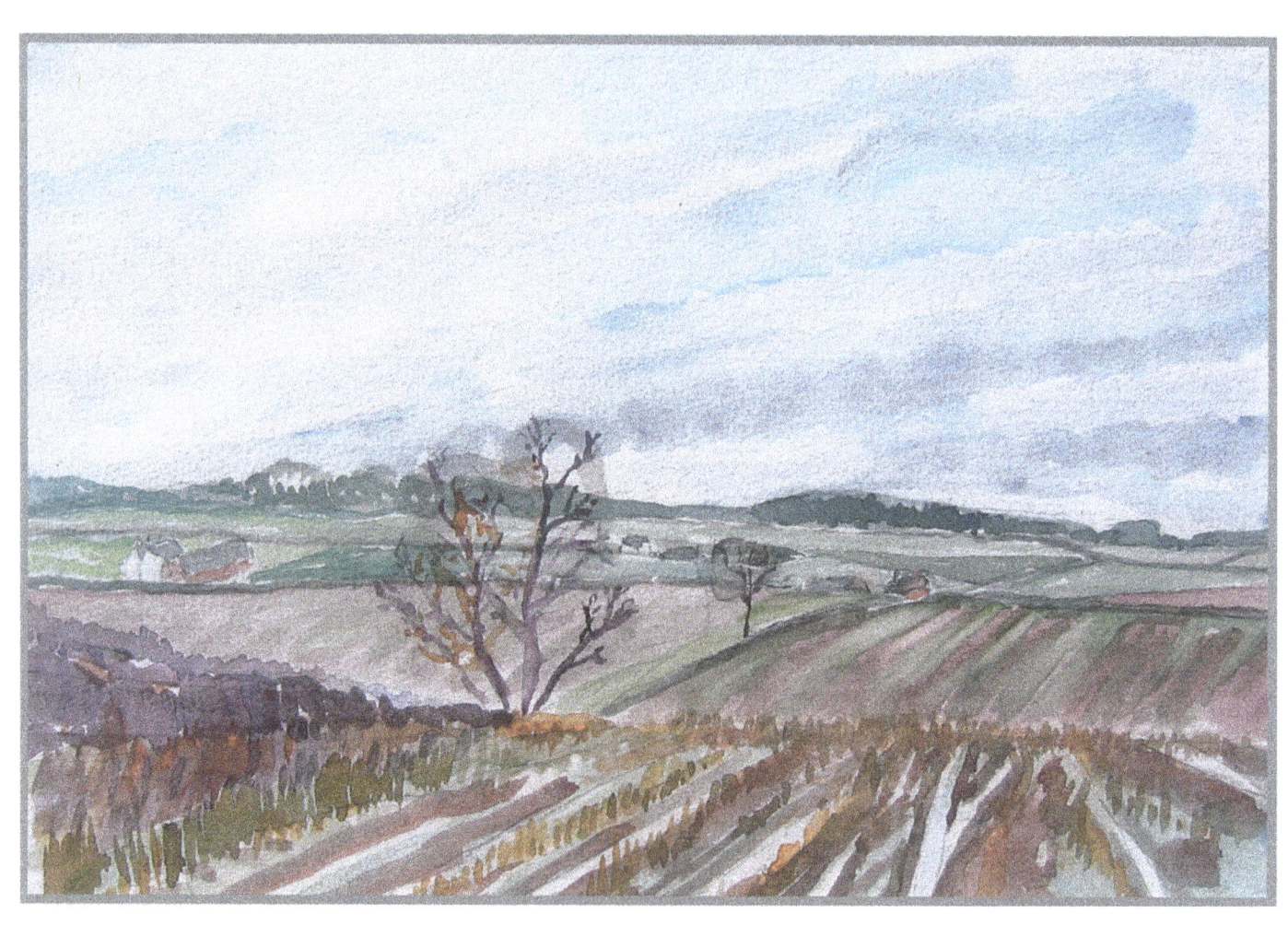

Yoxall
By Jane Robertson
2005 Watercolour 16" x 12"

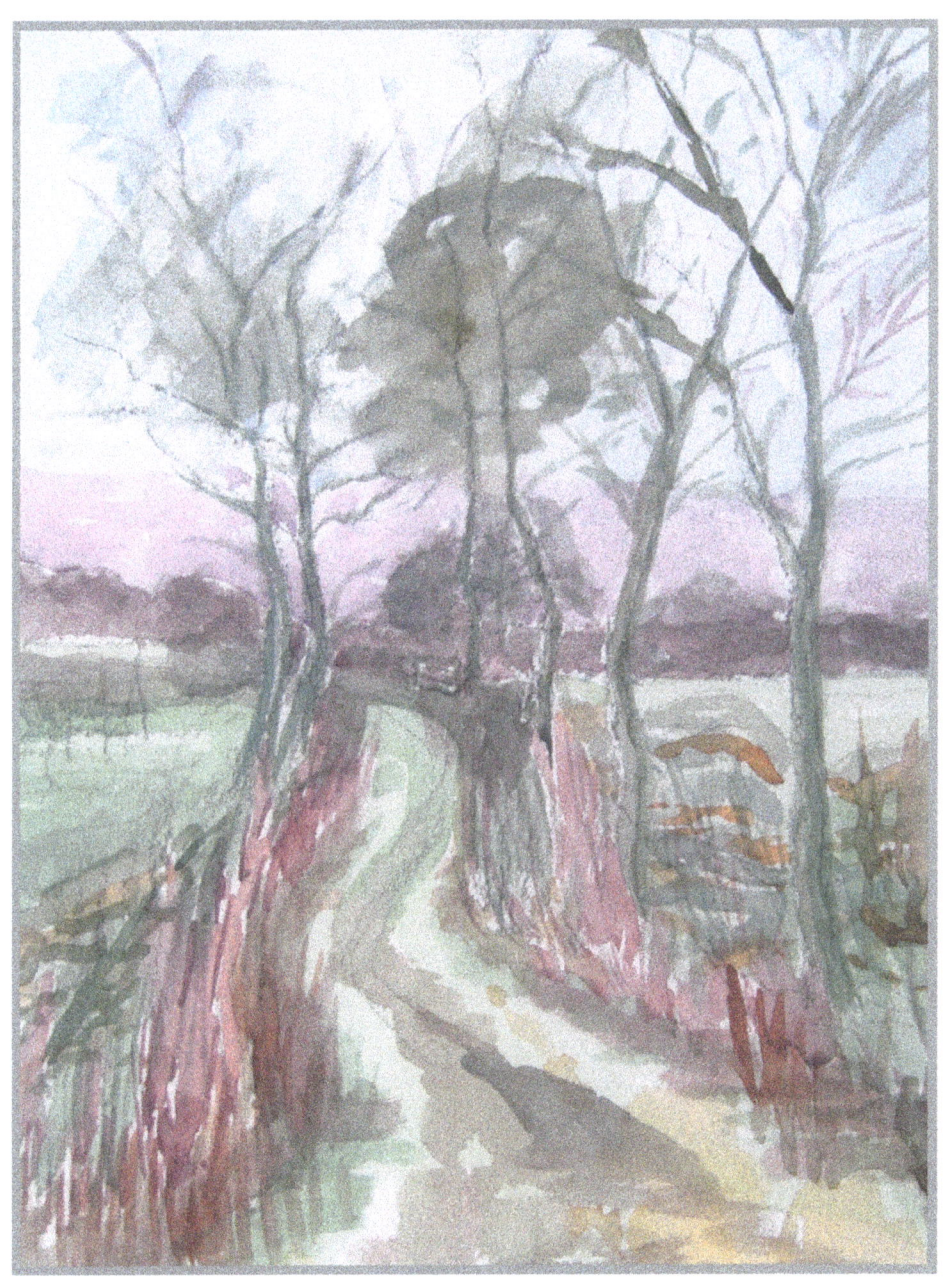

Meadow Lane
By Jane Robertson
2005 Watercolour 16" x 12"

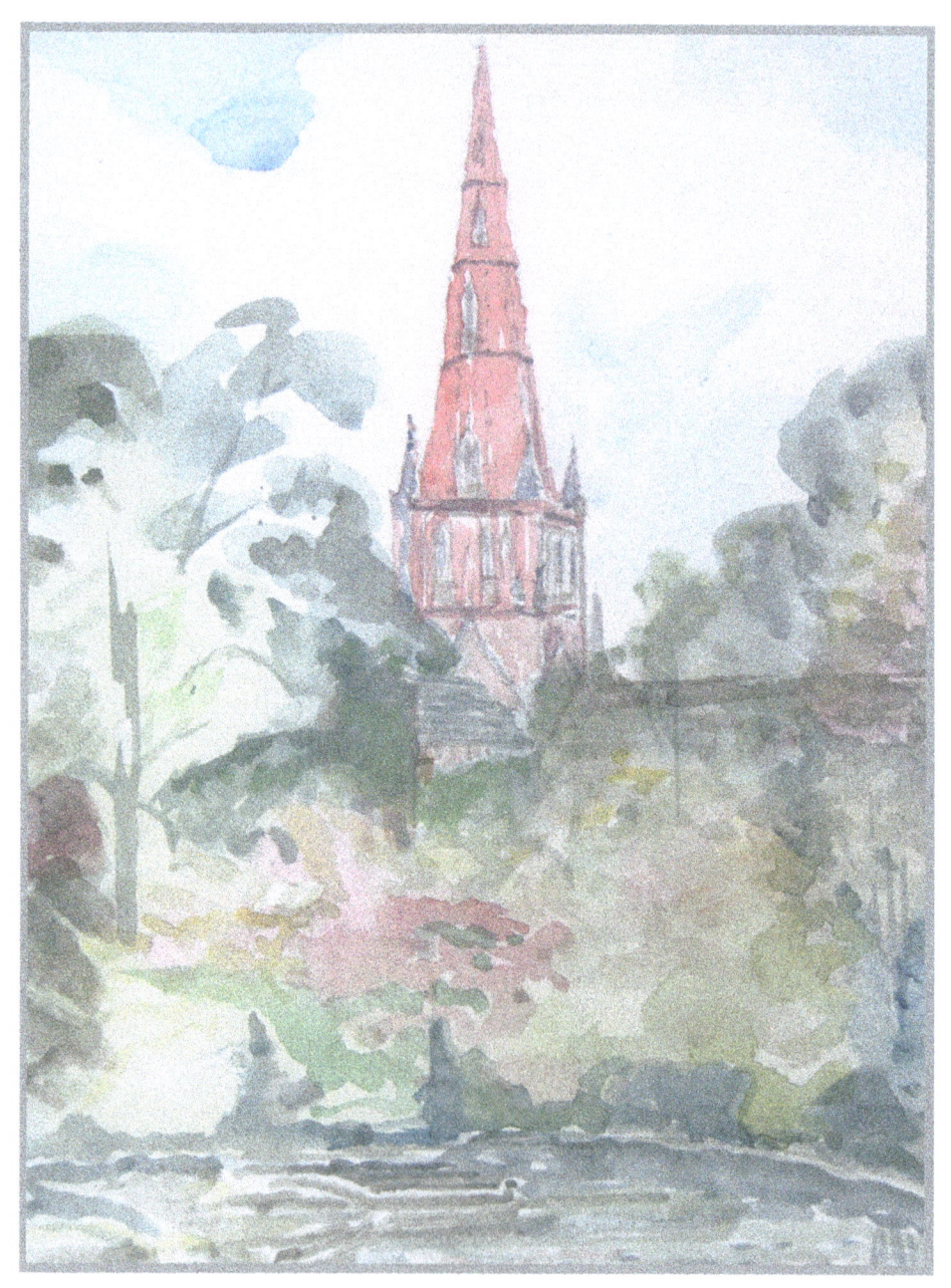

Lichfield
By Jane Robertson
2004 Watercolour 16" x 12"

Scottish Landscape
Jane

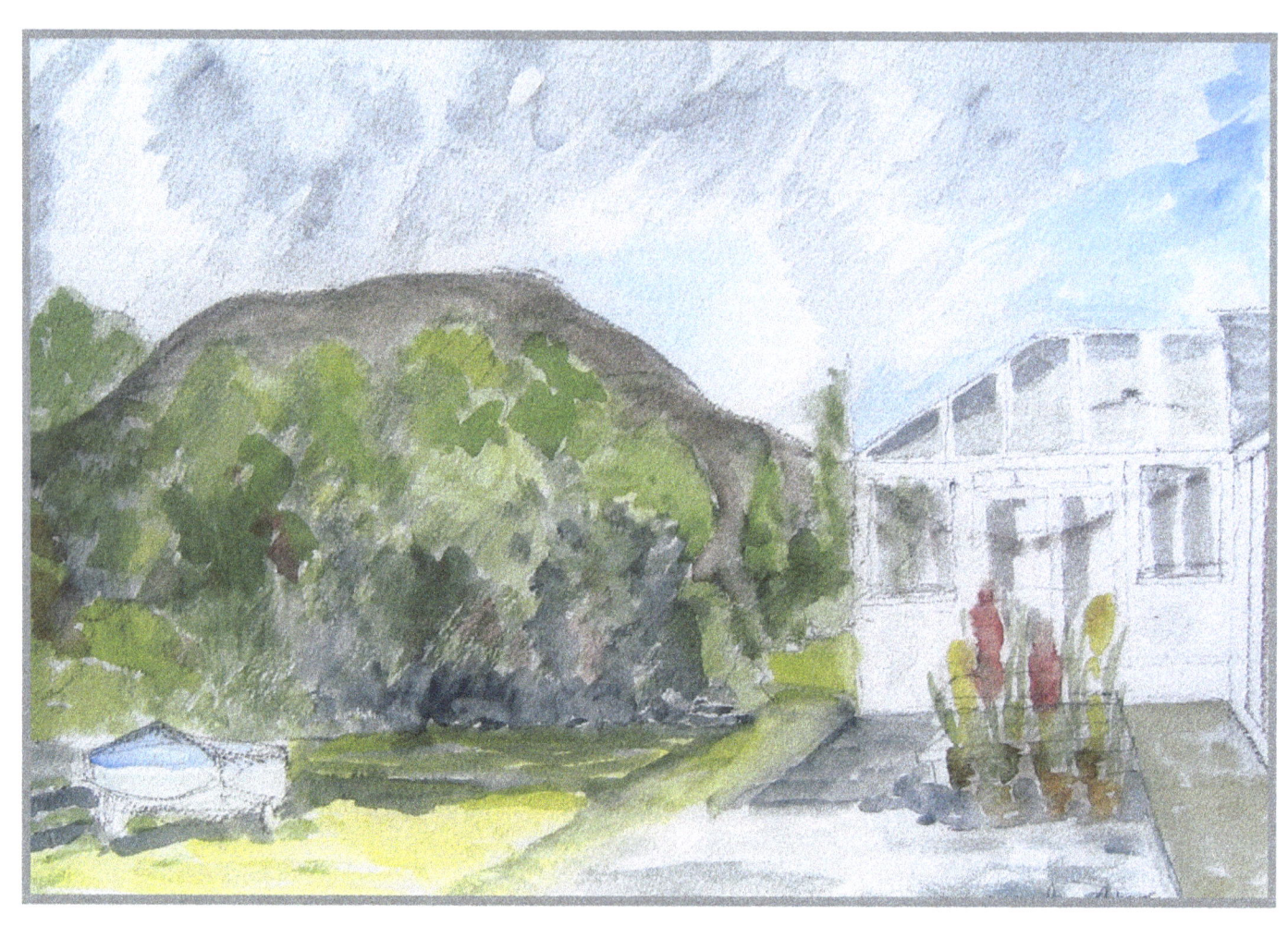

Green Gates
By Jane Robertson
2018 Watercolour 16" x 12"

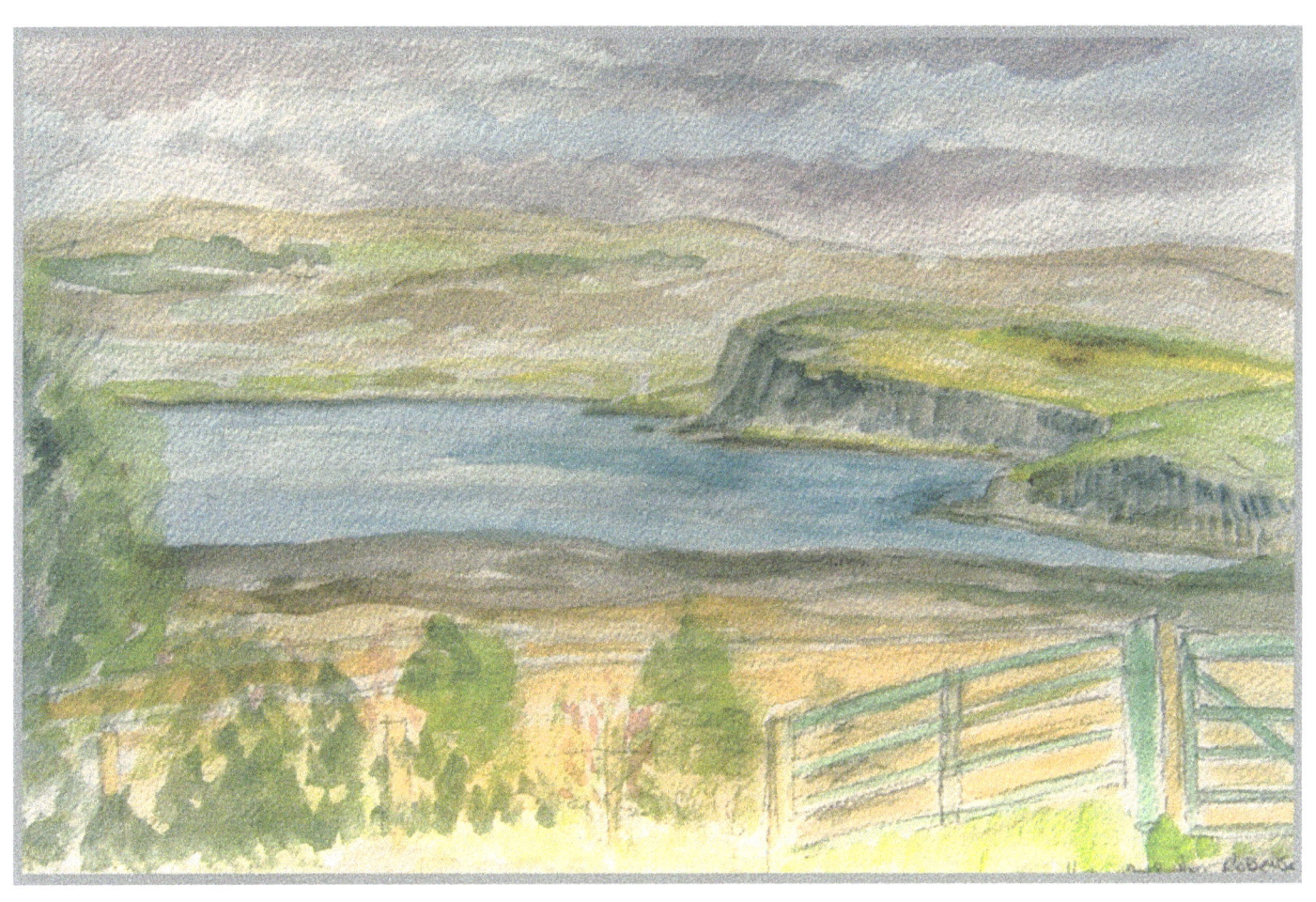

The View from Green Gates
By Jane Robertson
2007 Watercolour 16" x 12"

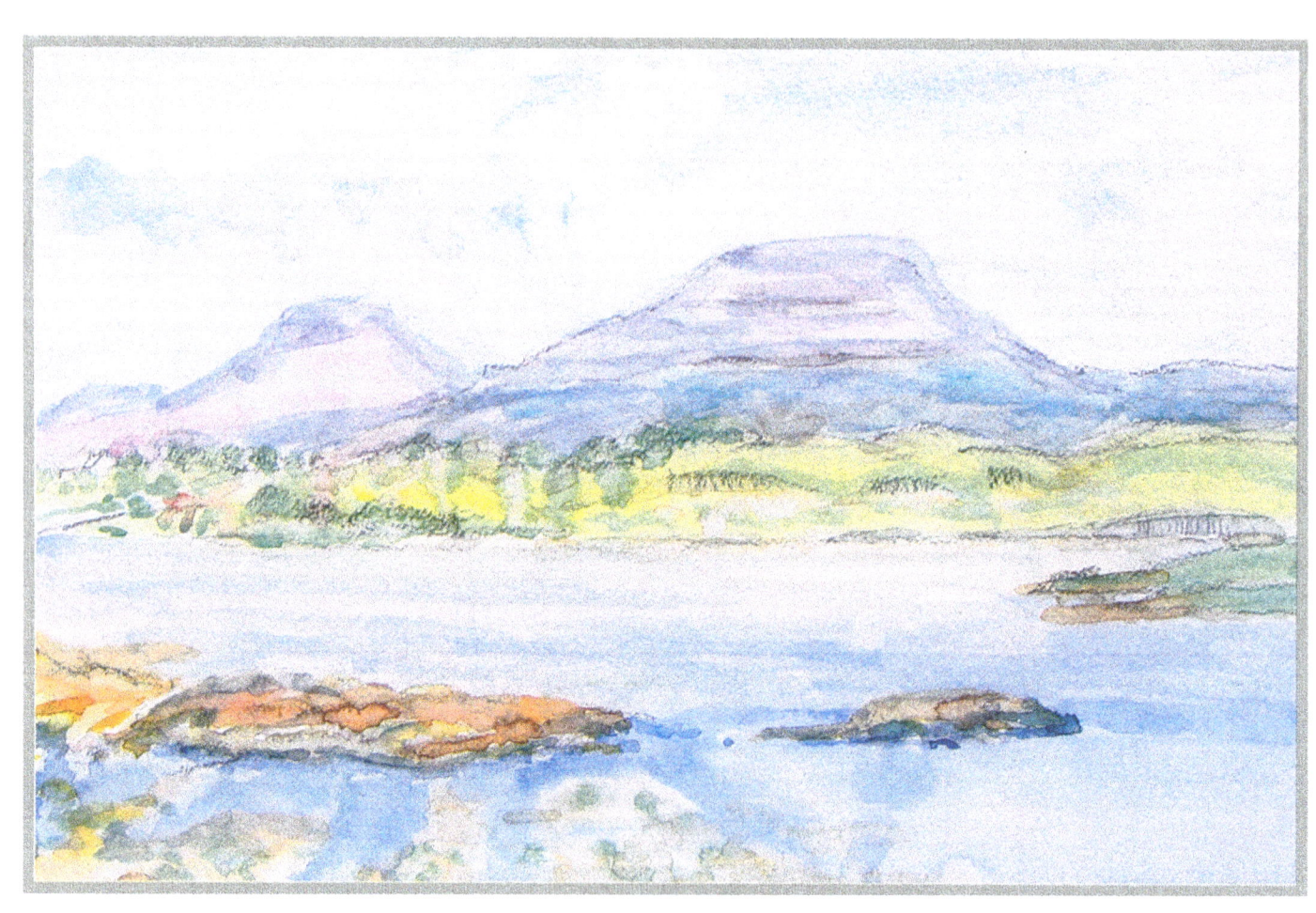

MacLeods Tables
By Jane Robertson
2007 Watercolour 16" x 12"

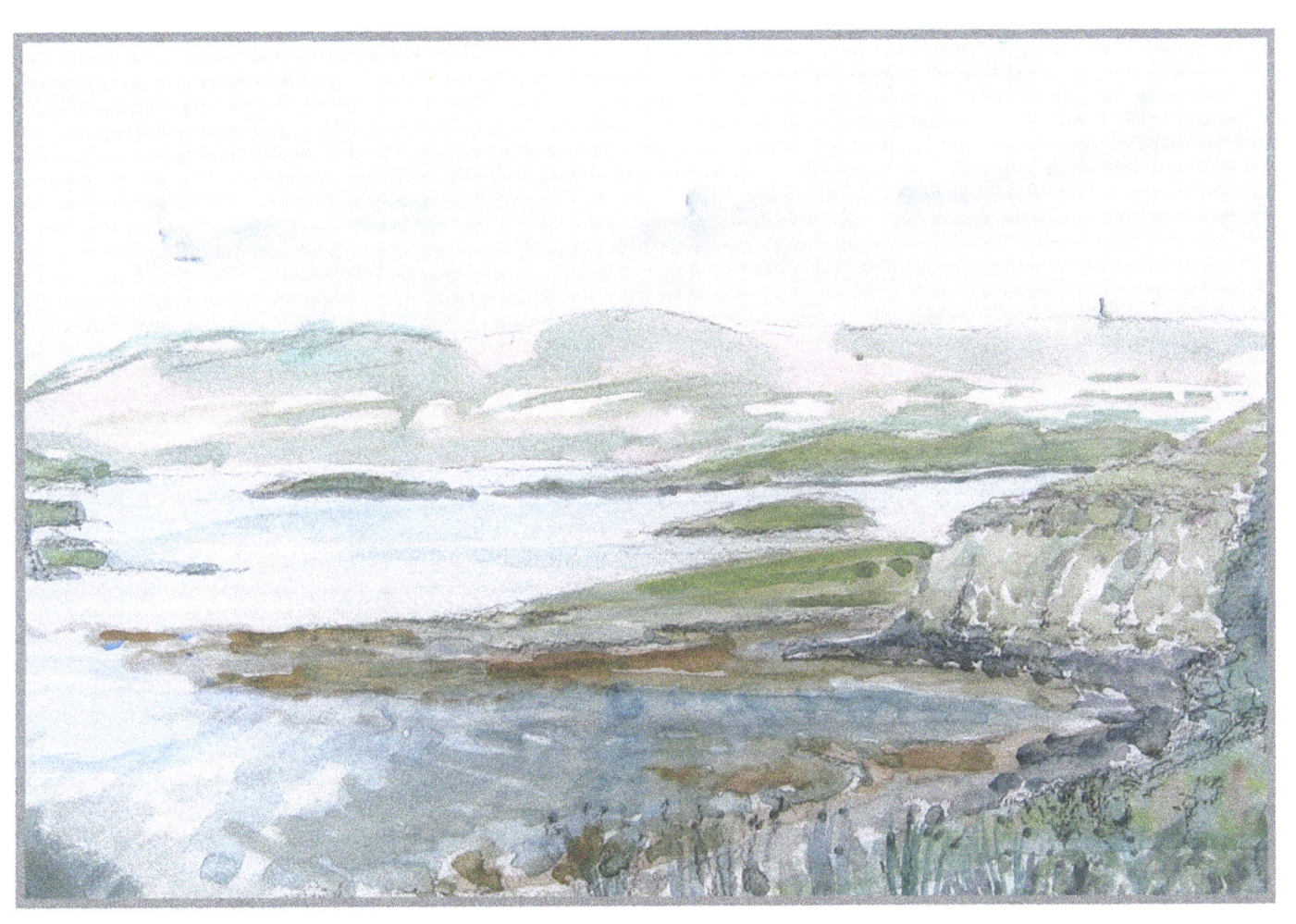

Beyond Dunvegan Castle
By Jane Robertson
2009 Watercolour 16" x 12"

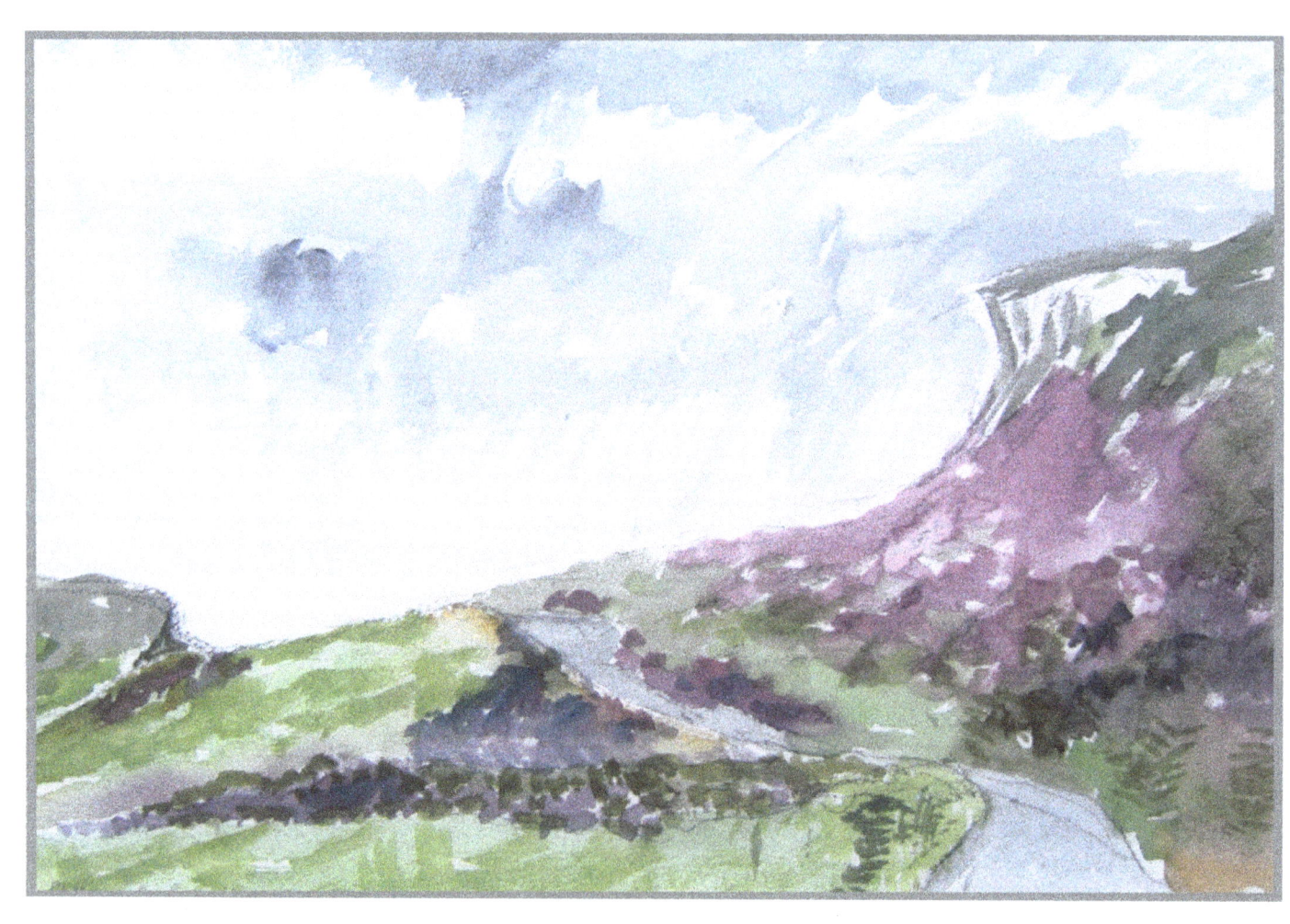

Cliffs near Dunvegan
By Jane Robertson
2011 Watercolour 16" x 12"

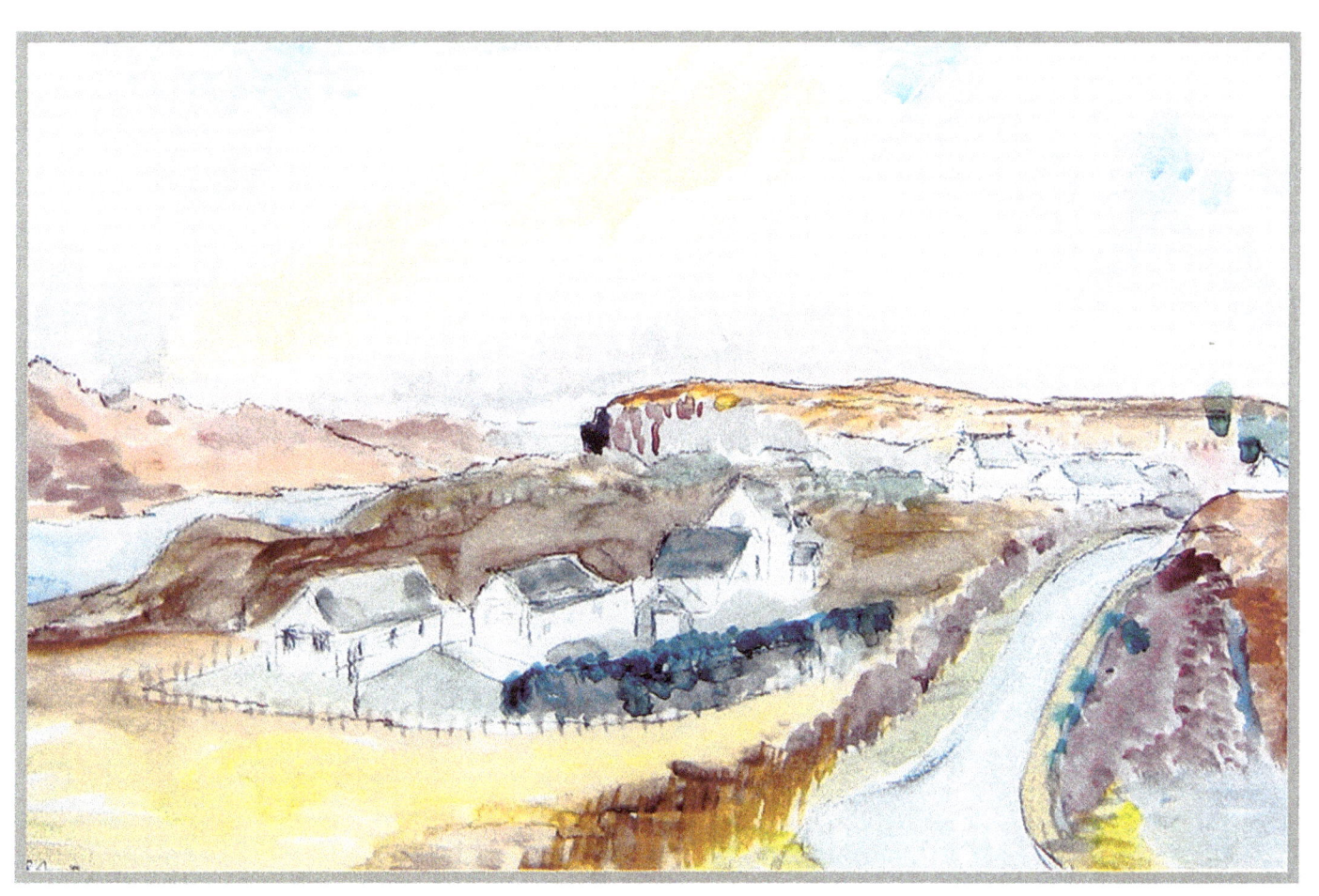

Flashader
By Jane Robertson
2016 Watercolour 16" x 12"

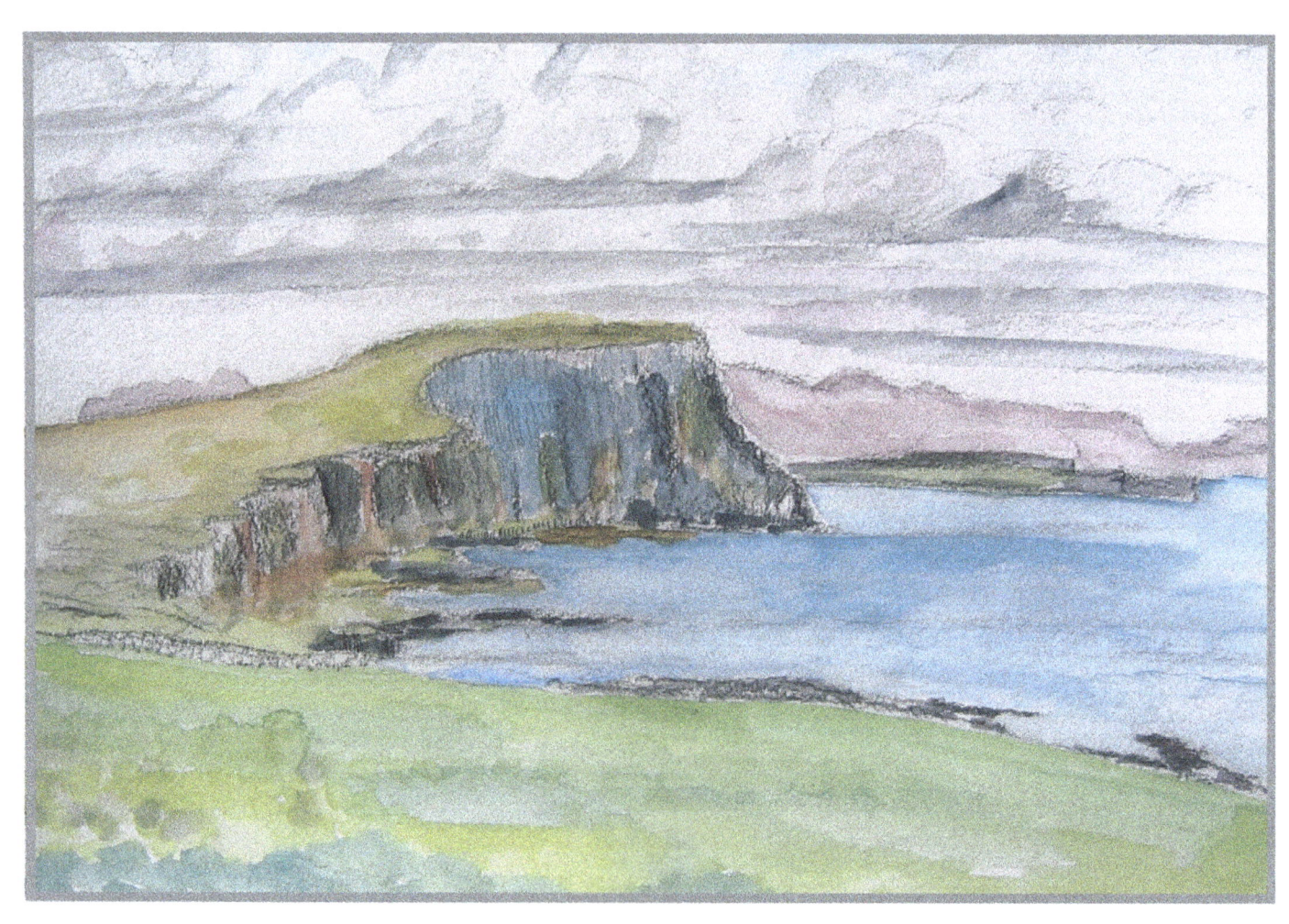

Orbost
By Jane Robertson
2015 Watercolour 16" x 12"

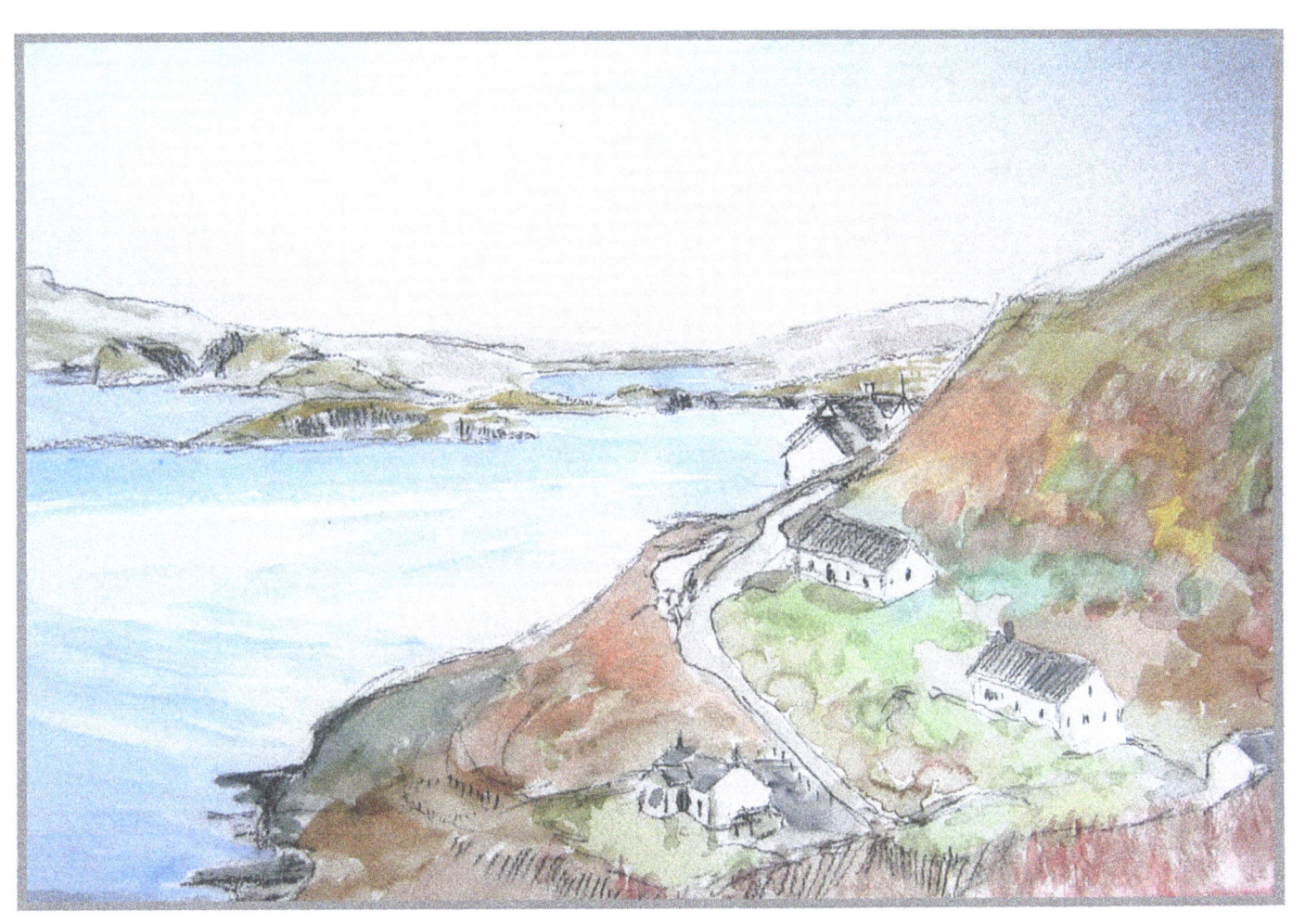

Fiscavaig
By Jane Robertson
12.02.2009 Watercolour 16" x 12"

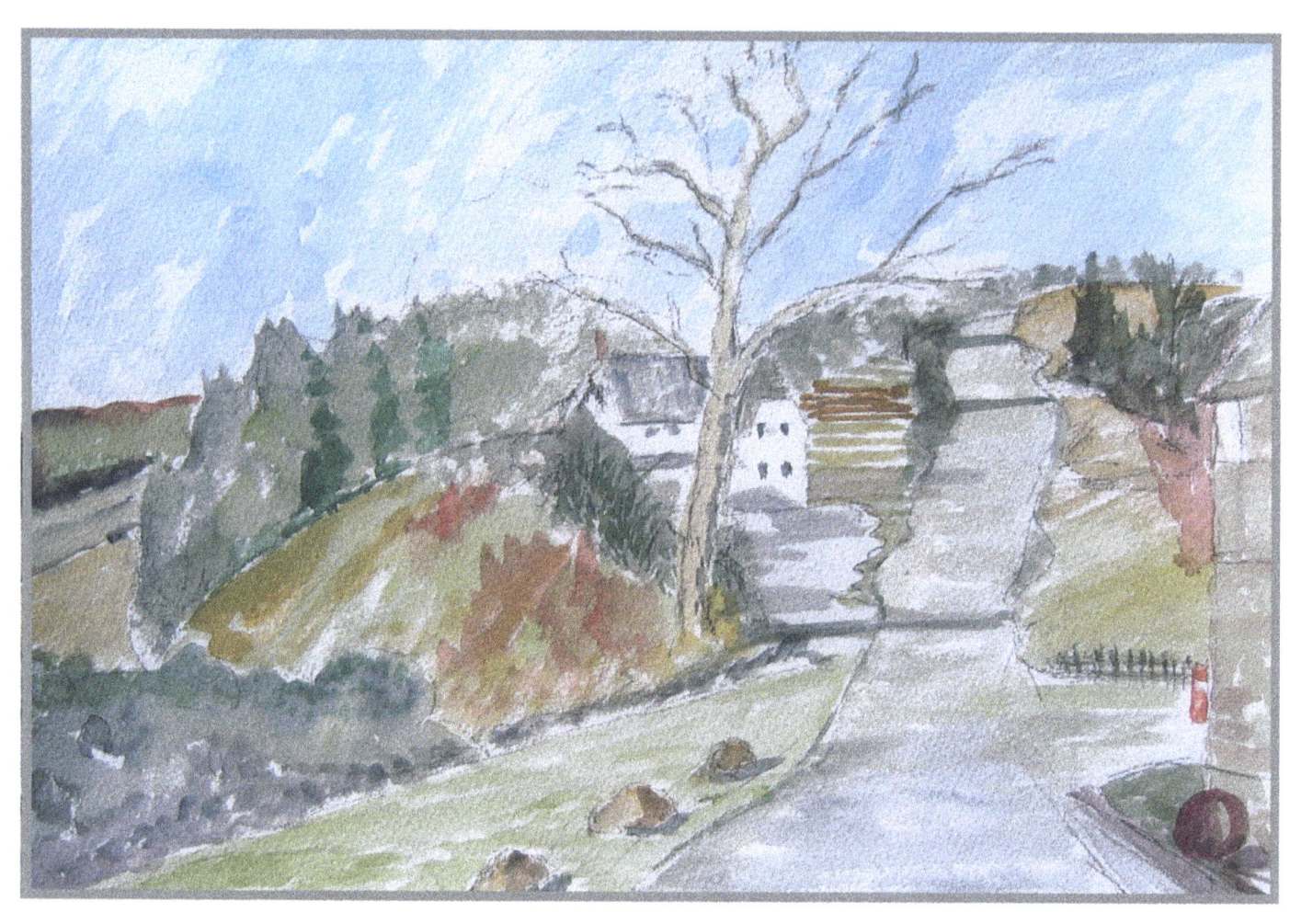

Stein
By Jane Robertson
2015 Watercolour 16" x 12"

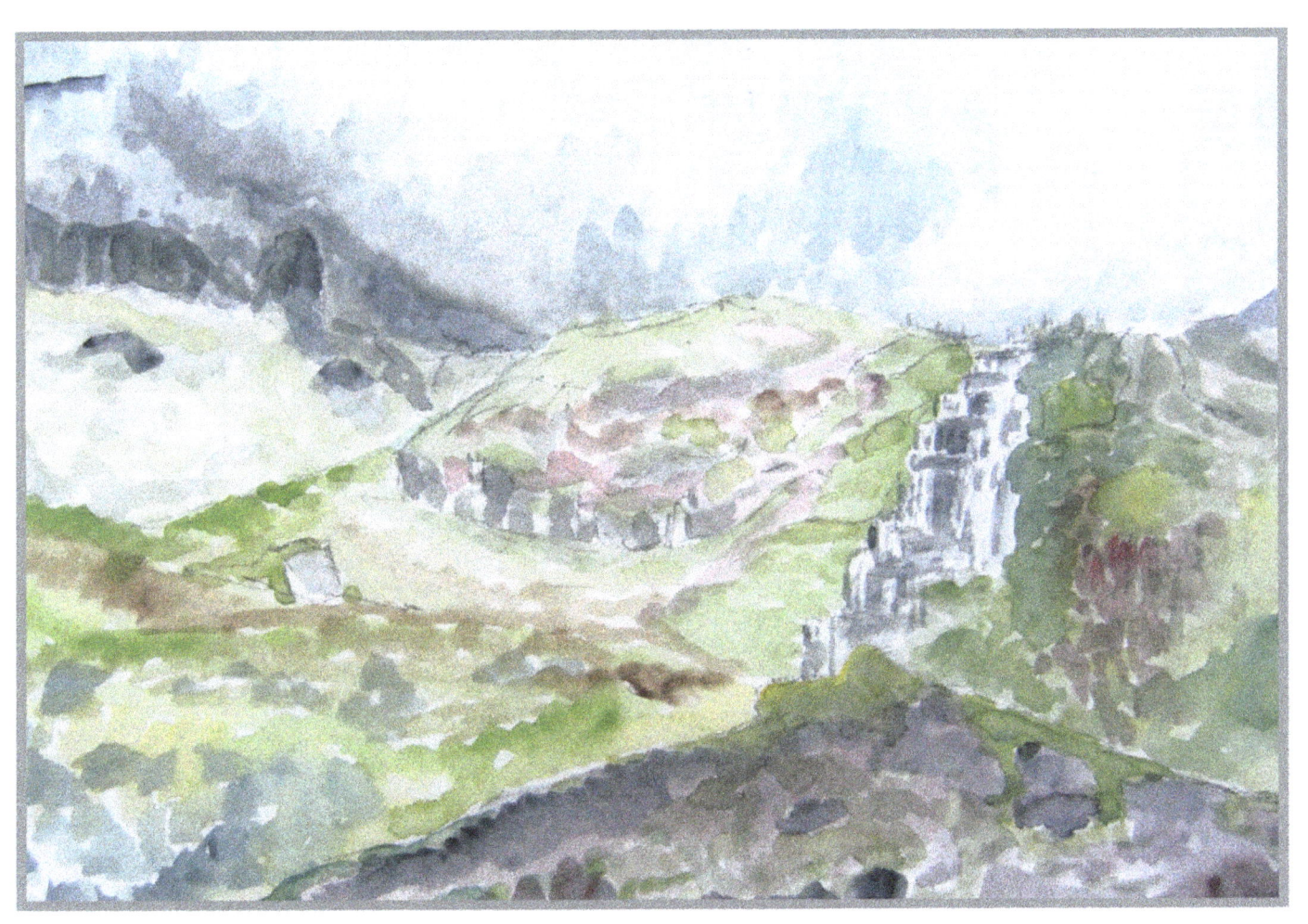

Waterfall, Storr
By Jane Robertson
2012 Watercolour 16" x 12"

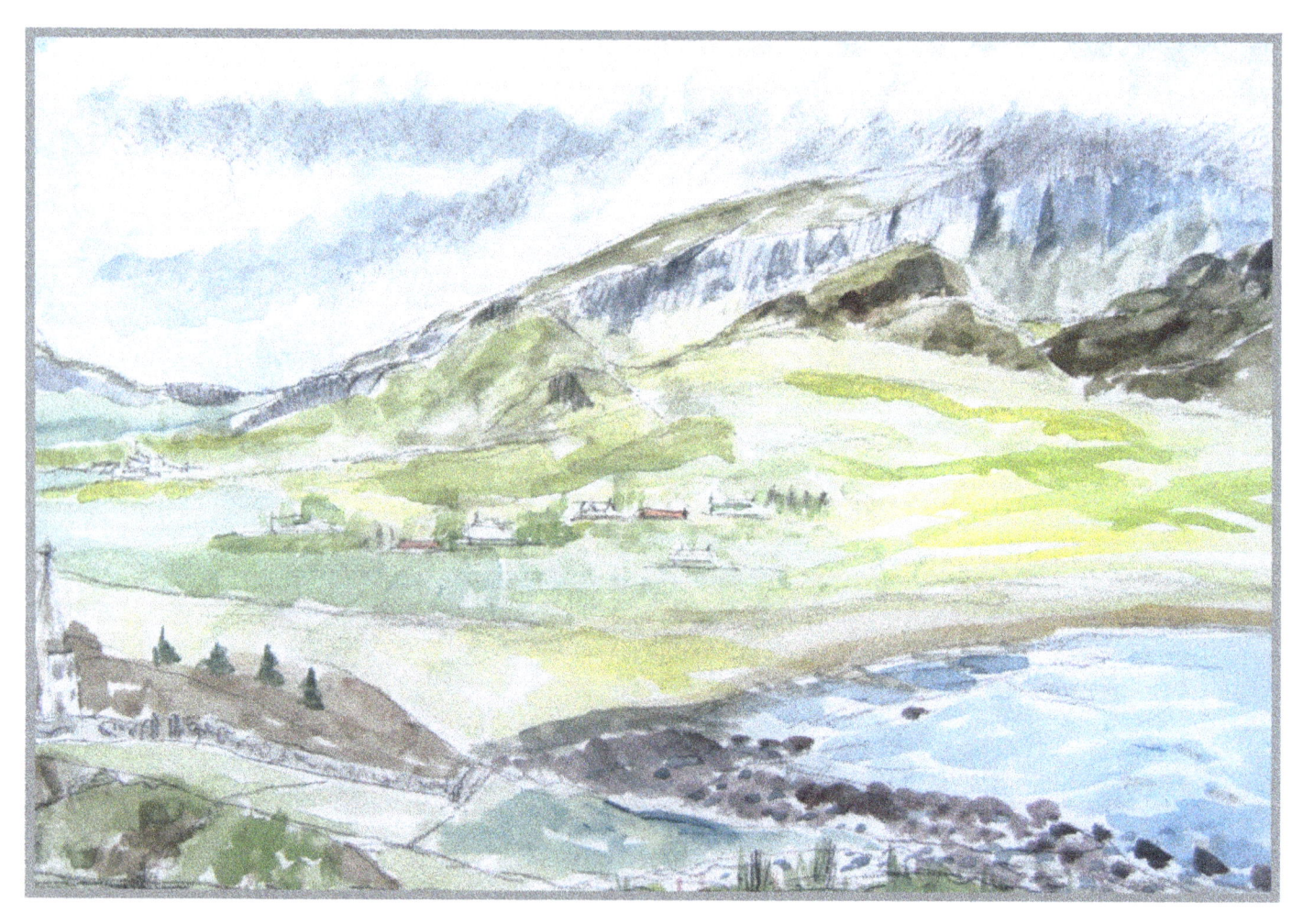

Staffin
By Jane Robertson
2018 Watercolour 16" x 12"

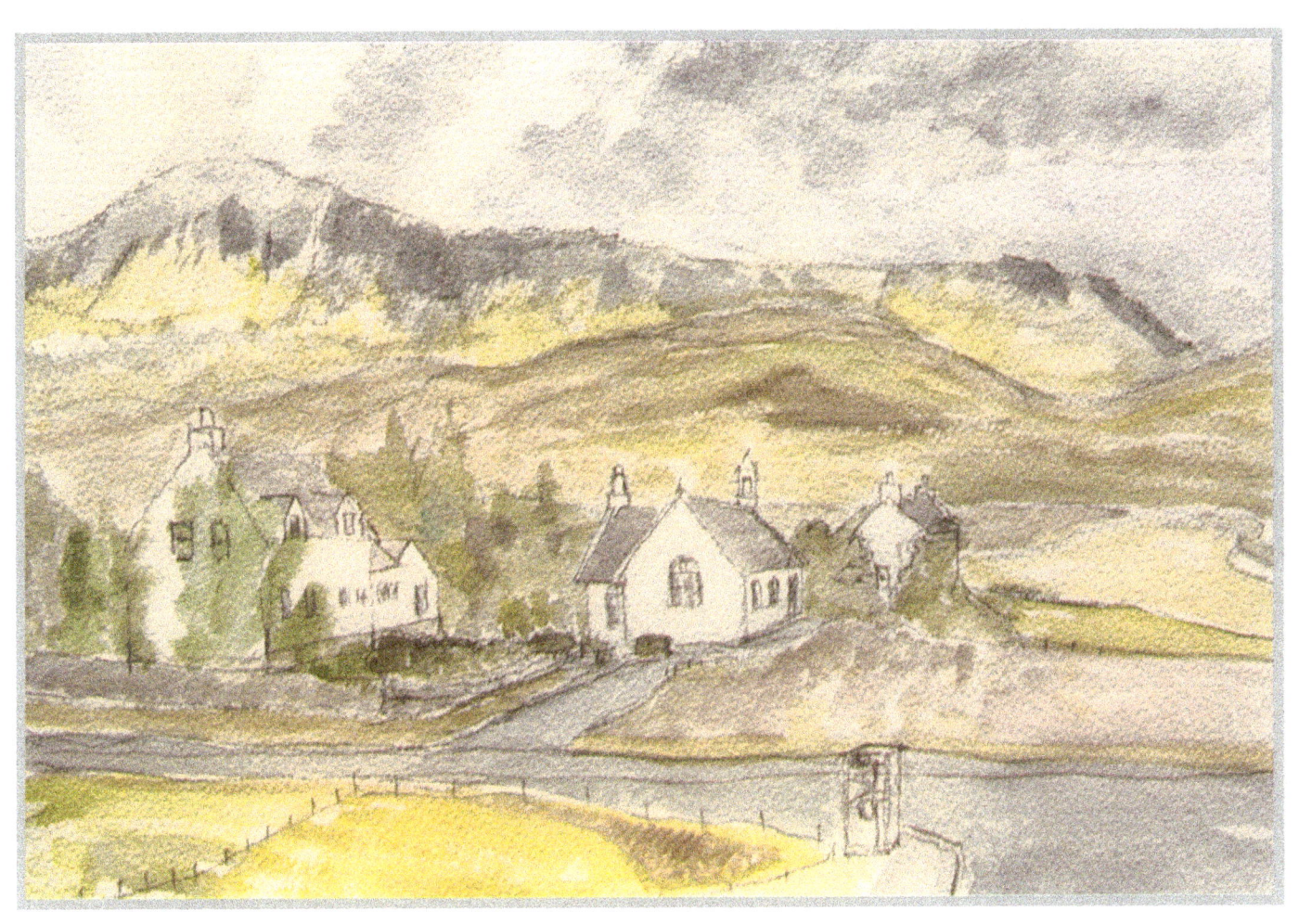

Staffin The Church
By Jane Robertson
2007 Watercolour 16" x 12"

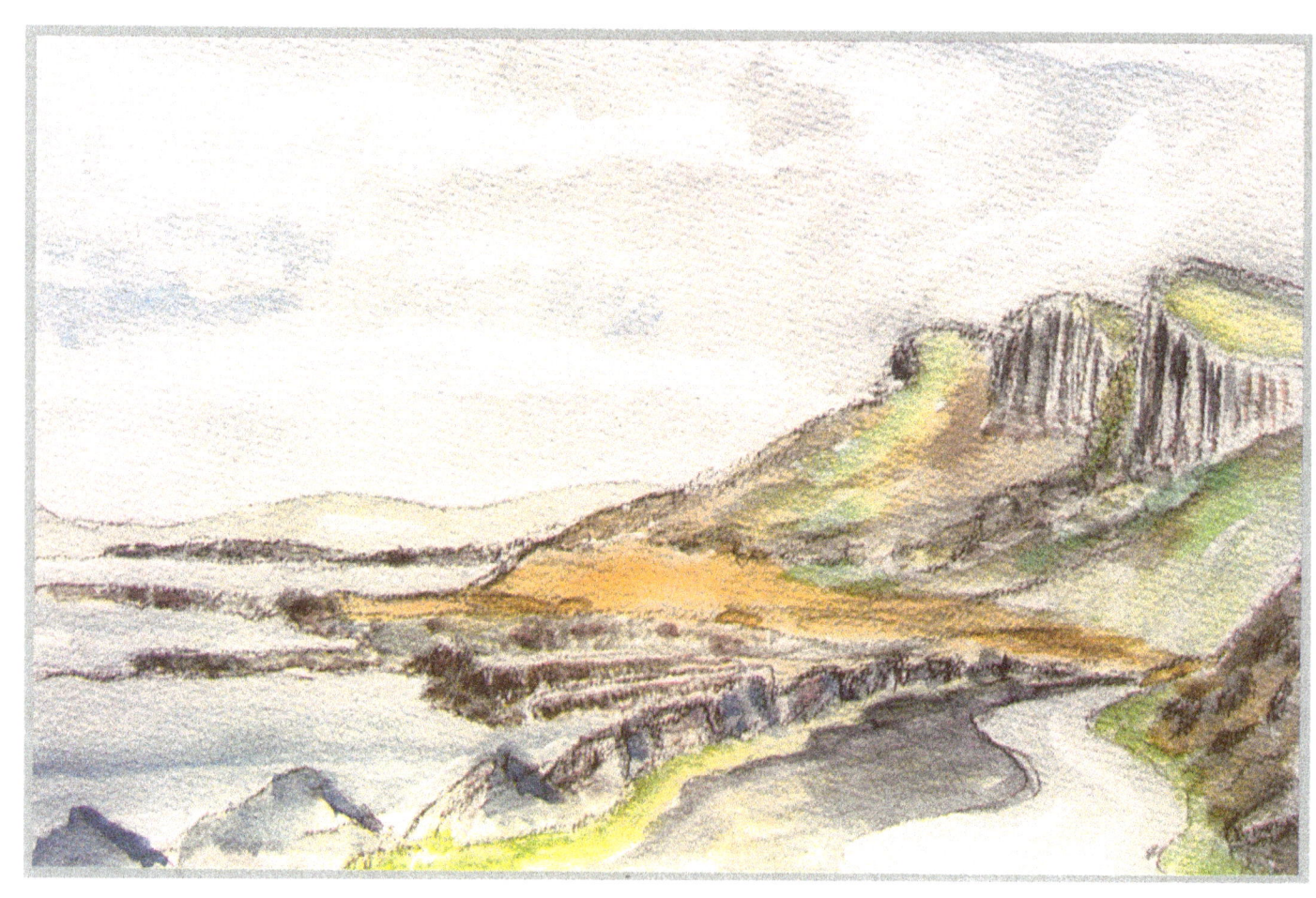

The Harbour at Staffin
By Jane Robertson
2007 Watercolour 16" x 12"

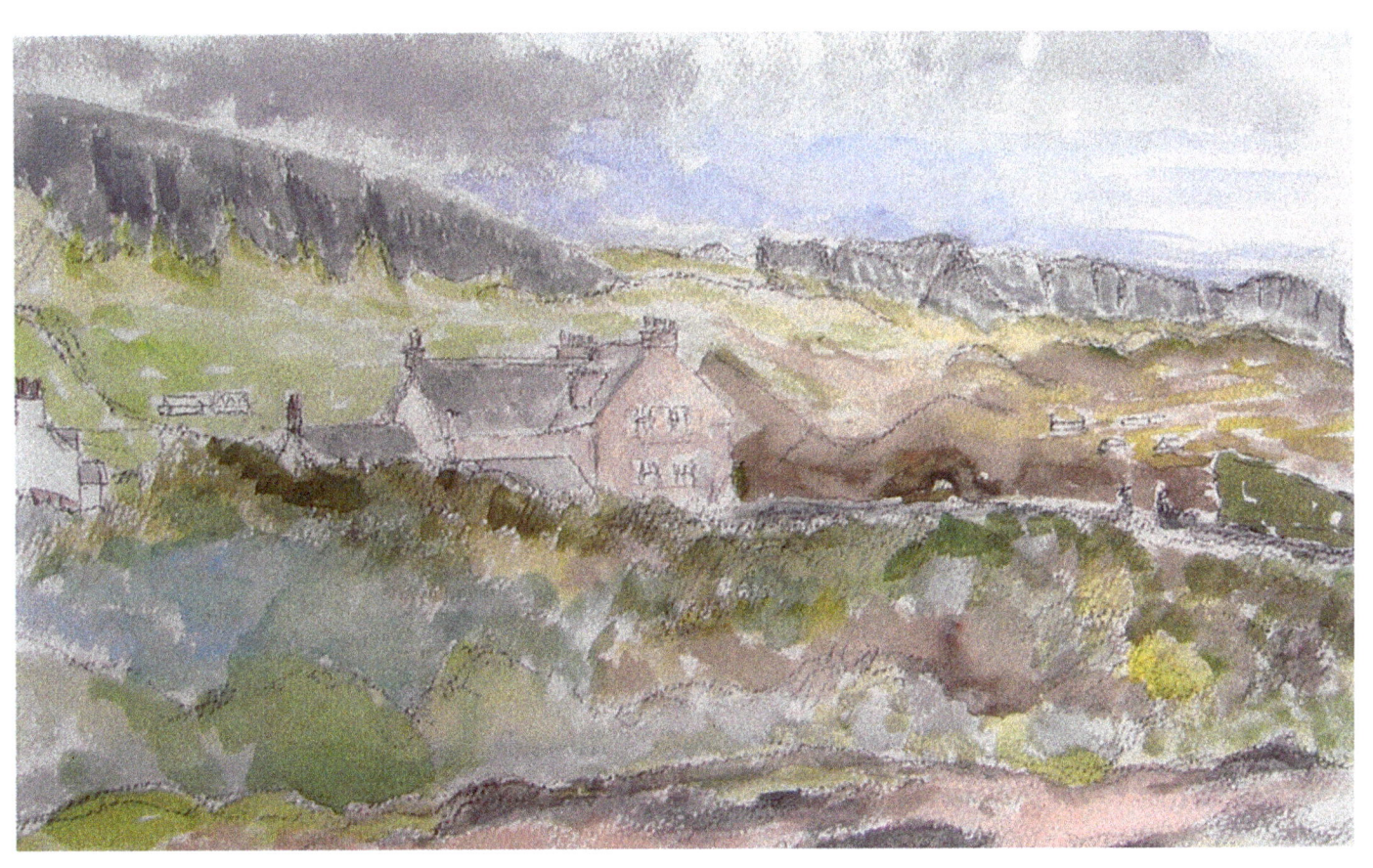

Staffin
By Jane Robertson
2007 Watercolour 16" x 12"

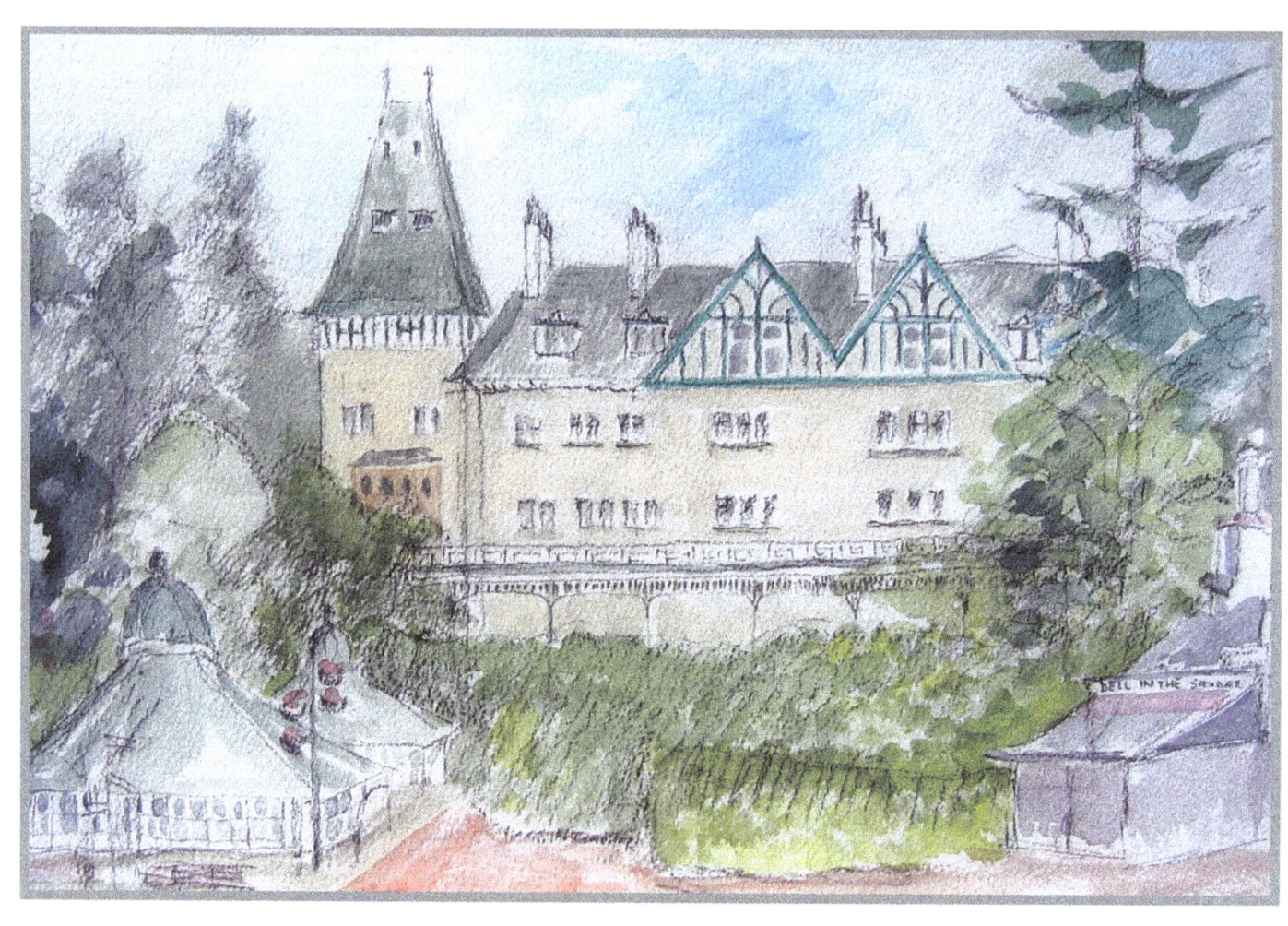

Strathpeffer
By Jane Robertson
2018 Watercolour 16" x 12"

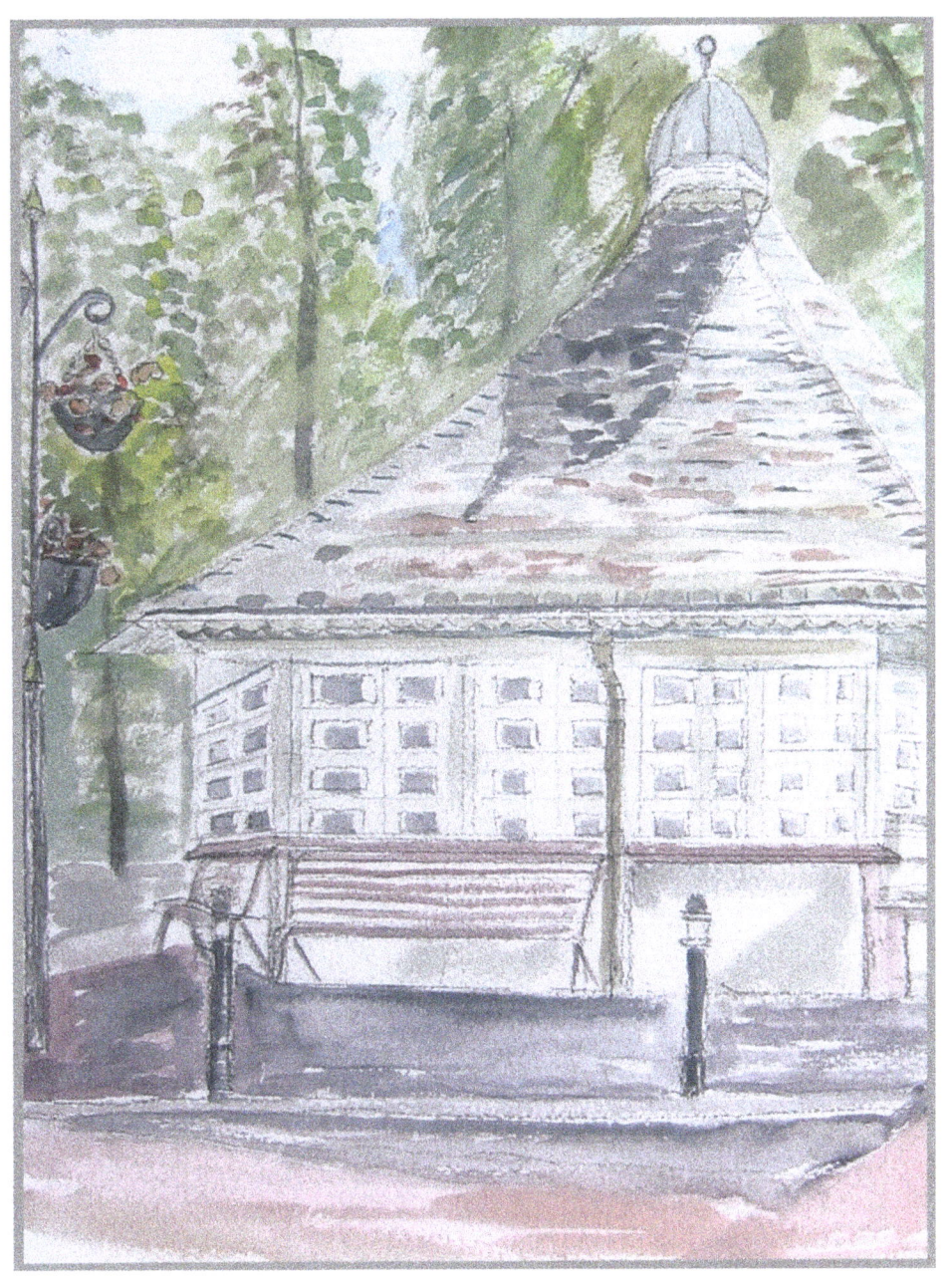

Pavilion Strathpeffer
By Jane Robertson
05.09.2014 Watercolour 16" x 12"

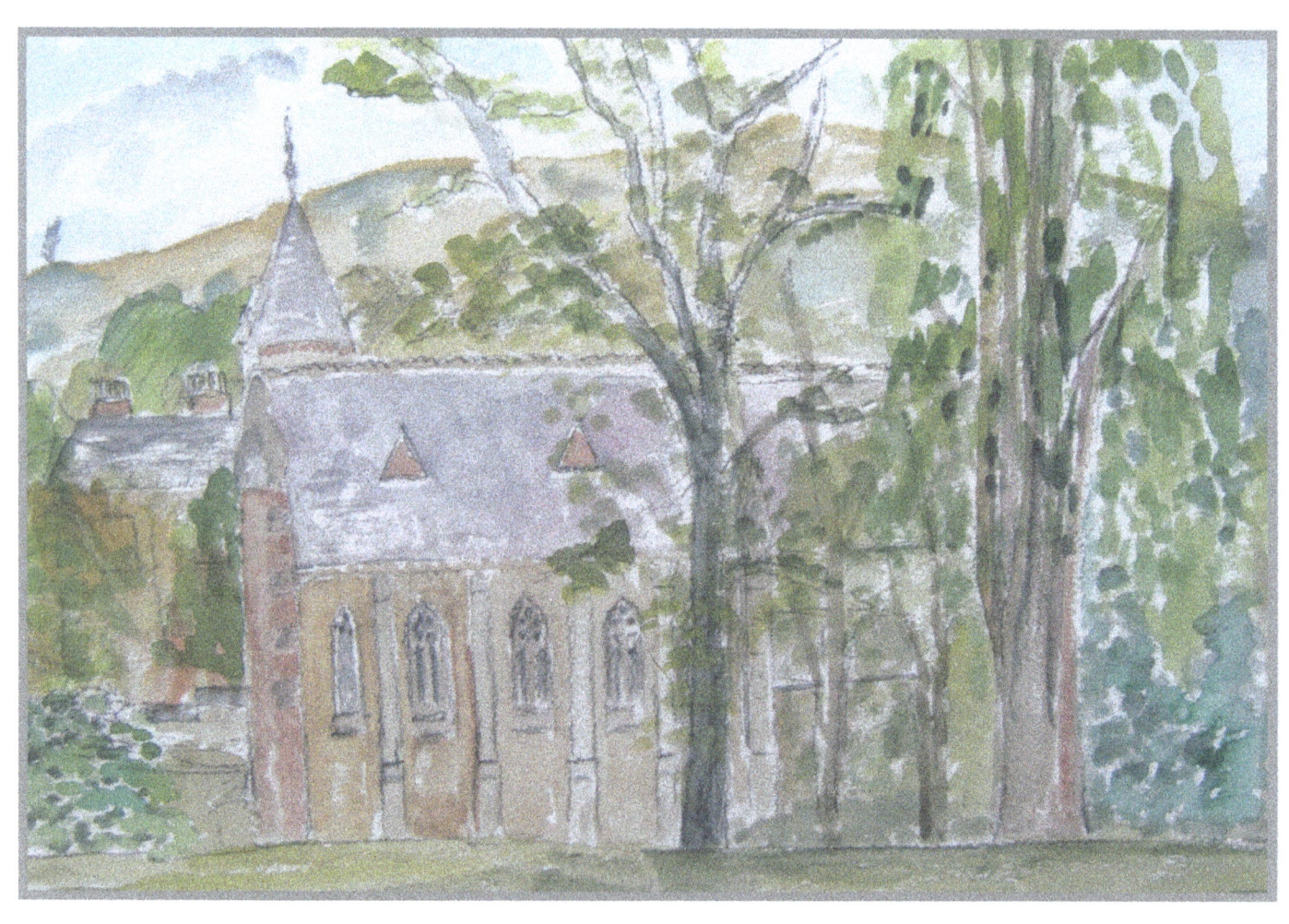

Strathpeffer
By Jane Robertson
2014 Watercolour 16" x 12"

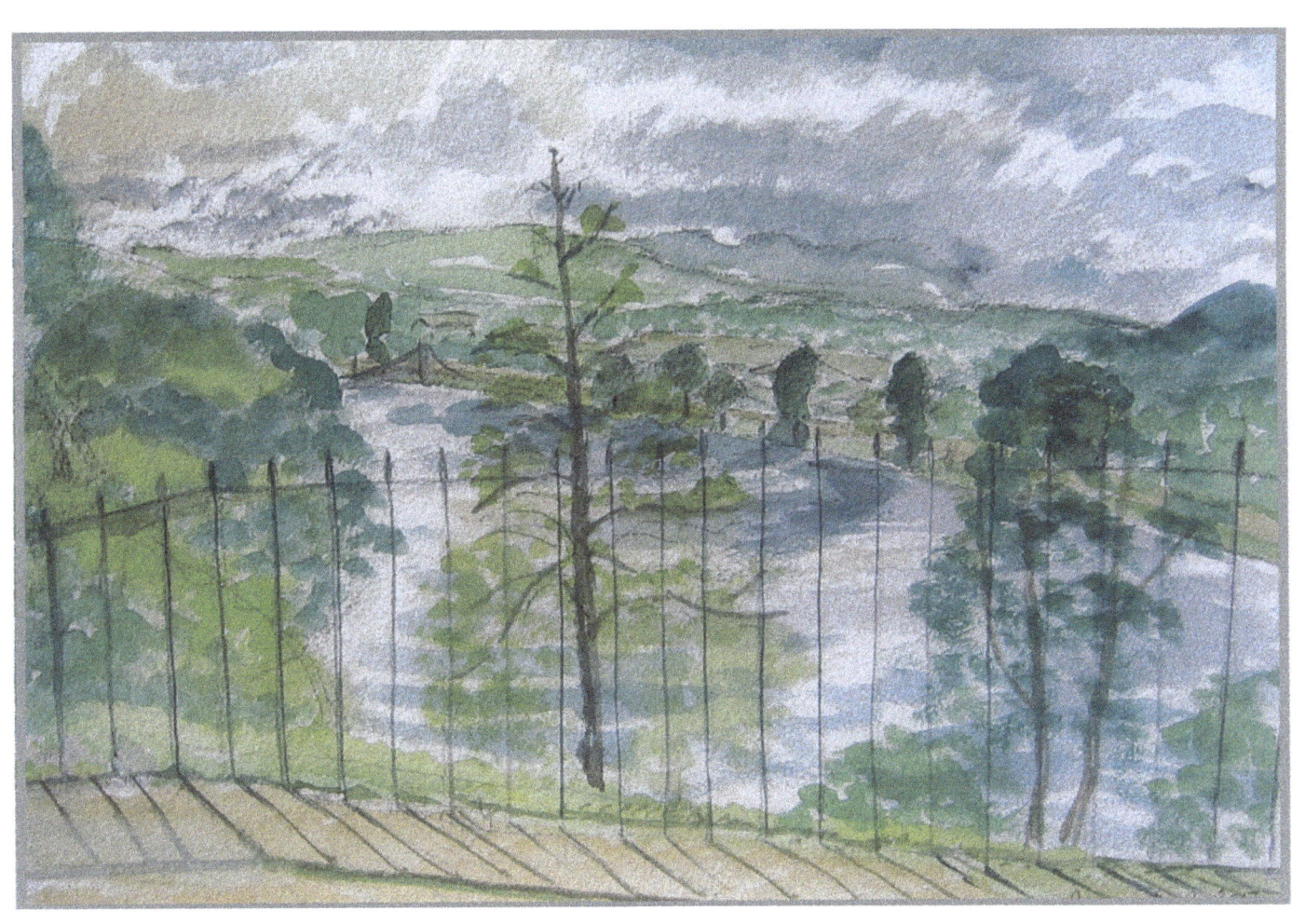

River Ness from the Castle
By Jane Robertson
2017 Watercolour 16" x 12"

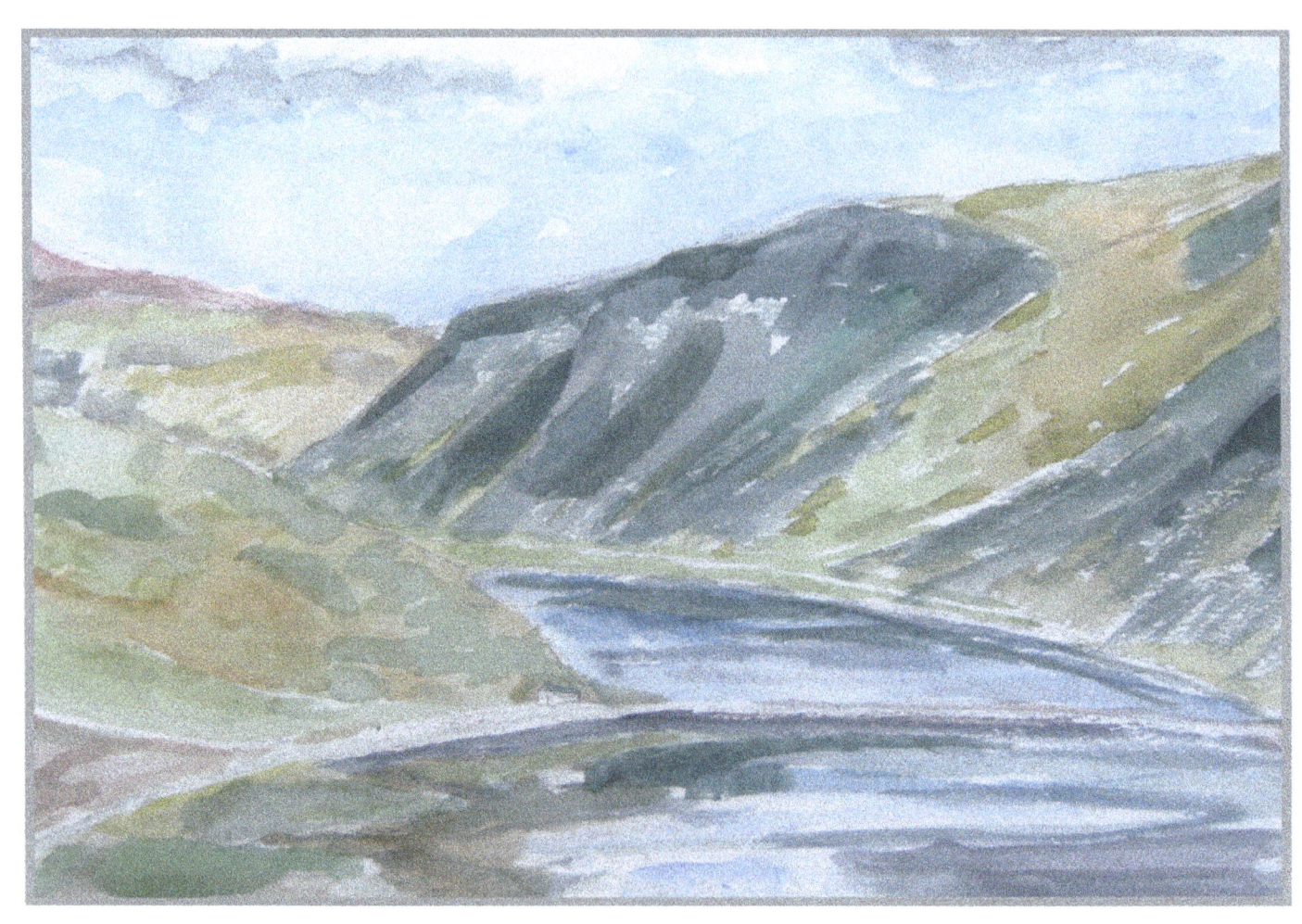

Bracadale
By Jane Robertson
2008 Watercolour 16" x 12"

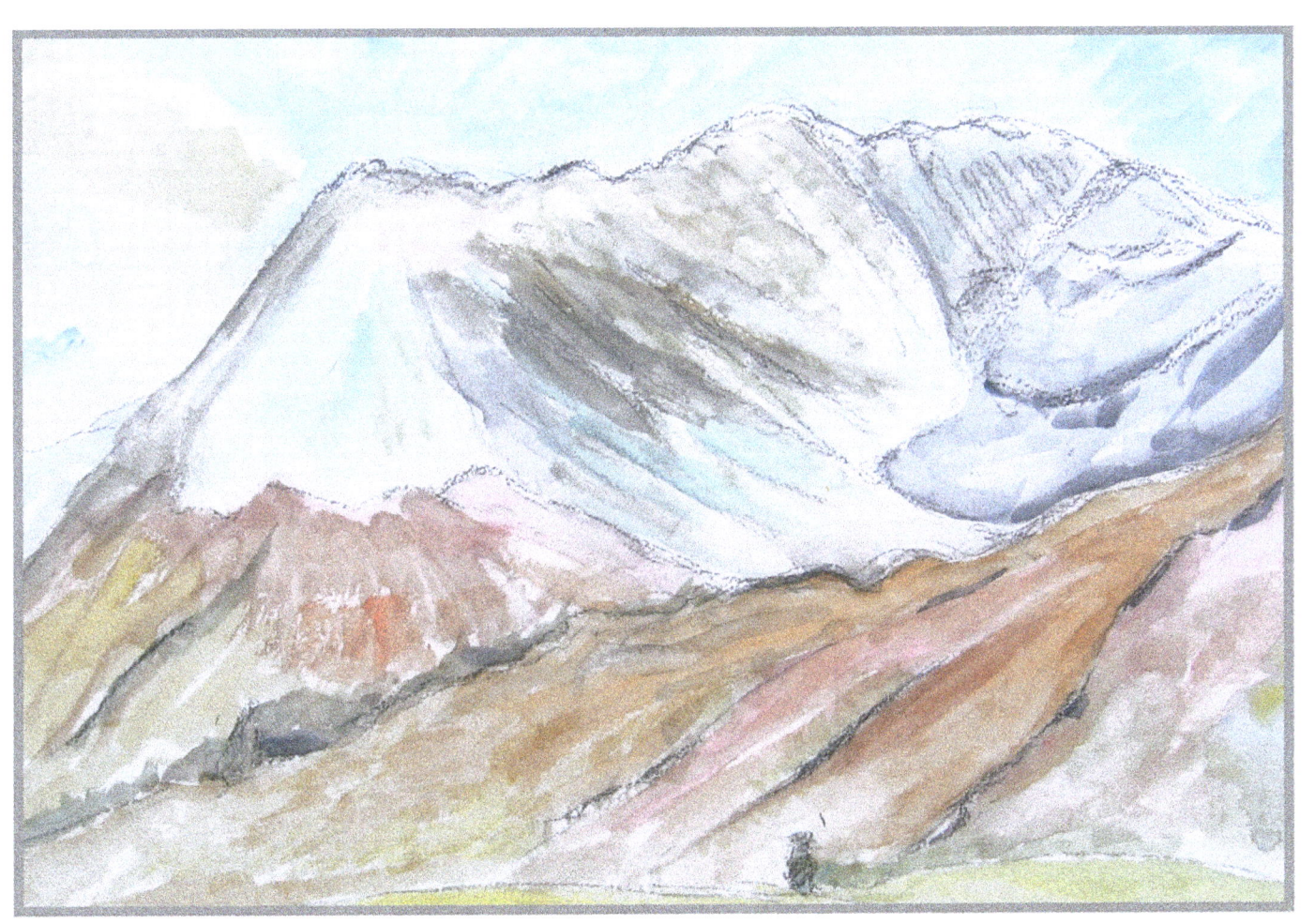

Glen Brittle
By Jane Robertson
13.12.2009 Watercolour 16" x 12"

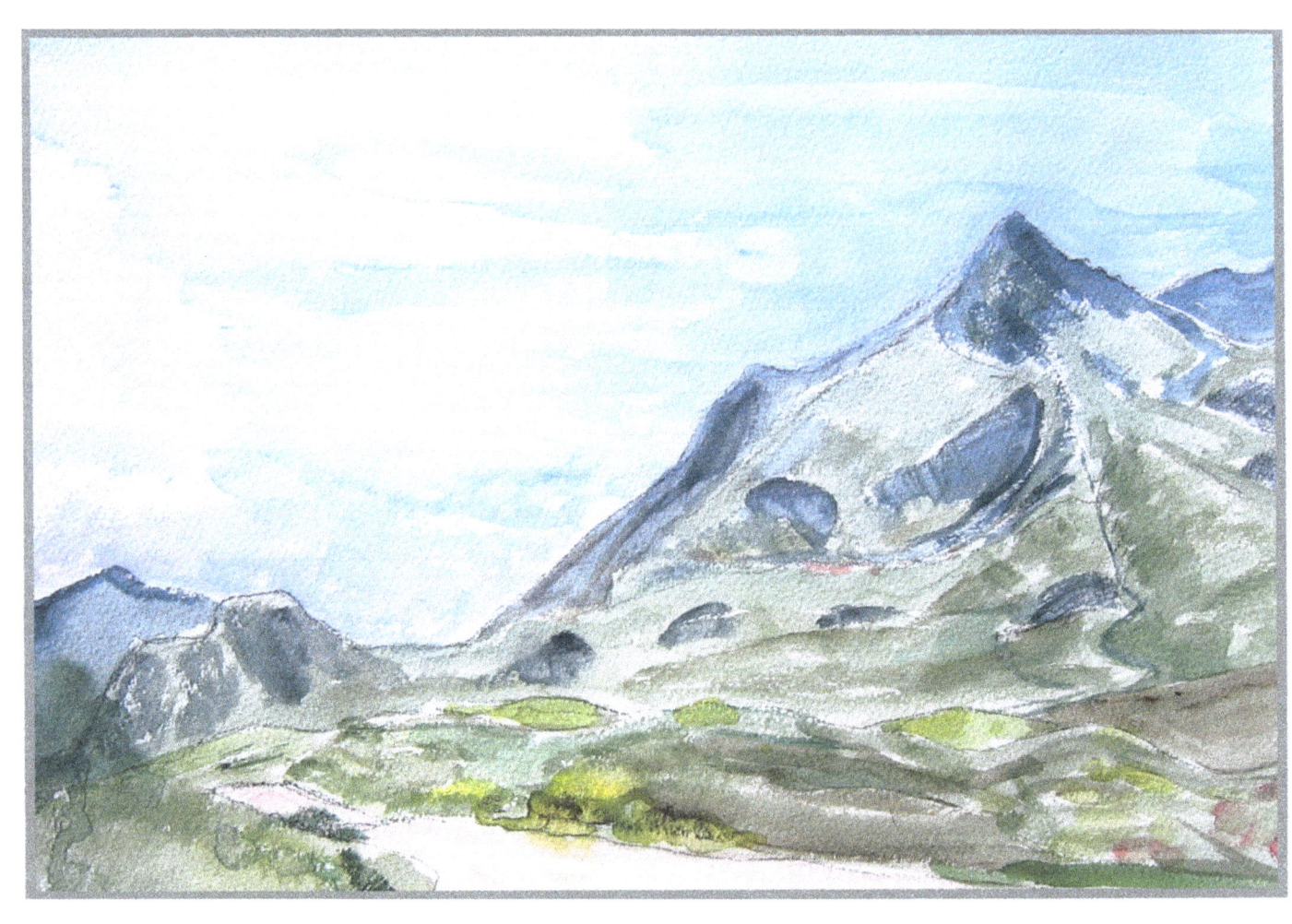

The Cuillins
By Jane Robertson
2014 Watercolour 16" x 12"

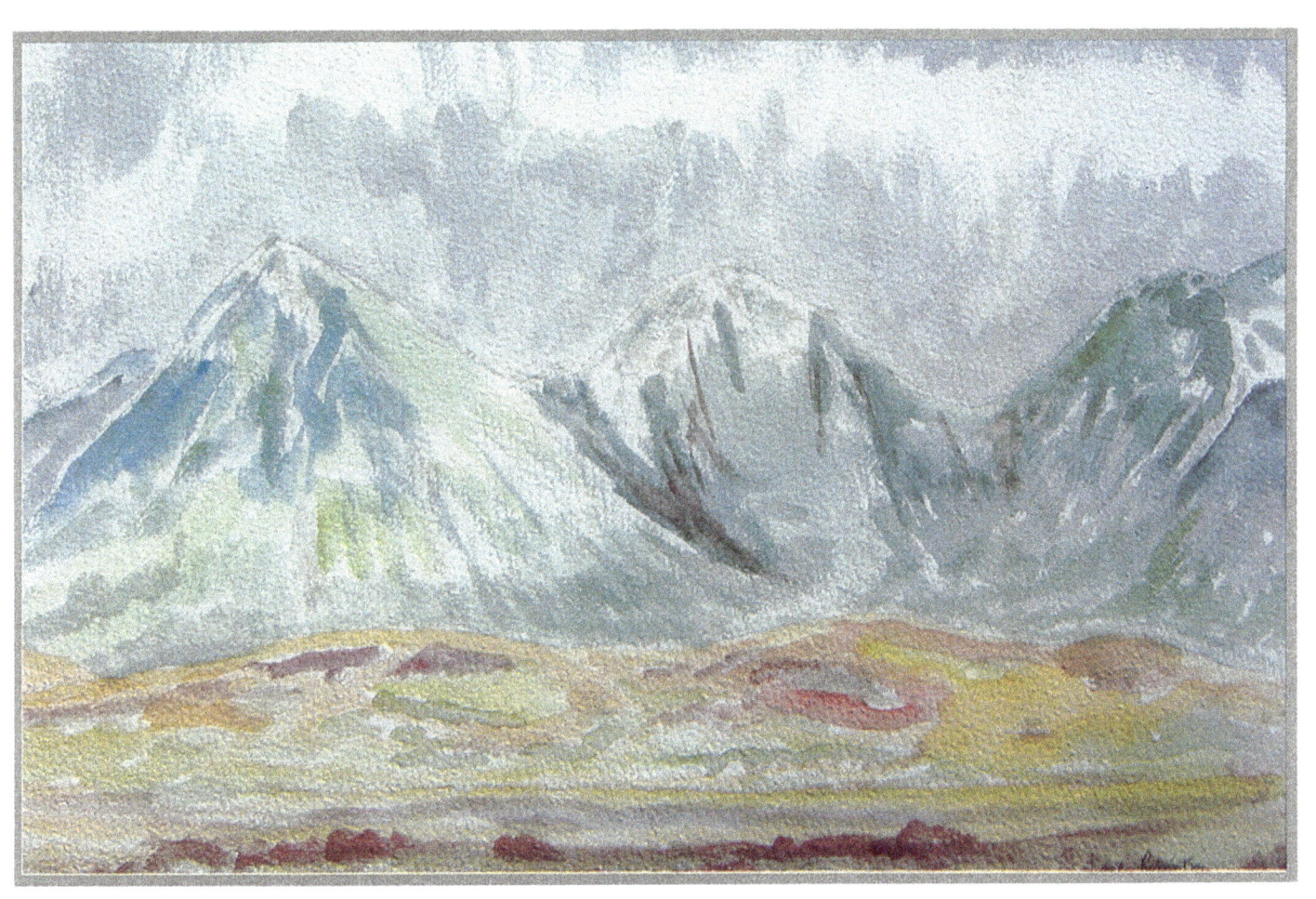

The Cullins
By Jane Robertson
2007 Watercolour 16" x 12"

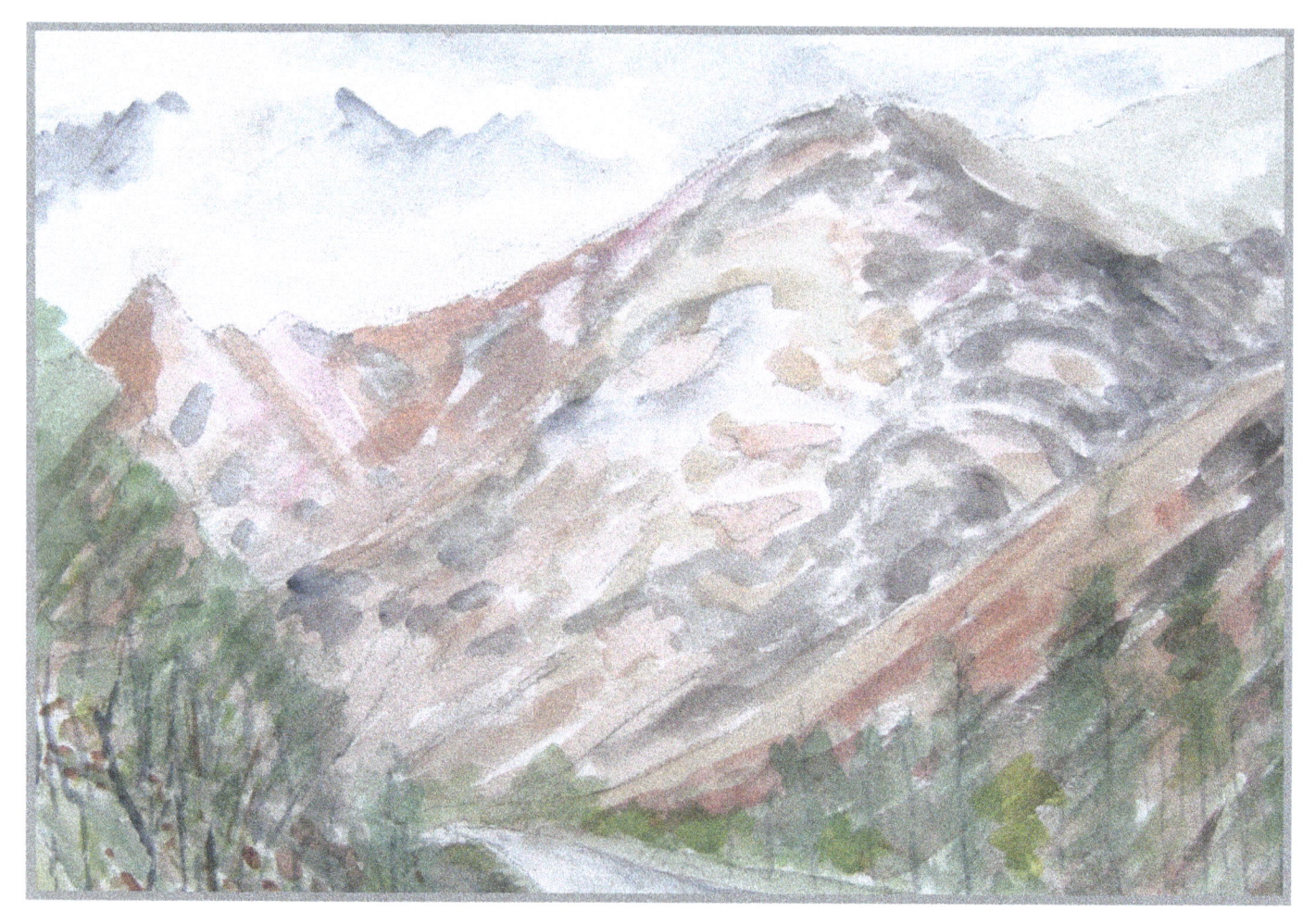

The Sisters
By Jane Robertson
2014 Watercolour 16" x 12"

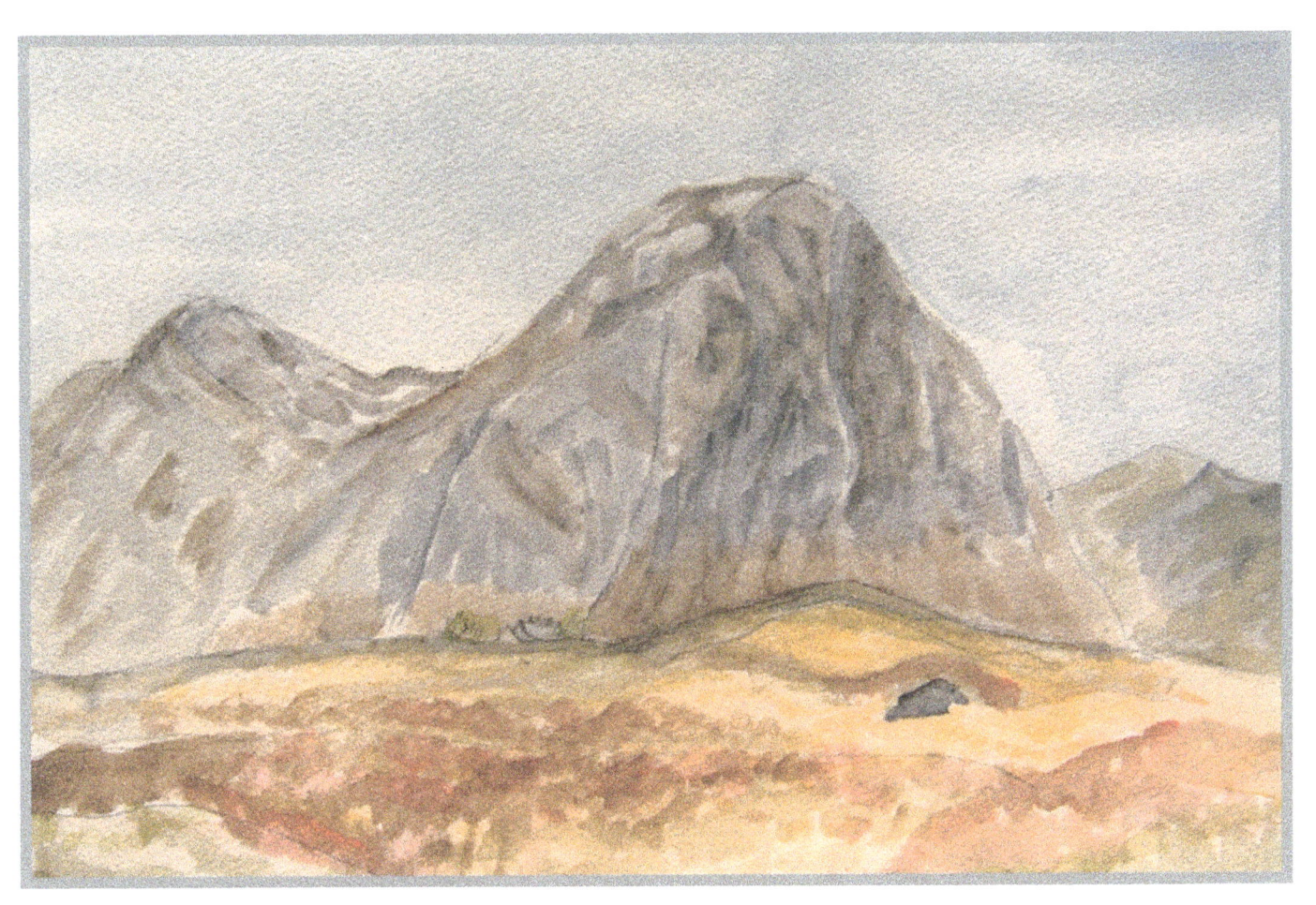

Buachaille Etive Mor
By Jane Robertson
2007 Watercolour 16" x 12"

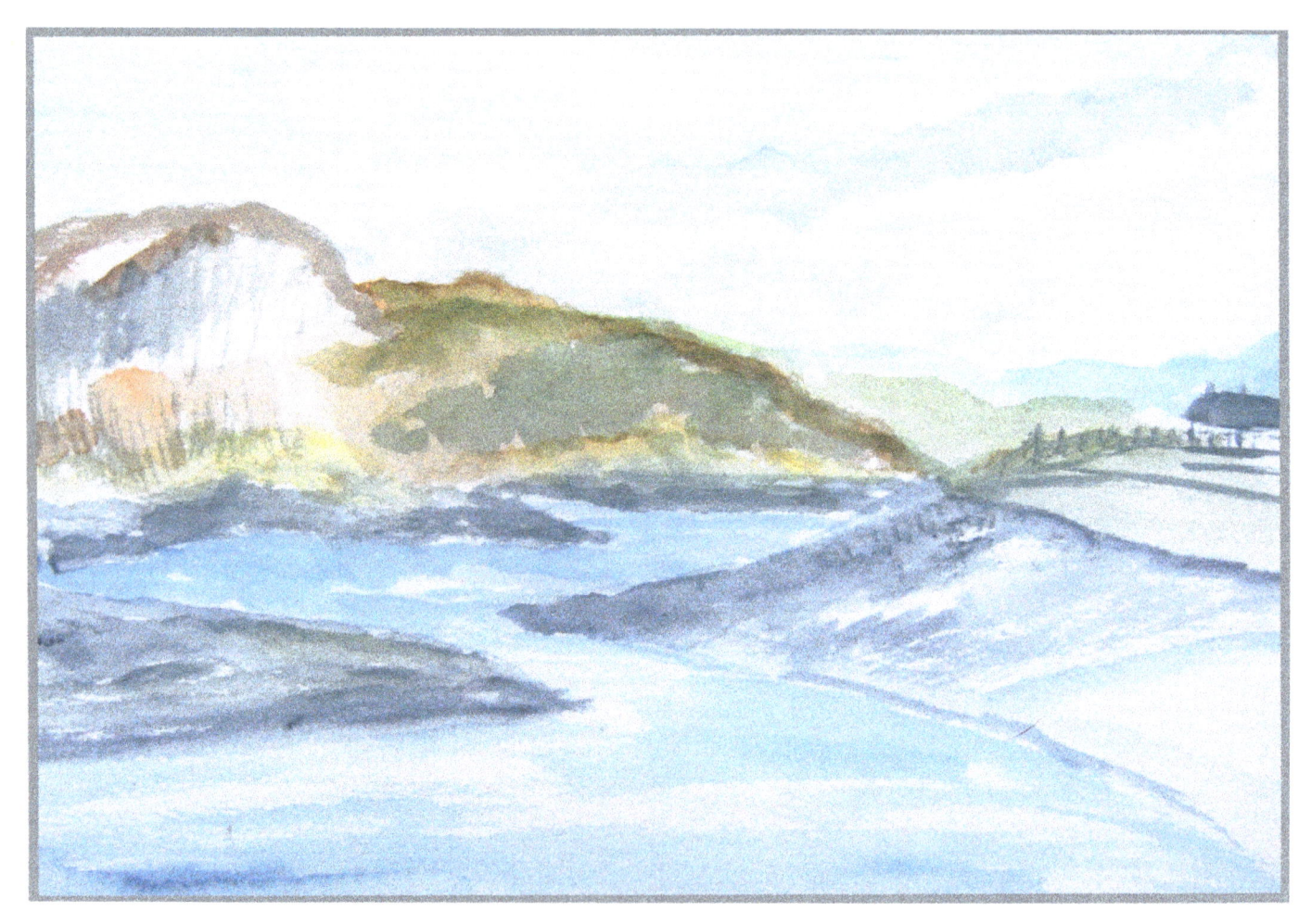

From Easdale Island
By Jane Robertson
2006 Watercolour 16" x 12"

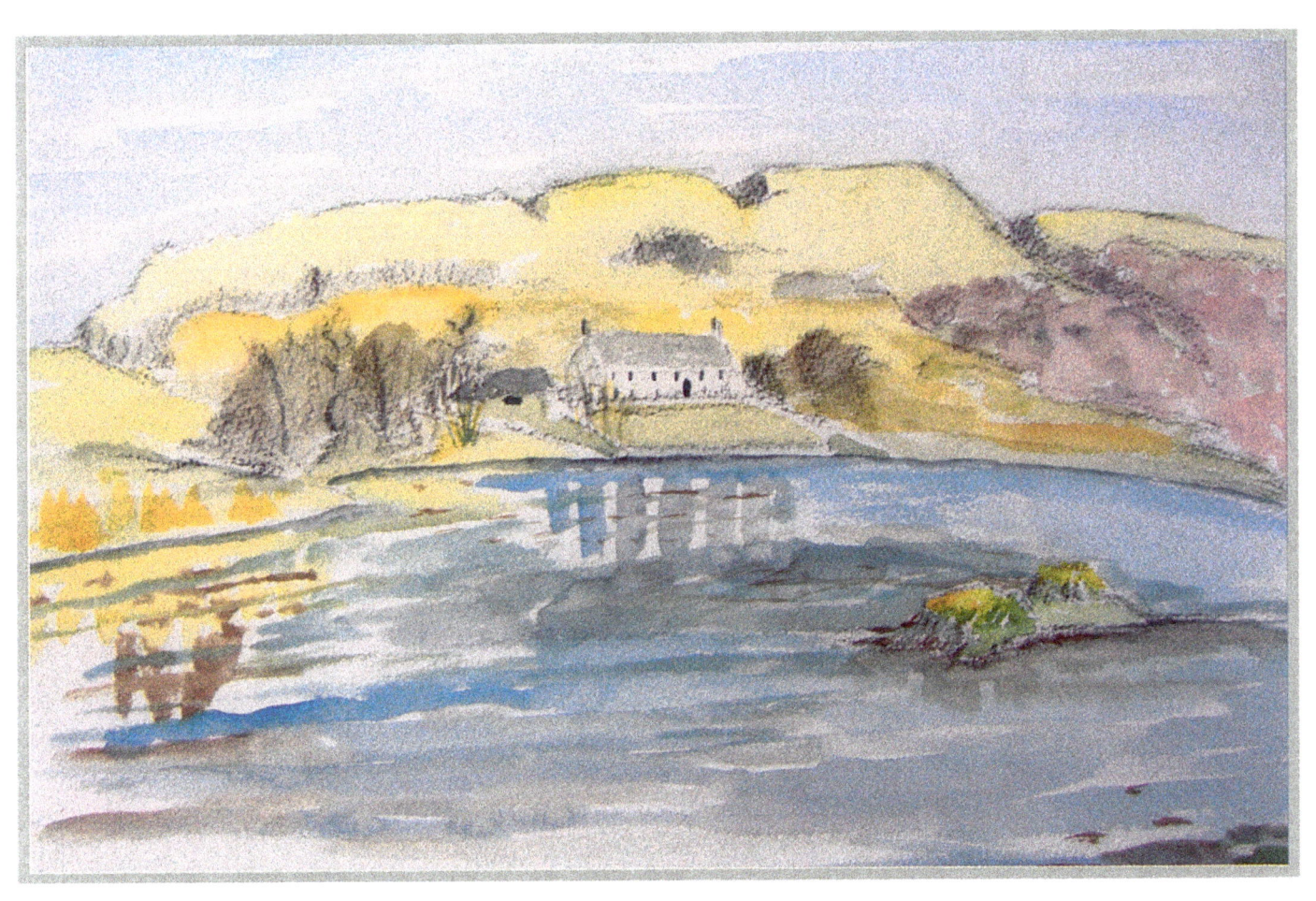

Clachan Seil
By Jane Robertson
2007 Watercolour 16" x 12"

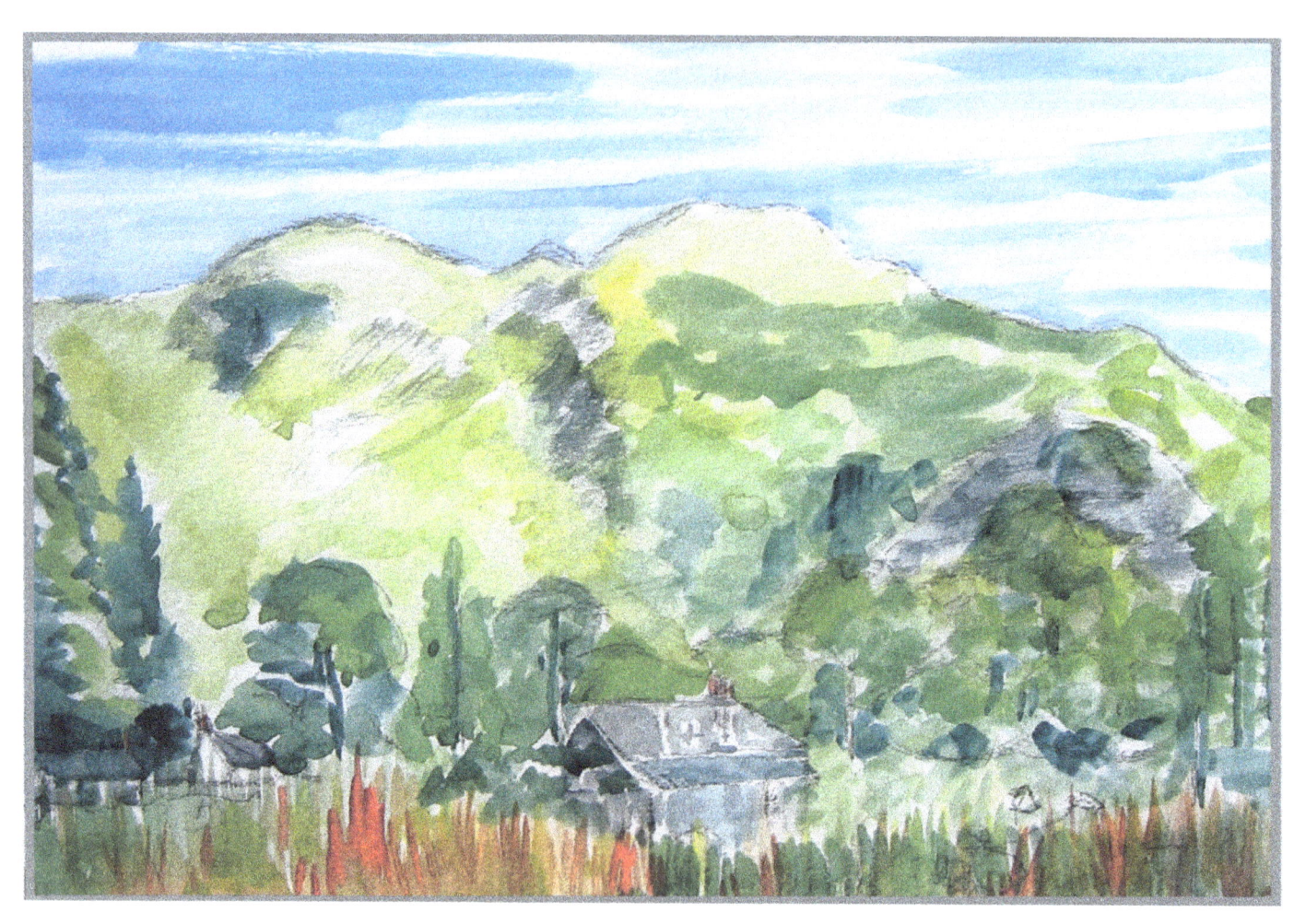

Ellenabeich
By Jane Robertson
2012 Watercolour 16" x 12"

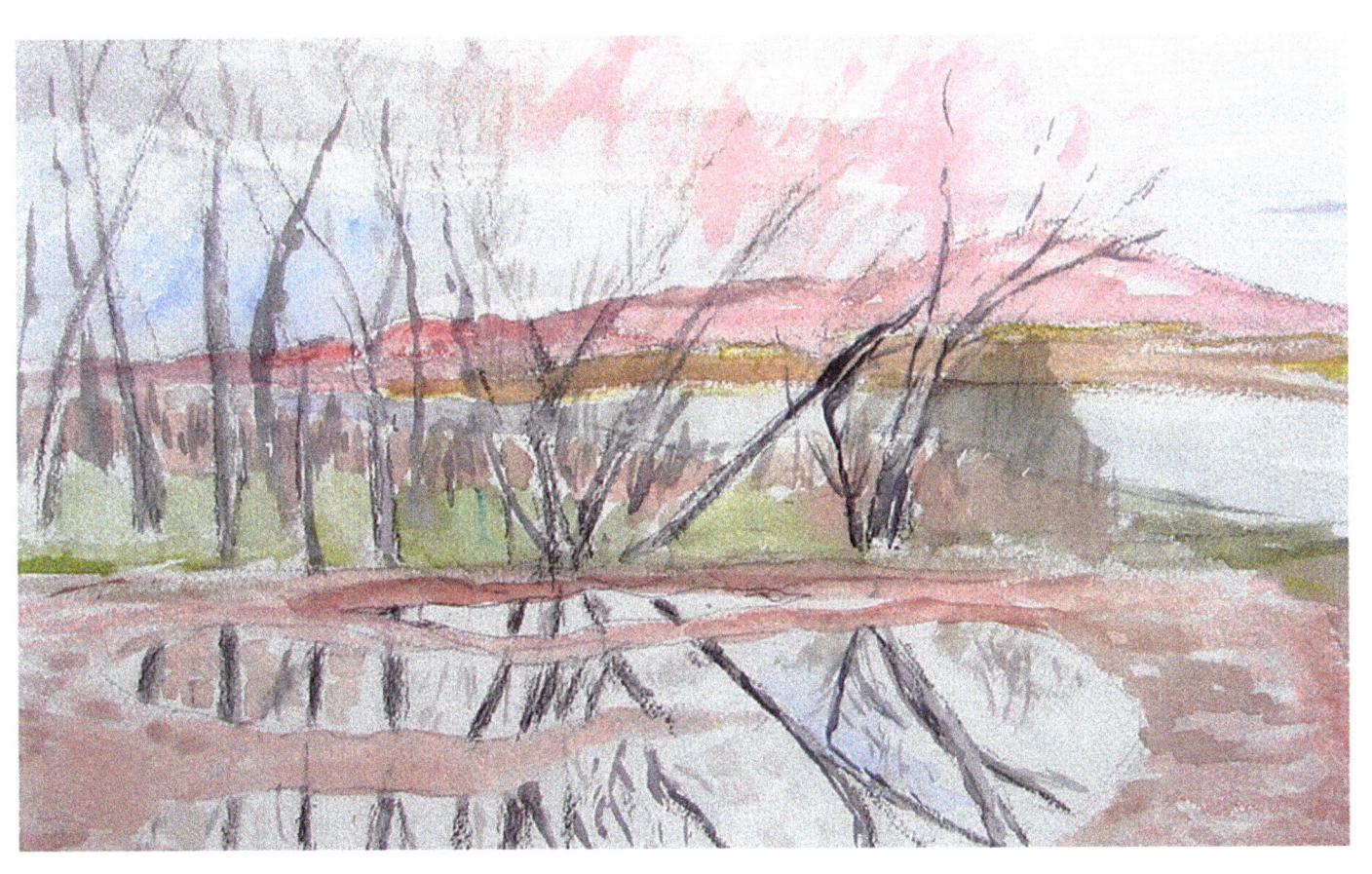

Refelections in Cromarty
By Jane Robertson
2007 Watercolour 16" x 12"

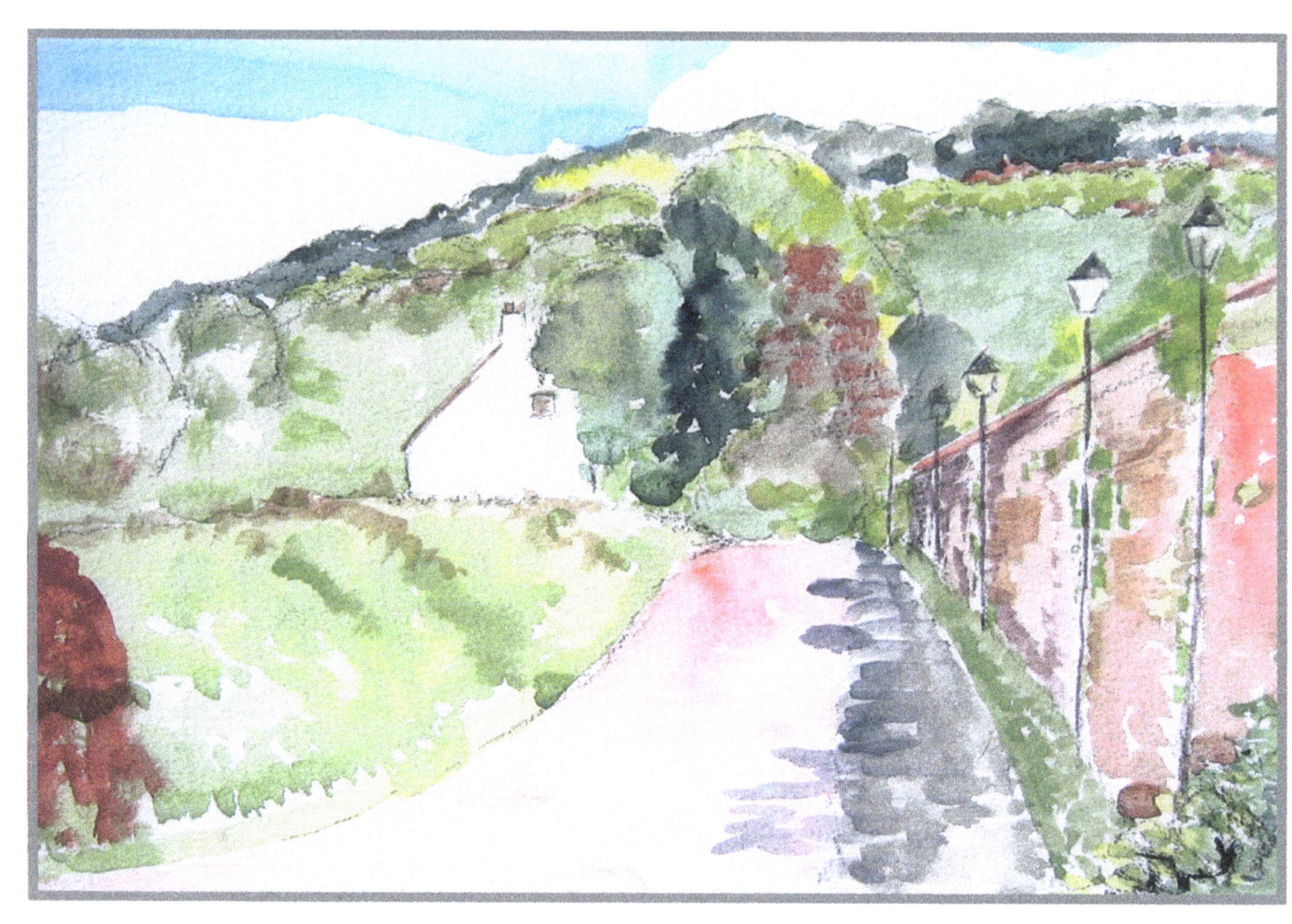

Cromarty
By Jane Robertson
2016 Watercolour 16" x 12"

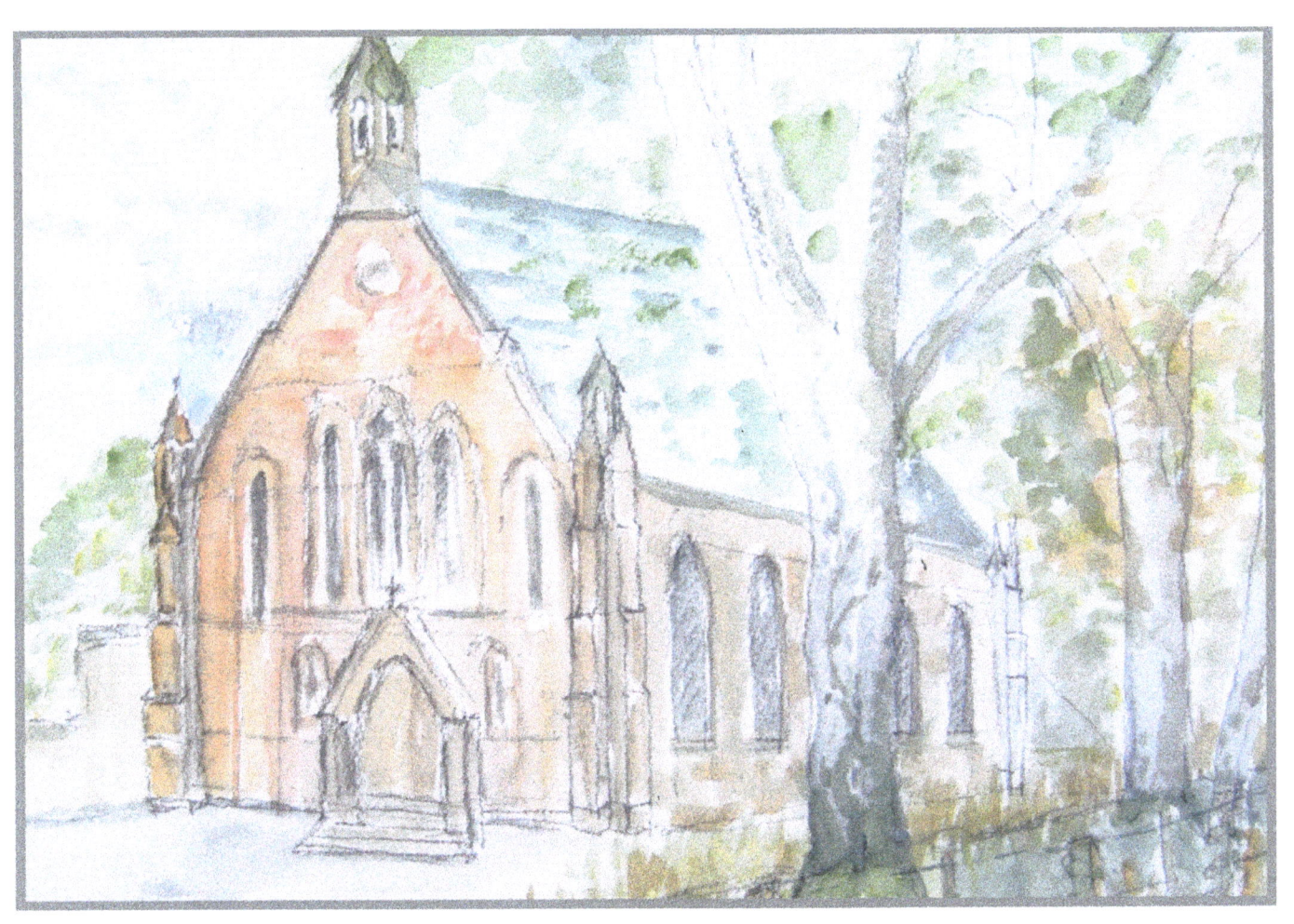

Munlochy
By Jane Robertson
2018 Watercolour 16" x 12"

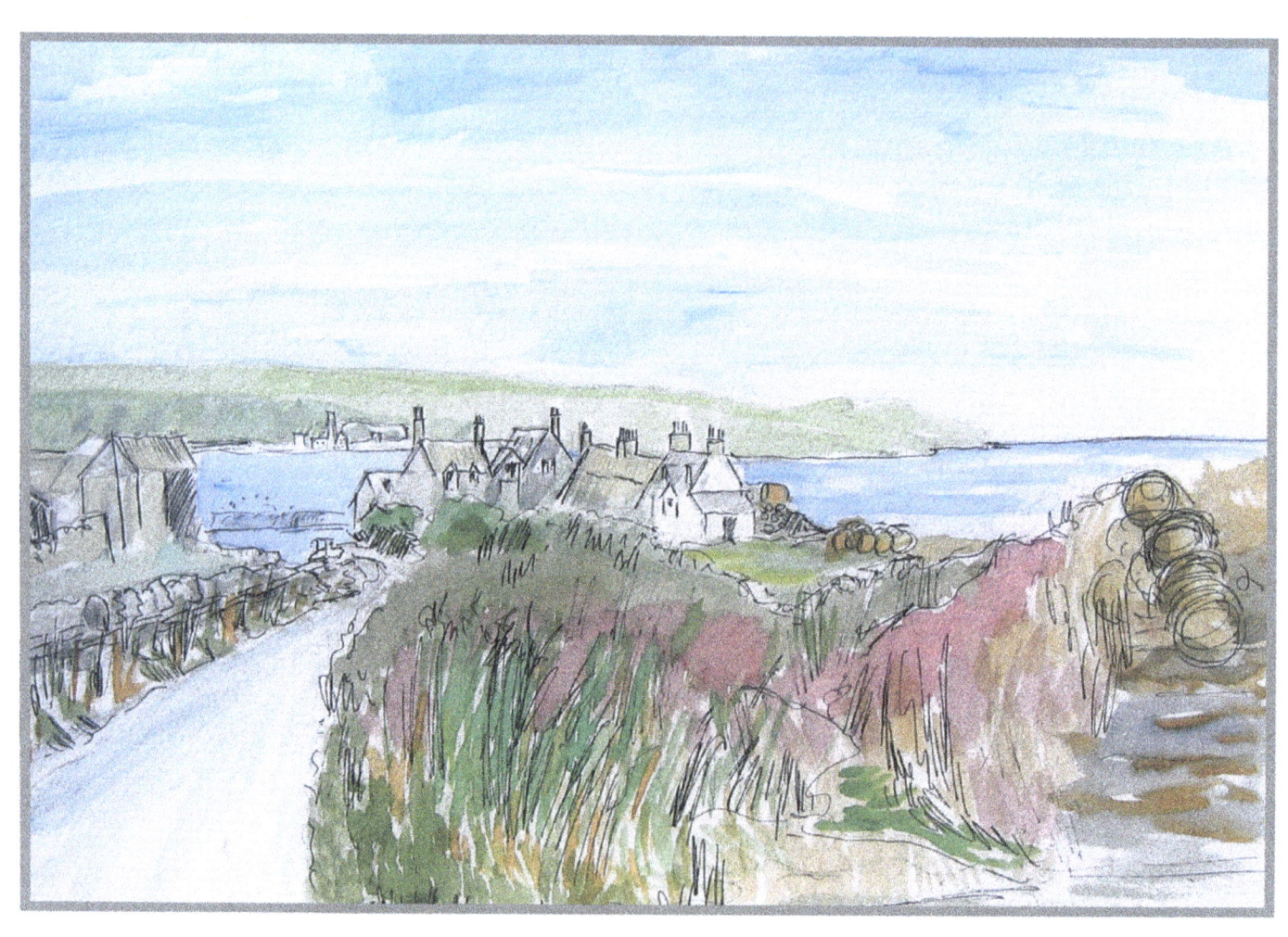

Thurso
By Jane Robertson
2008 Watercolour 16" x 12"

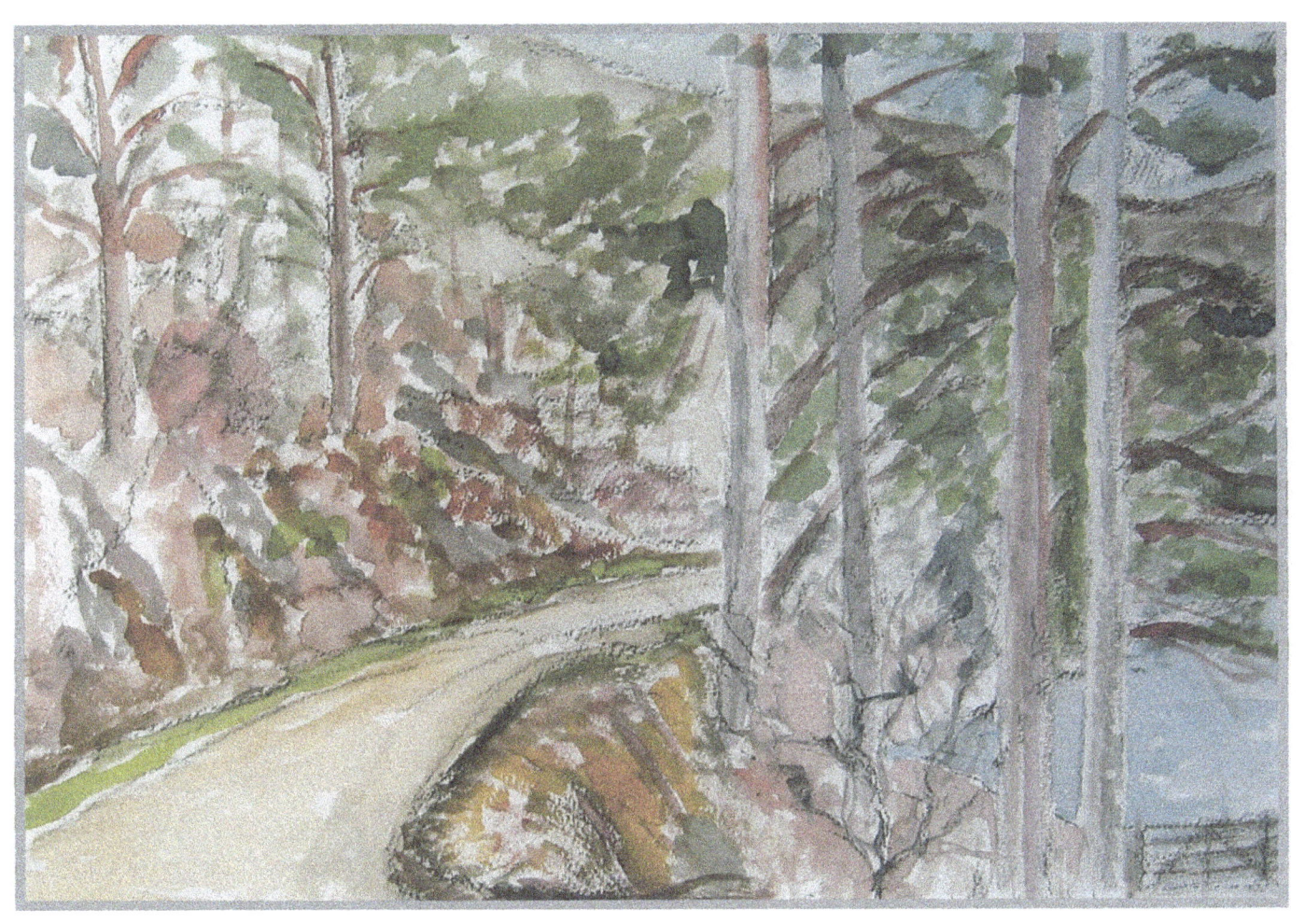

The Road to Shieldaig
By Jane Robertson
2013 Watercolour 16" x 12"

Portraits

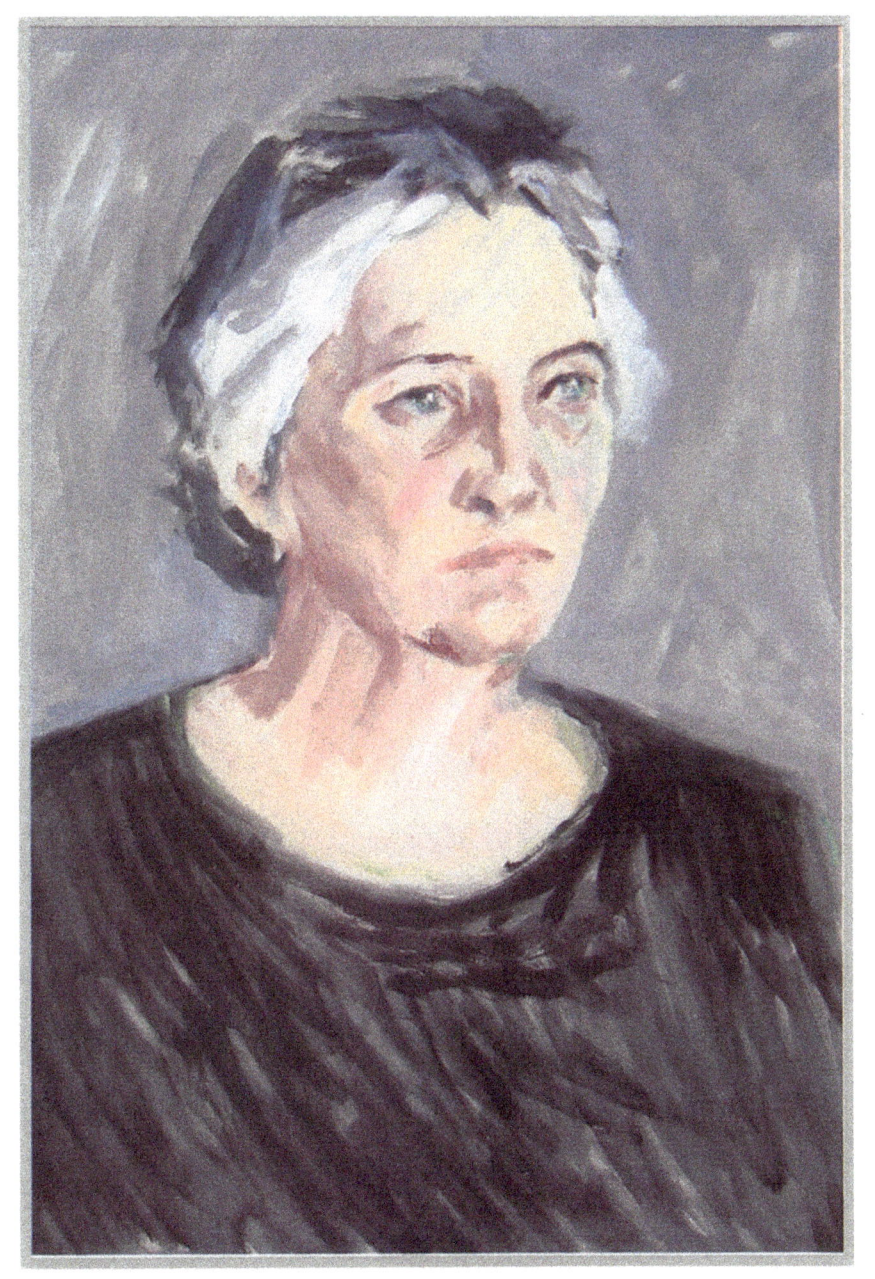

Jane
By John Robertson
Pre 2007 Acrylic 20" x 16"

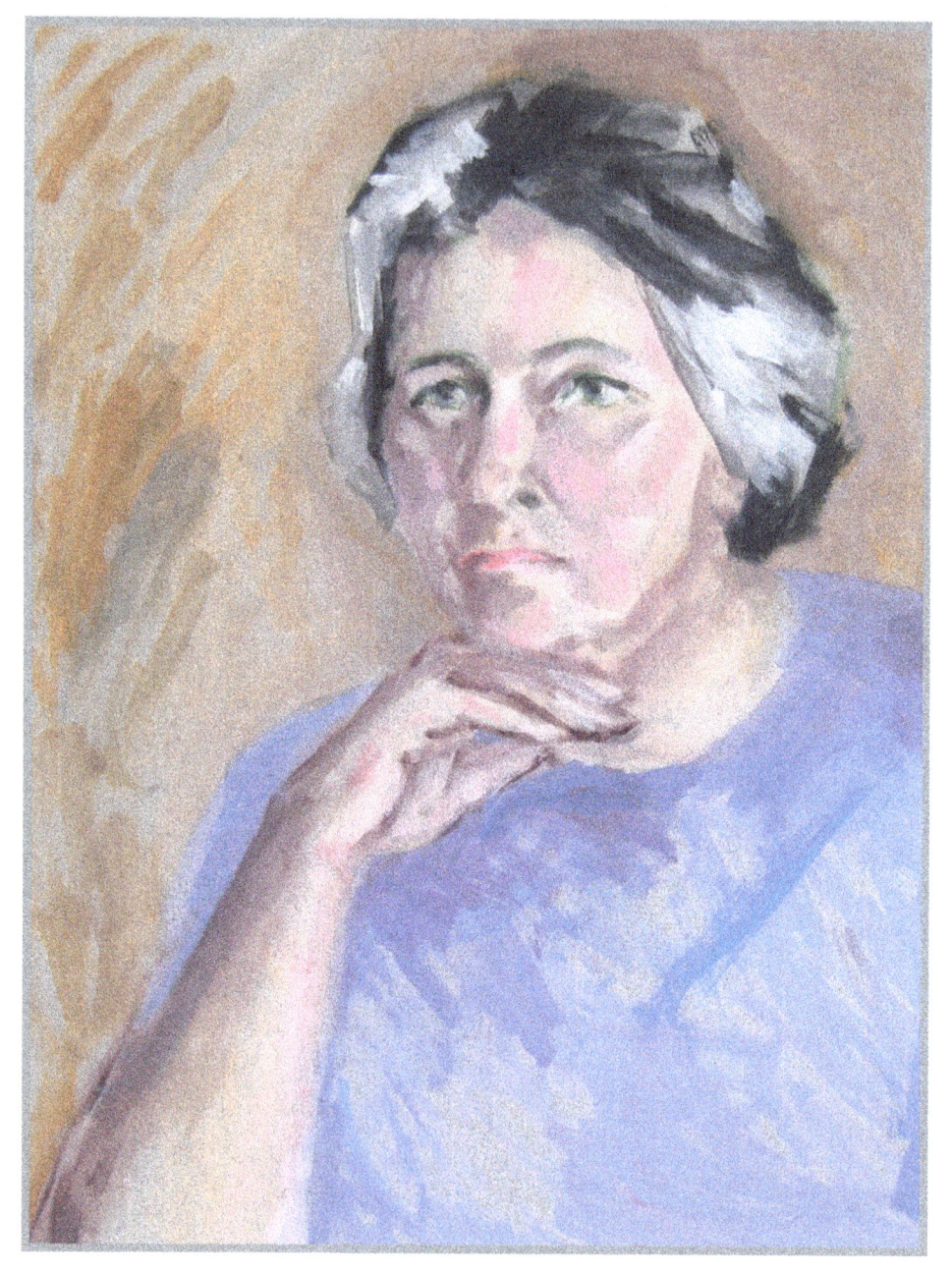

Jane
By John Robertson
2010 Gouache on Cardboard 20" x 16"

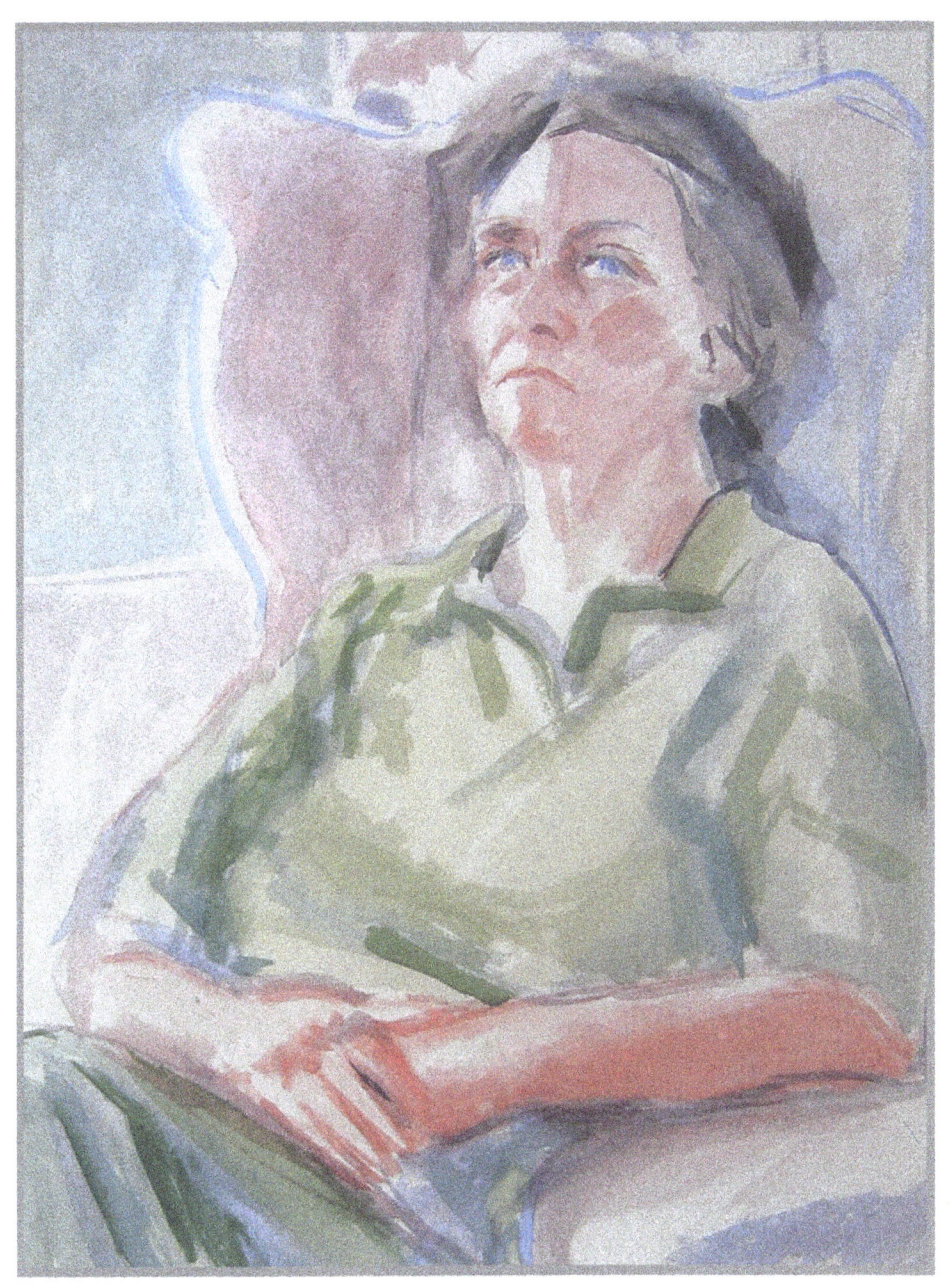

Reflections 1
By John Robertson
27.02.2000 Watercolour 27" x 20"

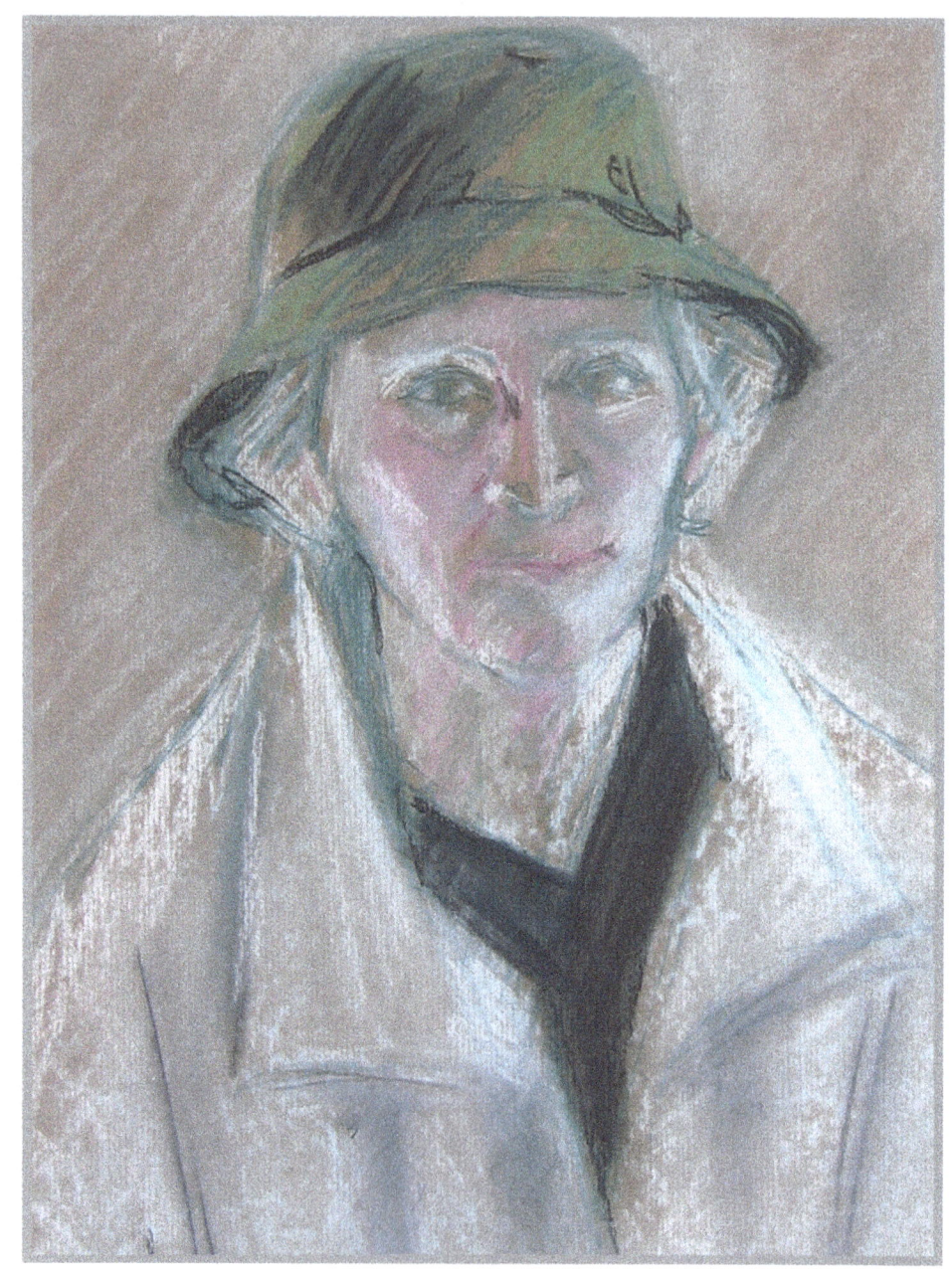

Green Hat
By John Robertson
01.12.2001 Pastel 20" x 16"

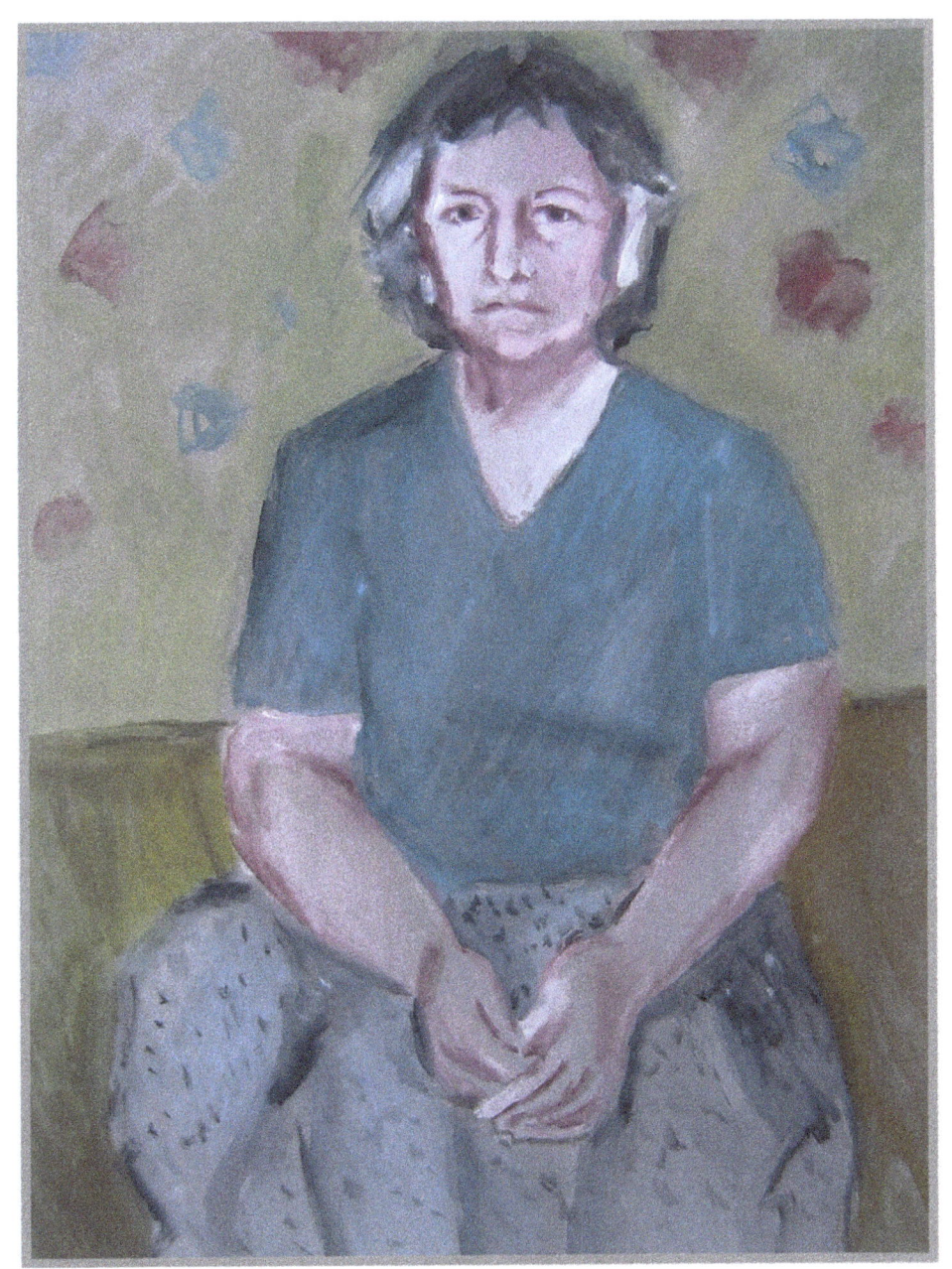

Jane in Blue
By John Robertson
23.08.2003 Acrylic 30" x 22"

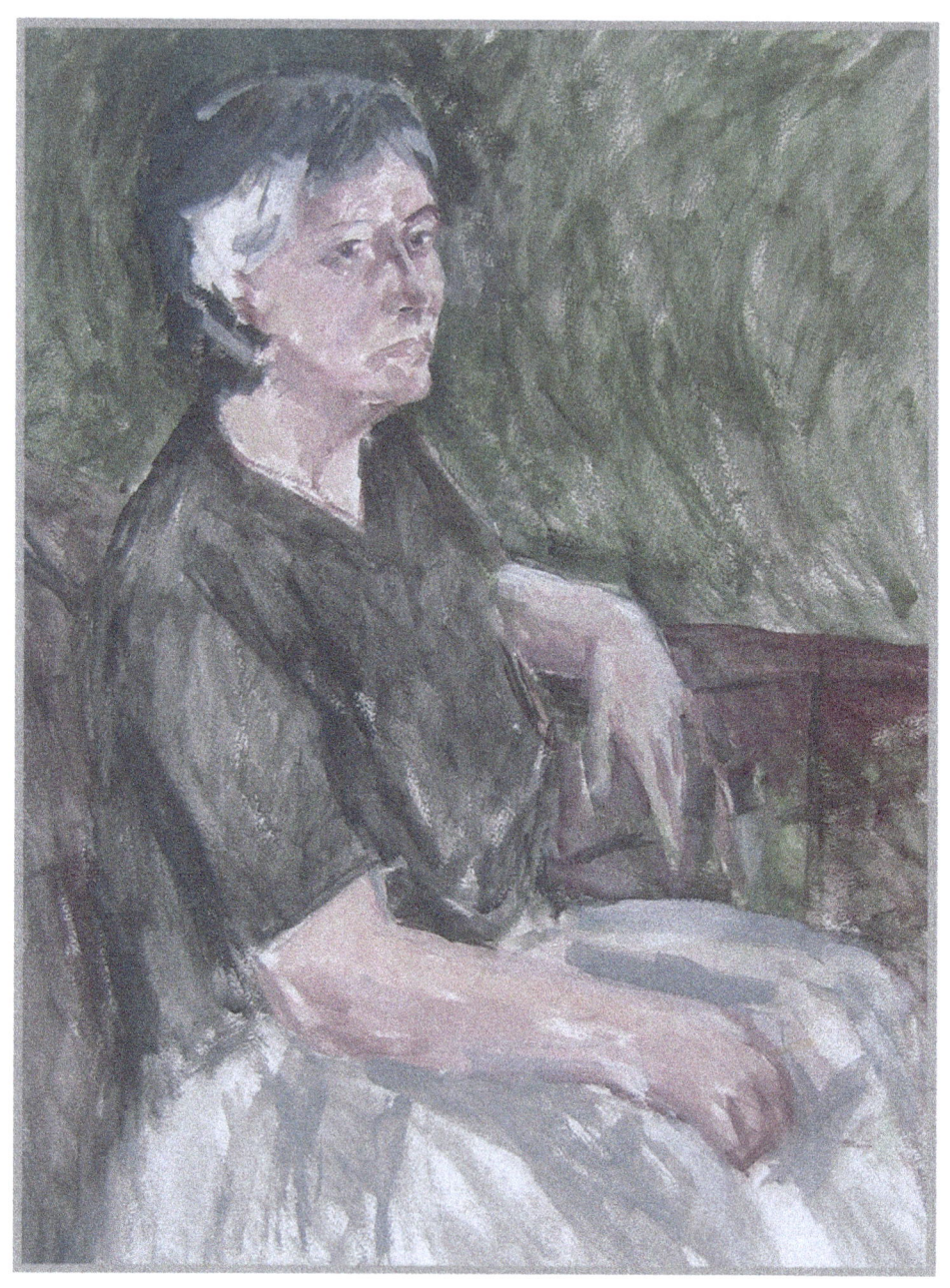

Jane Reclining
By John Robertson
07.09.1998 Acrylic 30" x 22"

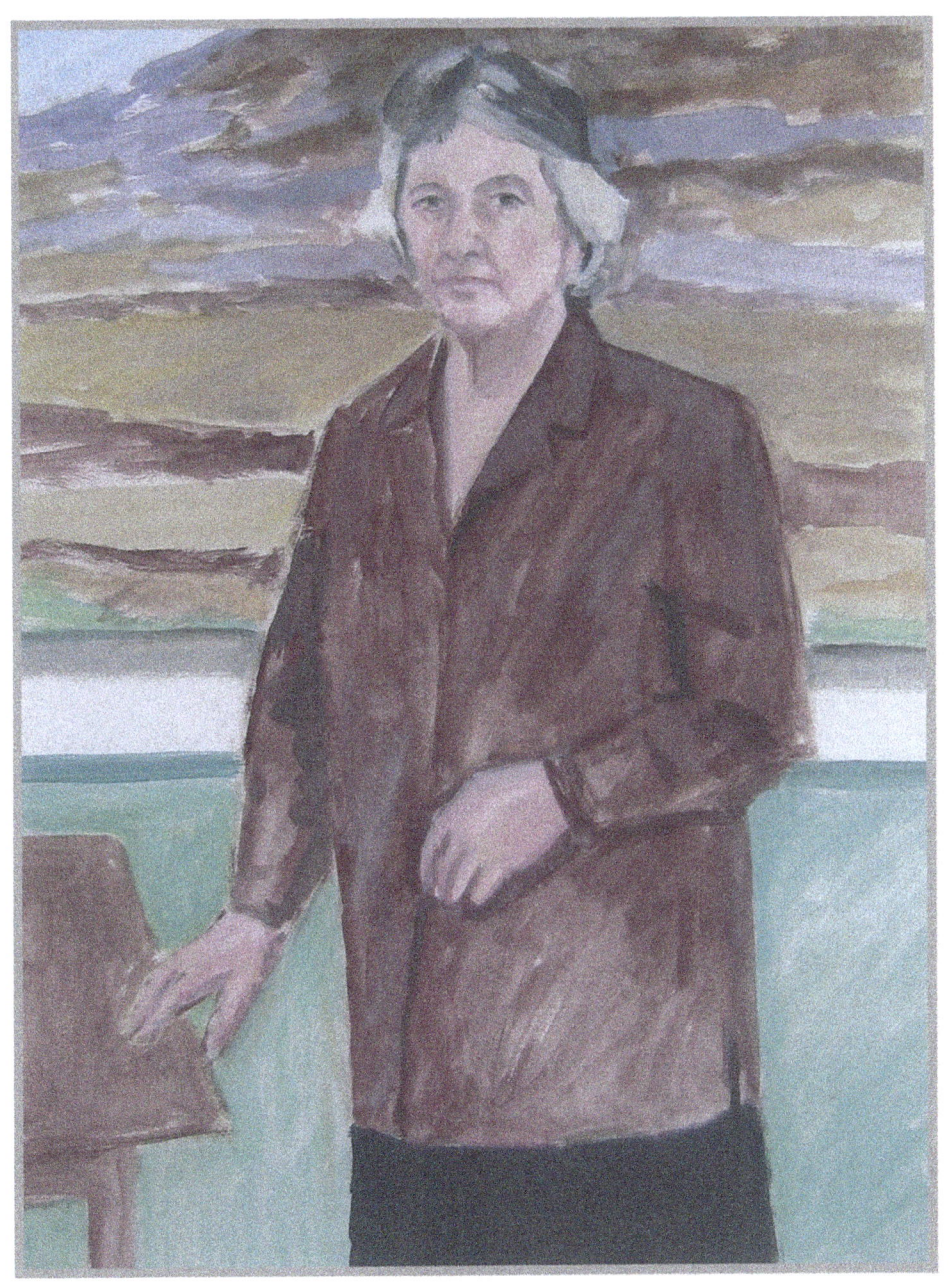

Jane in Skye
By John Robertson
2008 Acrylic 30" x 22"

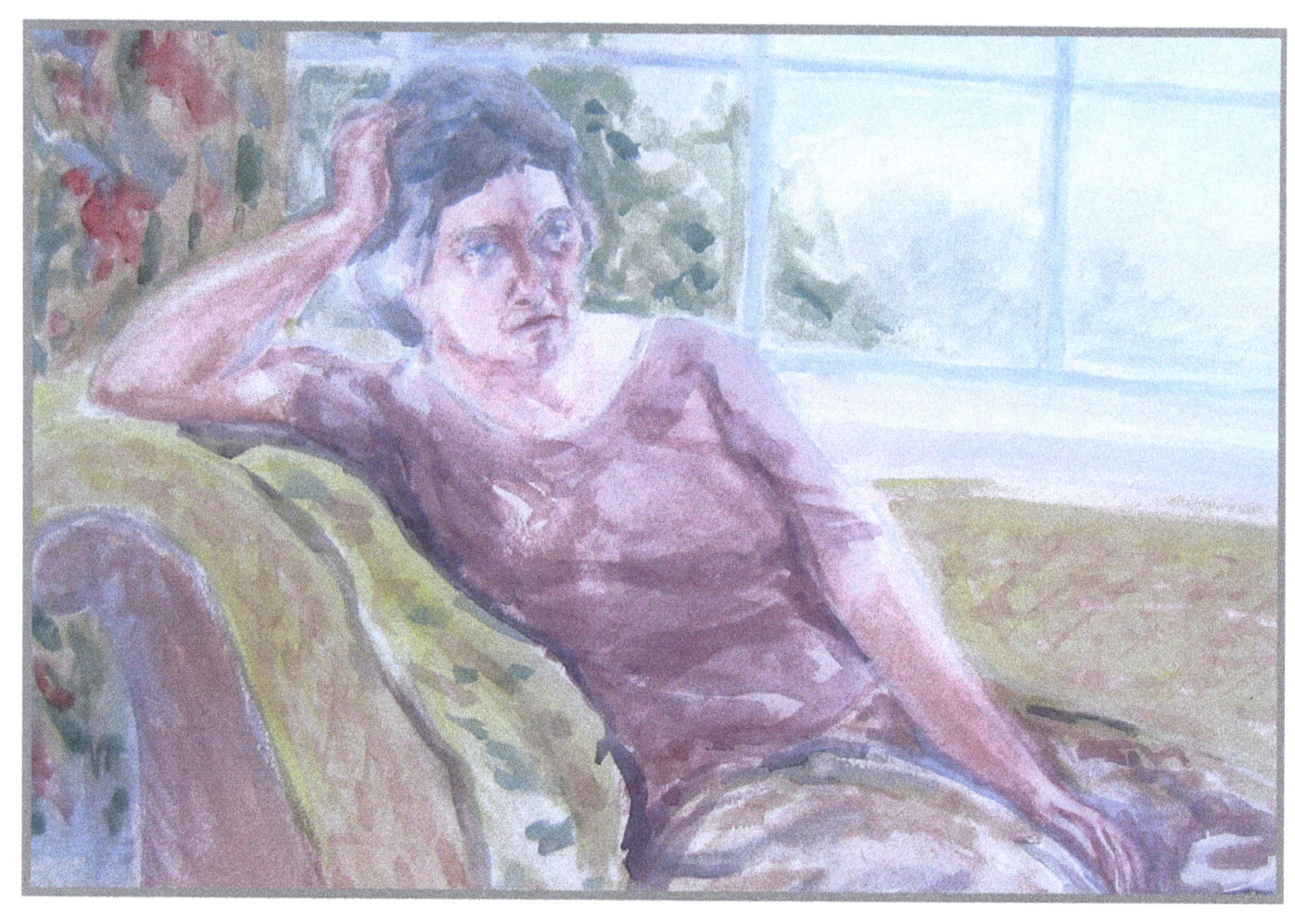

Jane, Chaise-longue
By John Robertson
01.01.2006 Watercolour 27" x 20"

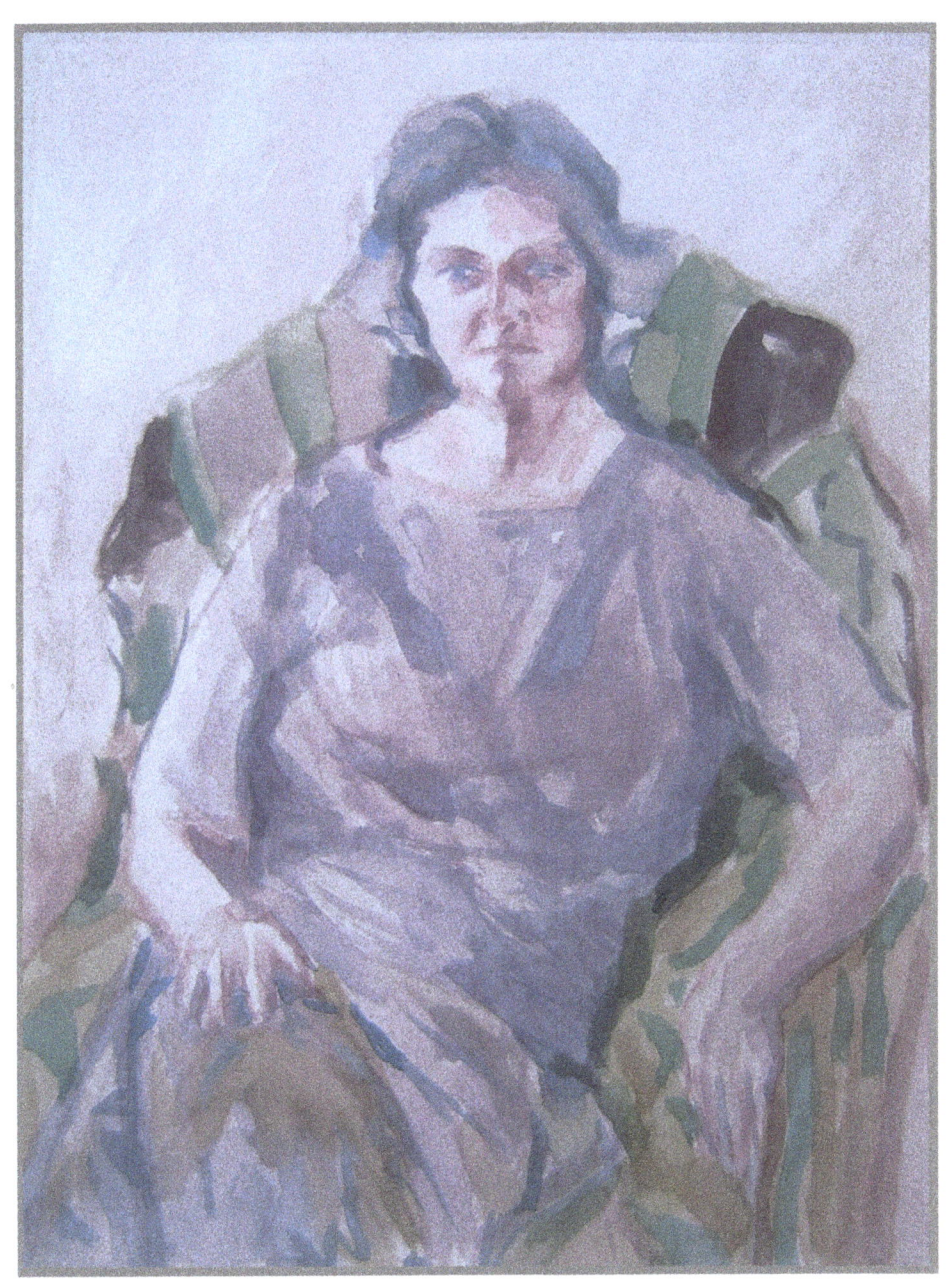

Jane in Purple
By John Robertson
24.03.2002 Watercolour 28" x 20"

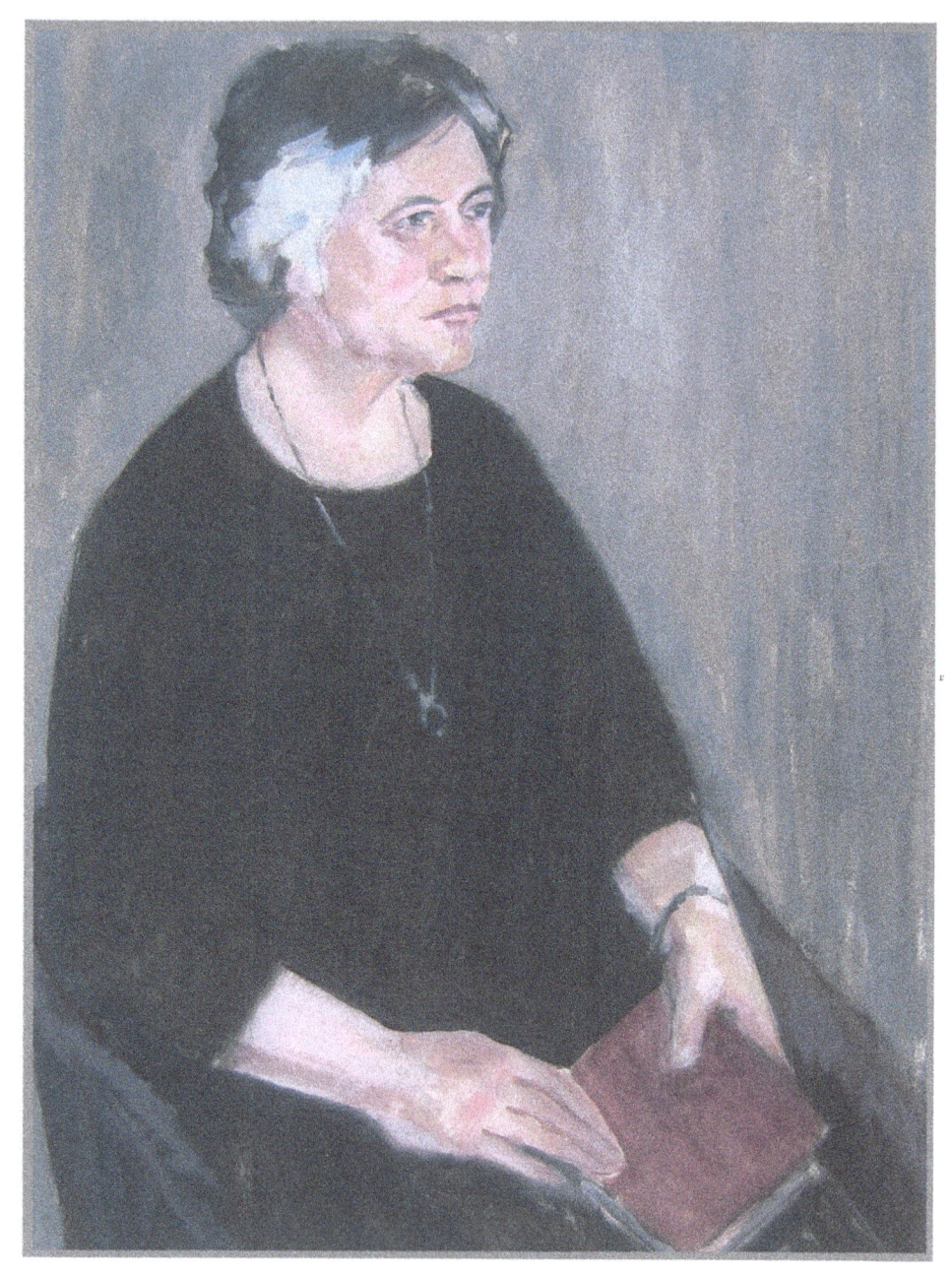

Jane with Book
By John Robertson
17.03.2008 Acrylic 30" x 22"

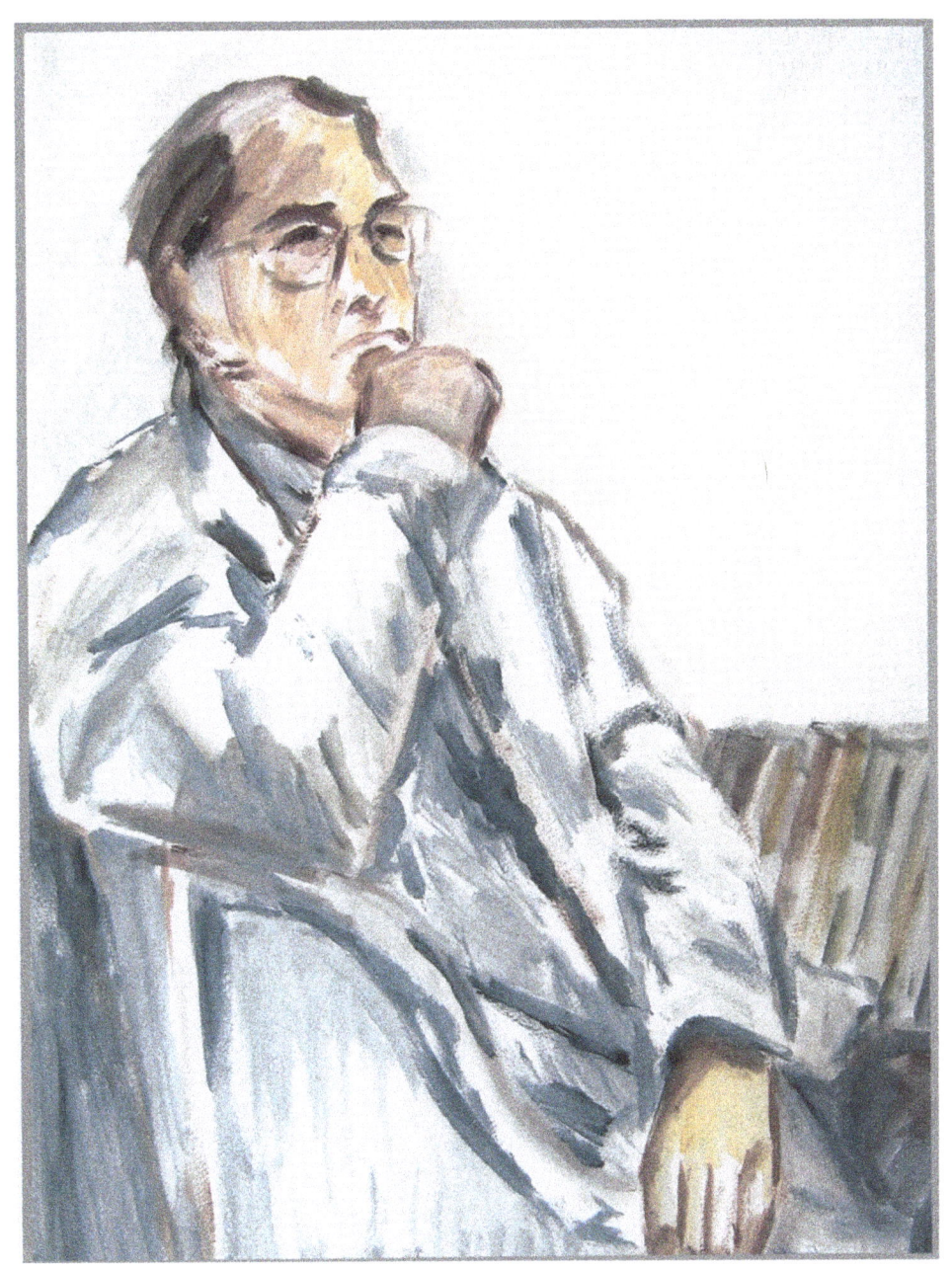

John with Books
By John Robertson
2009/2010 Acrylic 30" x 22"

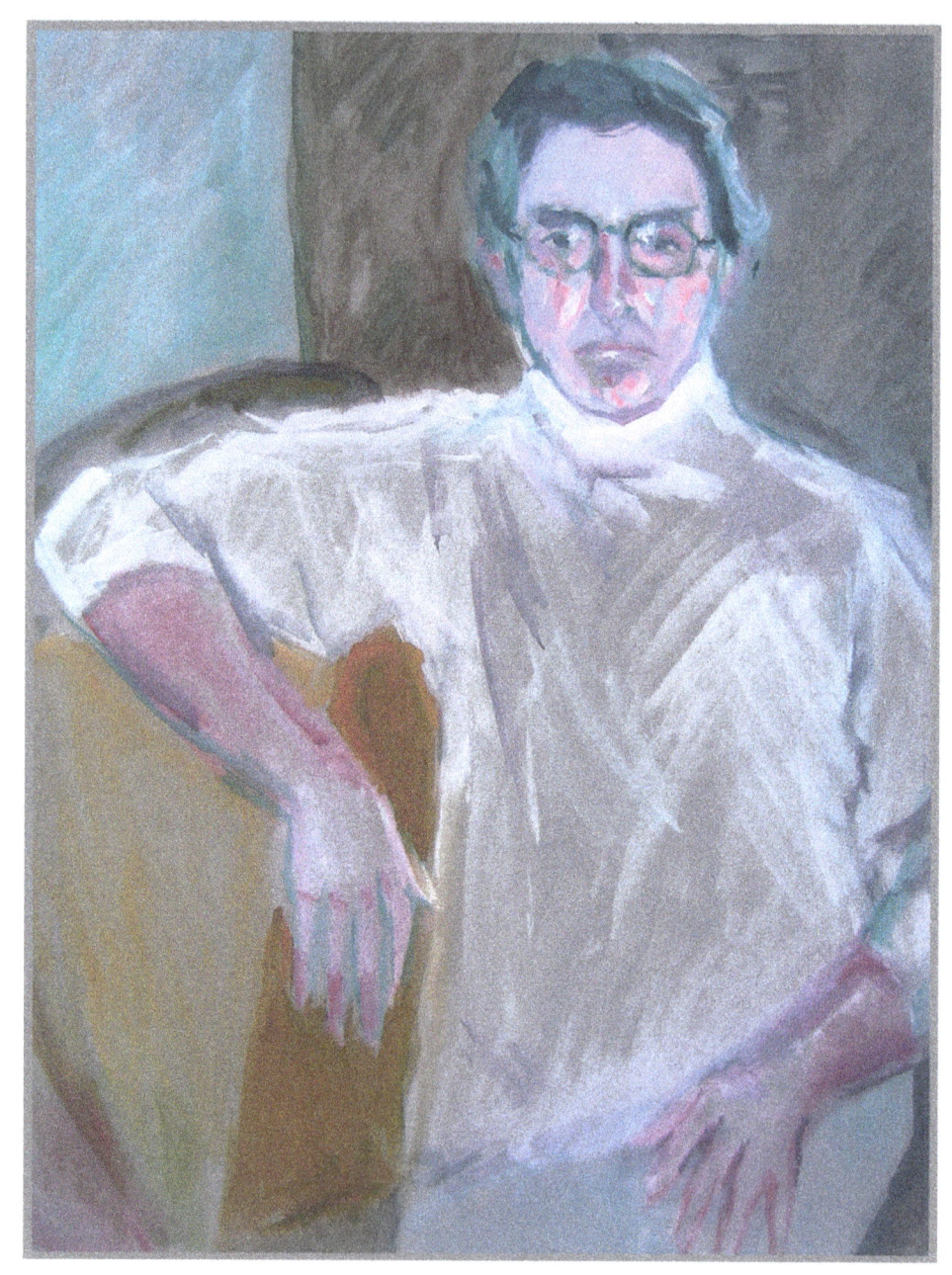

John with Glasses
By John Robertson
01.12.2001 Acrylic 30" x 22"

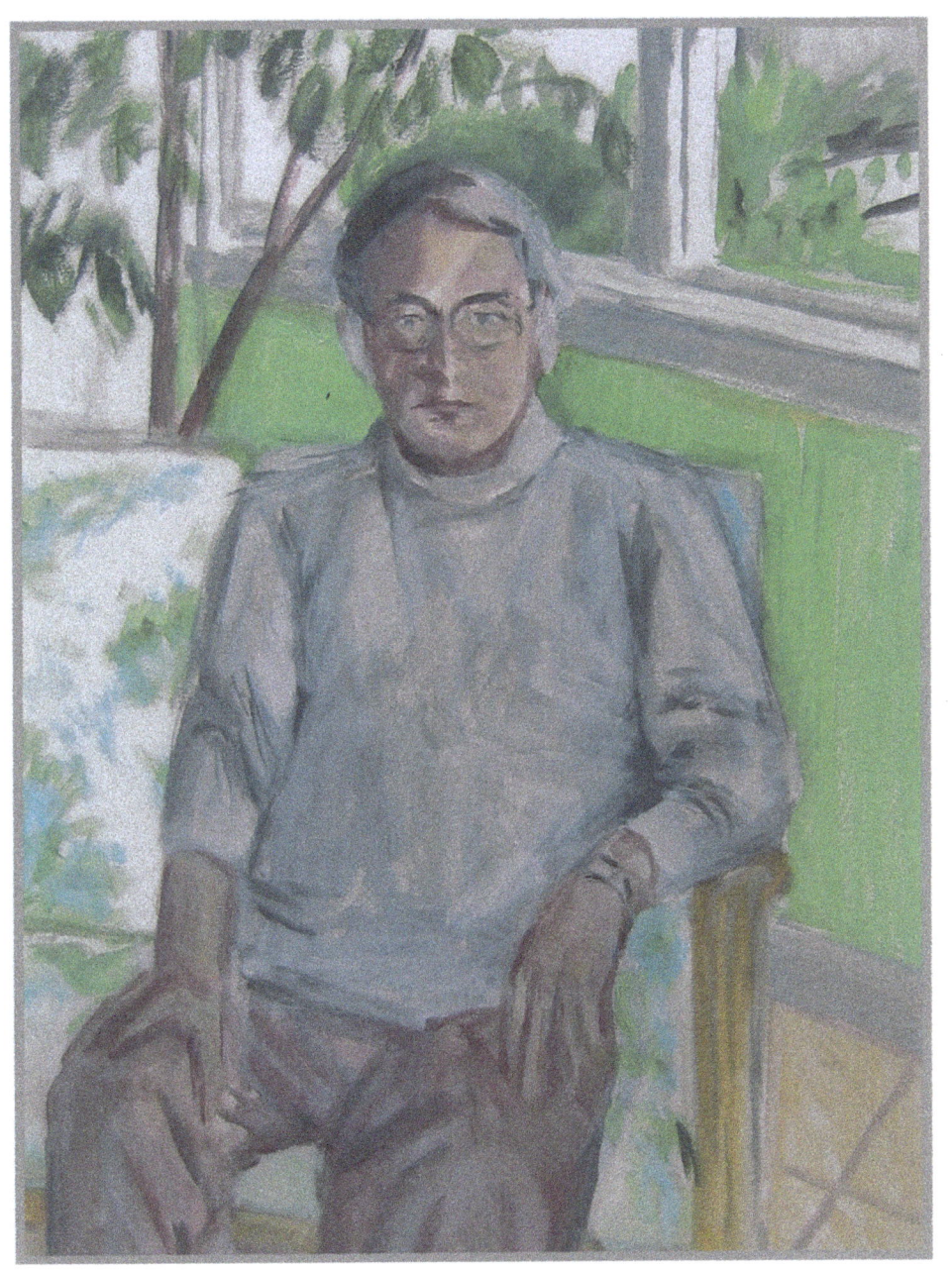

John at Strachur
By John Robertson
2010 Acrylic 30" x 22"

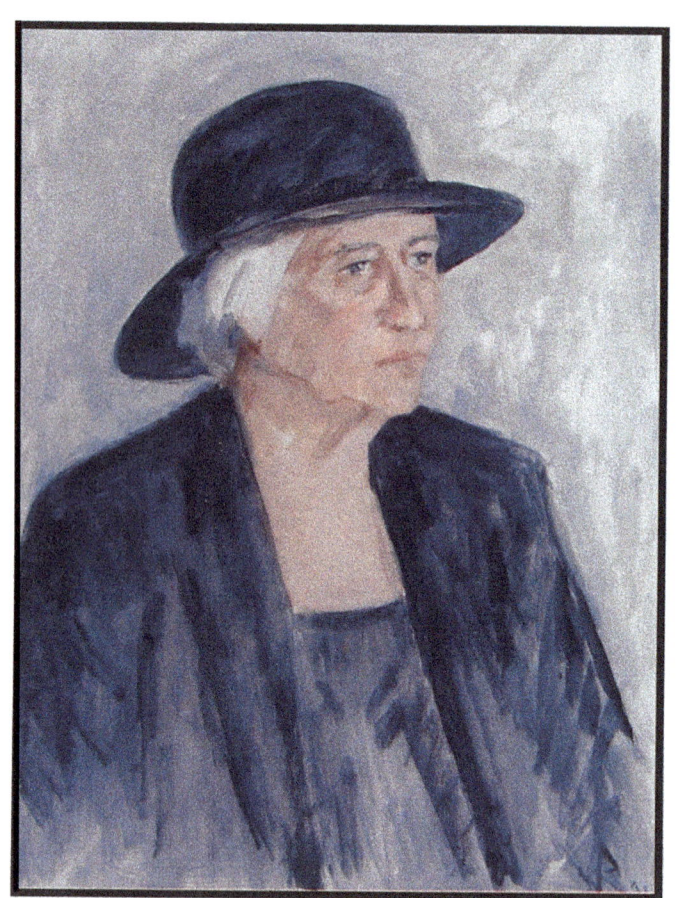 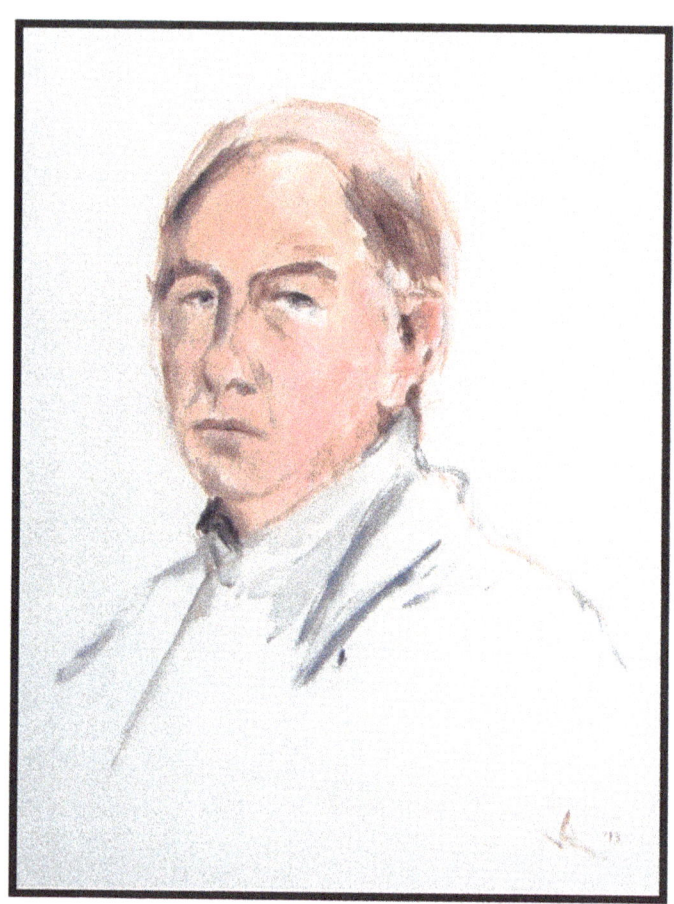

Jane and John
By John Robertson
2014 Acrylic 20" x 16"